JUST MEDICINE

Just Medicine

A Cure for Racial Inequality in American Health Care

Dayna Bowen Matthew

NEW YORK UNIVERSITY PRESS
New York and London

NEW YORK UNIVERSITY PRESS
New York and London
www.nyupress.org

© 2015 by New York University
All rights reserved

References to Internet websites (URLs) were accurate at the time of writing. Neither the author nor New York University Press is responsible for URLs that may have expired or changed since the manuscript was prepared.

ISBN: 978-1-4798-9673-8 (hardback)
ISBN: 978-1-4798-5162-1 (paperback)

For Library of Congress Cataloging-in-Publication data, please contact the Library of Congress.

New York University Press books are printed on acid-free paper, and their binding materials are chosen for strength and durability. We strive to use environmentally responsible suppliers and materials to the greatest extent possible in publishing our books.

Manufactured in the United States of America

Also available as an ebook

To my family

By justice a king gives a country stability.
—Proverbs 29:4 (NIV)

CONTENTS

ACKNOWLEDGMENTS

I suspect that many authors who complete their first book find themselves, as I do, with a list of people to thank that is longer, perhaps, than the book itself. Still, I am especially indebted to several whom I could not fail to mention briefly.

Although he will not ever read this work, my dean, mentor, and friend, David H. Getches, inspired this book. He believed in my ideas, and showed me how to be both a scholar and an advocate. I began this course of interdisciplinary study because he gave me the freedom to follow my heart, and I will spend my career in an effort to learn the lessons he taught me by his example. I must also thank Hal Bruff for allowing me regular access to his wisdom as a seasoned and remarkable author, and Chief Justice Michael Bender for his friendship, which sustained me as I began this project more than he will ever know. Fred Bloom, Aya Gruber, and Emily Calhoun stand out among the extraordinary group of colleagues who have supported my work at Colorado Law School and who read drafts, discussed my ideas, and encouraged me at important junctures during my writing. Also, encouragement from members of the academy whom I greatly admire—including Michelle Goodwin, Clare Huntington, Osagie Obasogie, and Angela Onwuachi-Willig—was invaluable to me.

One of my greatest joys has come from the welcome I received from the faculty at the University of Colorado's Institute of Behavioral Sciences as I embarked upon the journey to explore a new body of literature and knowledge when I began my sabbatical in 2011. I am grateful to Dick Jessor, Stefanie Molborn, and Michael Radelet especially for sharing their brilliance and passion for the social sciences with me. I will never be able to repay Jeff Luftig for taking the time to painstakingly review statistical methods and teach me to read social science literature critically, one article at a time. These are only a few of my university colleagues who have given true meaning to the importance and magic of interdisciplinary study.

I was able to interview the wonderful, national cross-section of physicians for this project in large part because of the help and access that Ceeya Bolman generously gave to me, sharing her incredible circle of influence. I also cannot adequately thank my friends from the Delta Eta Boulé who made calls, cajoled friends, and volunteered their time to ensure that I had patients from across the country to speak to about their experiences. Truly, their stories are the heart of this project.

I benefited greatly from the research assistance of several fine law and graduate students. Zach Ahmed, Michelle Brown, Jon Hoisted, Shannon O'Keefe, George Williams, IV, and Alex White, however, went above and beyond, helping me review earlier drafts line by line and test early versions of my ideas, precept upon precept.

I have a number of remarkable women whom I am privileged to count as my close friends. Among them, I thank Alicia Bassauk, Judy Erickson, Dr. Janet Palmer, and Amelia Peterson, who have been in so many ways my co-laborers in this project and without whom, I would not have completed this book. And finally, I thank Cecelia Cancellero for believing in this project from the beginning and for patiently sharing her talent to help me bring it to fruition.

I am blessed with three brilliant children—Griffin, Thomas, and Mari—who read and commented on my drafts, scowling at some ideas and cheering at others; they vigorously challenged my thinking, and celebrated my victories small and large along the way. I wrote in part to try to keep pace with their intellectual curiosity, social justice insights, and admirable development as scholars in their own right. I close my acknowledgment by thanking the people for whom no "thank you" could adequately convey my deep appreciation or affection for what they have given to me and to this project. First, my dear life partner and best friend, my husband, Thomas; second, my brother, Vincent, who has believed in me longer than anyone on earth; and third my parents, Marion and Vincent Bowen, who imparted an optimistic desire to contribute to justice for all in America and modeled the belief that every one of us is responsible to contribute to making that vision a reality. I am eternally grateful.

PREFACE TO PAPERBACK EDITION

Many important social and scientific changes relevant to achieving a just and equitable health care system have occurred since this book was first published in 2015. Some are positive. First, a broad commitment to health equity has emerged on the part of health care providers. Health equity goals, programs, and strategies have been adopted by virtually every organization that delivers medical care in the nation. Providers now, with near unanimity, articulate a commitment to ensuring that everyone has a fair and just opportunity to be healthy. This goal means different things to different actors. At minimum, it means mitigating illness and death from avoidable and clinically unnecessary differences among people and populations. Broadly, it means creating the "Culture of Health" that not only identifies health disparities but implements policies, systems, and laws to reduce unequal access to social determinants such as fair-paying jobs, basic education, decent housing, safety, and quality health care. A second set of changes has to do with our understanding of implicit bias. The term "unconscious racism," as well as a basic understanding of the phenomenon it describes, has made its way from the annals of social psychology and philosophy textbooks into the cultural discourse of employers and employees, politicians, teachers, police officers, journalists, and of course, health care providers, payers, and consumers. It is now generally understood that everyone thinks negatively about some other people without intending to. The habit of assigning people to groups and then reacting according to the traits associated with those categories is now accepted as a given, even if we cannot agree on the extent to which these thoughts influence, affect, or harm others, or how to measure the biases themselves.

Some of the changes pertinent to finding a cure for inequity in American health care are decidedly negative. Chief amongst them is the dreadful resurgence of racism—overt and covert—which has made a comeback in America. Over the past two years, violent and deadly mobs have felt at liberty to terrorize people on the streets of cities like Charlottesville, Virginia; the incidence of hate crimes directed at Jews, Muslims, immigrants, and LGBTQ communities has spiked; and hate-filled rhetoric fills the airways, social media, and even passes for public policy in governments that appeal to the fears of an increasingly segregated public. Finally, by every conceivable measure—education, employment, income, wealth, poverty, arrests and incarceration, and food security— inequities that separate those with advantages from the disadvantaged in America are severe and worsening to levels not experienced in this country since the Great Depression of the 1930s.

All this means that this book—and a fresh look at the lessons it contains—is more important today than ever before. With one final, important difference: the lens now must be population-based. To eradicate inequity in American health care, it is no longer sufficient to look at discrimination only in health care. We must look at how racism, bias, and discrimination infect *all* of the social determinants of health, both historically and contemporarily. Providers must understand that their patients who belong to racial and ethnic minorities are affected by discriminatory housing practices—mortgage lending, maintenance of substandard conditions, properties, evictions, accommodations—all aspects of housing for minority residents and homeowners have been infiltrated by ugly, health-harming racial and ethnic biases. Inequitable discipline in schools, disproportionately high arrest rates, sentencing, and exposure to violence scar children and adults for life. We are only now beginning to fully appreciate how stress, anxiety, and serious mental illnesses associated with discrimination and racial violence adversely impacts the health of vulnerable communities. Those wishing to implement the health care delivery model outlined in this book must make room for these structural concerns. Training a generation of de-biased providers is an essential and necessary component of reducing health disparities. However, those de-biased individuals must appreciate their roles as care-givers within a social context where racial and ethnic biases adversely impact every facet of their patients' lives and health—particularly their patients who are members of black, Latinx, and Native American communities— if these providers hope to deliver quality health care, and give these patients a fair opportunity to live healthy lives. In short, to cure racial inequality in American health care, doctors, nurses, administrators, social workers, psychologists, dentists, physician assistants (PA's), and all of us who are patients, must now account for and take aim at the impacts of racial and ethnic inequality in health care, and in each of the social determinants of health. This book offers a way to approach this task by providing a framework for critical self-evaluation and reform within the health care delivery system and a prescription for changes beyond health care. Now, more than ever before, we need the tools offered in *Just Medicine*.

Introduction

The New Normal

For the past thirty years, medical doctors, social scientists, psychologists, policy analysts, jurists, and a wide spectrum of health care providers have been studying and discussing health inequality in America. Meanwhile, by one estimate, 83,570 minority patients die annually due to health care disparities.[1] Black and brown patients consistently receive inferior medical treatment—fewer angiographies, bypass surgeries, organ transplants, cancer tests and resections, less access to pain treatment, rehabilitative services, asthma remedies, and nearly every other form of medical care—than their white counterparts. Yet minority patients are sicker and more likely to die than whites from a wide range of diseases and illnesses for which we have data.[2] Certainly, this picture is complicated. For example, health and illness for all racial and ethnic groups follow a social gradient so that minority populations, which disproportionately occupy low socioeconomic strata, also predictably suffer relatively worse health outcomes than whites do.[3] Although it is popular to blame the poor for their poor health by pointing to risky health behaviors, careful studies of nationally representative populations conclude that the significantly higher prevalence of cigarette smoking, alcohol consumption, obesity, and physical inactivity are only one aspect of the relationship between lower socioeconomic status and poor health.[4] Moreover, behavioral disparities must not be taken out of their societal context where unequal exposure to the stress of discrimination, inequitable access to healthy food and built environments, and inferior access to resources generally are integrally associated with many racial and ethnic differences in health behavior.[5] In fact, racial and ethnic differences in health treatment and outcomes persist in multiple studies even after controlling for differences in insurance status, income,[6] education, geography, and socioeconomic status.

Researchers have identified numerous structural and individual determinants of these disparities at all levels. These include socioeconomic circumstances such as poverty, inferior education, and segregated housing conditions along with lack of access to healthy food choices or recreational facilities; systemic and organizational contributors such as medical practice settings and sources of insurance; and geographic proximity to care. The economic and social conditions called "social determinants of health" often drive patient-specific contributors to poor health such as poor family health history, diet, and low physical activity. All have been shown to contribute to the disparity of health outcomes experienced by ethnic and racial minority patients in the United States. However, this book is about the single most important determinant of health disparities that is *not* being widely discussed in straightforward terms: this determinant is racial and ethnic discrimination against minority patient populations, an uncontrovertibly significant contributor to health inequality.

The evidence that the majority of Americans involuntarily harbor anti-minority prejudices makes it impossible, even immoral, not to examine the impact of unconscious racism on health and health care. Therefore, this book makes a thorough examination of the scientific evidence that does exist to confirm that providers discriminate against patients and patients discriminate against providers. This cycle of discrimination produces inequality throughout the health care system. The inequality itself is not news. But the fact that it is avoidable challenges the complacency that allows the racial and ethnic discrimination that produces them to persist. This book calls for providers, patients, scientists, and jurists to face the uncomfortable truth that although overt racism, prejudice, and bigotry may have subsided in America, racial and ethnic injustice, unfairness, and even segregation in American health care have not. The most tragic proof that racial and ethnic injustice is alive and well is the phenomenon we politely call "health disparities." The message of this book is that a significant cause of these health disparities is the unconscious racial and ethnic bias that infects our delivery system. Implicit racial and ethnic biases in health care are harmful, avoidable, and unjust. This book charts a way to deal with health and health care disparities as injustices, not merely as inevitable byproducts of human nature or a phenomenon subordinate to biological and social differences. Instead, the argument made here is that health inequality due to unconscious discrimination is a structural malady in need of a systemic cure.

This book lays bare a disturbing contradiction. On one hand, injustice and inequality are anathema to our professed national identity. Yet on the other hand, unconscious bias has become an entrenched and acceptable social norm, empirically demonstrated to control decision-makers not only in health care, but in civil and criminal justice proceedings, law enforcement, employment, media, and education. Unconscious racism has become the new normal. Thus, to defeat inequality due to unconscious racism in health care, individuals as well as institutions must realign themselves away from this social norm that is incongruous with the core underlying values to which our nation's doctors, patients, and health care professionals expressly aspire. The solutions this book proposes are comprehensive; they have their origin in law, and to some this may seem radical. But they are solutions grounded in a historical and empirical record. The solutions are further supported by original, qualitative interviews reported here. These narratives allow doctors, nurses, and patients to bring their voices and real-life experiences to bear on a worthy cause: achieving justice and equity in American health care.

Chapter 1 recounts the historical origins of legally enforced discrimination that have laid the structural foundations for African, Asian, Hispanic, and Native Americans to suffer inferior health outcomes in the United States since this country's inception. I argue that law has directly influenced the differences in health and health care experiences between minorities and whites throughout our nation's history. When laws enforced slavery, segregation, and nationalism, minority health fared poorly. During the periods of our history when civil rights laws were effectively used to desegregate health care and promote equal access, health care disparities improved. Today, however, traditional civil rights laws have become irrelevant in the effort to bring justice to health care. Those antidiscrimination laws punish only outright bigotry and the most virulent forms of racism. Now that these forms of overt racism are out of vogue and mostly absent from the health care system, the rule of law has been neutralized and no longer controls racial discrimination. Therefore, the great American tradition of running two separate and unequal medical systems for white and non-white patients is back.

Chapter 2 explains the nature and evidence of discrimination in contemporary health care. The quantitative and qualitative data gathered in this chapter explain that health care providers *unintentionally* discriminate against racial and ethnic minority patients—and that their unintentional discrimination directly and substantially contributes to ethnic and racial health care disparities. Moreover, the evidence also shows that patients hold implicit biases and thus react to providers' discrimination through the lens of their own experiences with race bias and inequity. The result is a viciously reciprocal cycle of miscommunication between doctors and patients that ultimately harms patients' health. When patients perceive or experience discrimination arising from implicit biases, they respond rationally by seeking to minimize the reoccurrence of the offense. Thus, minority patients are more likely to switch providers, less likely to follow up on or adhere to their doctors' advice, and more likely to generally distrust their providers. Decreased patient satisfaction and decreased continuity of care follow, to the detriment of minority health outcomes. Much of the current discourse on health disparities "blames the victim," charging patients with non-adherence and with poor diet and living choices or alleging the existence of biologically based justifications for inequality. My analysis of patient bias does not belong to this genre. Instead, I employ the evidence that patients unconsciously react negatively to unconscious racism to explain how implicit bias is a culprit on both sides of the clinical encounter, which occurs within a structurally unsound environment that in turn reinforces bias.

Chapter 3 presents a preponderance of evidence showing that providers' disparate treatment of their minority patients is closely associated with their implicit racial and ethnic biases. This chapter identifies physicians' unconscious racism as a primary contributor to health disparities. Chapters 4, 5, and 6 present the Biased Care Model, one of this book's core contributions to advance our understanding of health and health care disparities. The Biased Care Model organizes the best social science literature on implicit bias into a conceptual framework to answer important, but hitherto unresolved questions raised by the Institute of Medicine in its landmark 2003 report on American health disparities. Specifically, the Biased Care Model identifies the mechanisms by which implicit biases affect disparate health outcomes. The model explains how health providers continue to discriminate against minority patients even as polls and surveys tell us that most Americans, especially doctors, are decidedly not racists. The model's mechanisms are grounded in empirical literature and are supported by the voices of doctors and patients whose interviews confirm the presence and influences of implicit biases in their clinical experiences. Thus, the rich qualitative and quantitative data that supports the Biased Care Model spans three chapters. Chapter 4 describes the impact implicit biases have before a physician and patient meet, chapter 5 discusses the role of implicit biases during the clinical encounter, and chapter 6 examines the mechanisms that permit implicit biases to continue contributing to health disparities even after the clinical encounter ends. The questions these chapters confront are tough, and the facts are uncomfortable. The answers the Biased Care Model provides fill an important void in our understanding of the way health inequalities evolve, and thus they lay the foundation for fashioning evidence-based policy solutions.

Chapter 7 introduces an evidentiary "game changer" in the discourse about addressing implicit bias in health care. This chapter explains the social science evidence that implicit racial and ethnic biases are malleable. Contrary to popular fiction, unconscious racism is neither inevitable nor unalterable. This chapter is full of evidence that confirms that the habit of acting out of one's implicit racial biases can be changed. Therefore, the chapter concludes, health care providers and the institutions that employ them can be held morally responsible for addressing the inequities these biases cause. This chapter opens the way for structural responses to the health disparity crisis. The next chapter explains why responding to this crisis is not only a moral responsibility, but also appropriately a legal one.

Chapter 8 answers the question that will plague many health care providers who read this book, especially those who are sympathetic to the cause of justice and equality in health care: Why do we need a law to deal with implicit bias? The short answer is that other avenues will simply not work. Political efforts at universalizing access, regulatory efforts at enforcing cultural competency, and private efforts at "doing the right thing" have all failed. At best, these well-intentioned efforts have only reinforced the culture in which it is assumed that explicit racial motives have little remaining influence on health disparities today. Implicit biases are not entirely impervious to these programs and policies, but the public health policy literature helps to explain why they are insufficient solutions. The more complete answer is that health care disparities are rooted in structural inequities and therefore require a structural solution. Consequently, the legal reforms I propose will change the context in which health care is delivered and shift the social norm that has tolerated health inequality for far too long. The policy problem presented by health care disparities has both the good and bad fortune to be a late-comer to the list of complex practical conundrums that fundamentally challenge broad constitutionally protected American values such as racial equality and justice, but require interventions at the intersection of law and science to solve. For example, law has joined with scientific expertise to help regulate the evolving challenges presented by climate change, genetically modified foods, and pharmacogenomics, just to name a few examples. Accordingly, chapter 8 makes the case for strengthening legal interventions to promote health equality.

Chapter 9 proposes concrete reforms founded on legal and scientific solutions to the problem of racial and ethnic health disparities. This chapter challenges current antidiscrimination law's "naive" assumption that humans act solely in accordance with their explicit and conscious intentions. In fact, the scientific evidence indicates that we all act much more consistently with our unconscious and implicit intentions. I compare the assumptions about human behavior that underlie the current law to what we know about real human behavior as it impacts health and health care, and I argue that antidiscrimination law should better match reality. I conclude with an appeal for action directed towards the four stakeholder groups I hope to impact most: social scientists, health care providers, law- and policy-makers, and patients. I ask each group to consider its role in eradicating health inequality and to consider this book's broader implications for the fight for racial and ethnic equality beyond health care.

While my focus here is on unconscious racism, I do not overlook other determinants of health disparities that will not succumb to legal remedies. Changing only the law will not solve the socioeconomic disparities that lie at the foundation of our society and produce the poor health experienced by many poor people. Yet neither do I use the complexity of the problem and its causes as an excuse to avoid forthrightly addressing the pervasiveness of discriminatory health care. I also cannot shrink from confronting implicit racial bias due to a seemingly paralyzing fear that doing so is the equivalent of charging health care providers with outright racism and bigotry. The cure for this paralysis is an accurate understanding that implicit and unconscious biases are facts of American life that contradict and work against most Americans' true intentions. Physicians are no exception; they need not be racist to discriminate against racial minorities. Nevertheless, discrimination due to implicit bias must be addressed because it unnecessarily decreases the quality and length of life of people in this country who are not white. Distinguishing overt from unconscious racism frees us to honestly and candidly address the problem of providers' implicit bias. In the process, we will see that the scientific evidence is legally sufficient to warrant or even mandate reform of antidiscrimination law.

I reach one primary conclusion in this book. It is that the presently available social science evidence associating implicit racial and ethnic bias with health disparities provides a morally compelling and legally sufficient basis for legal action. A sufficient stack of "further research"— the social scientist's beloved refrain—could not be generated fast enough to slow the devastating effects of implicit bias on the lives of tens of thousands of minority patients each year. Ignoring health disparities due to discrimination is costly. In addition to the nearly 84,000 people of color who needlessly lose their lives annually due to health disparities, there are significant economic burdens imposed by health care discrimination. A 2009 report by the Joint Center for Political and Economic Studies estimated that eliminating health disparities would have reduced direct medical care expenditures by $229.4 billion and indirect costs due to illness and premature death by approximately $1 trillion during 2003–2006.[7] Therefore, the pages that follow unite the medical, neuroscientific, psychological, and sociological expertise on the issue of implicit bias and health disparities with the powerful influence of explicit and enforceable rules of law to devise an effective and innovative plan to reduce implicit biases in health care and eliminate the inequity they cause, so that all in America can enjoy a just, humane health care system, regardless of color, race, or national origin.

1

Bad Law Makes Bad Health

Sickness is not just an isolated event, nor an unfortunate
brush with nature. It is a form of communication—the language of the organs—through which nature, society, and
culture speak simultaneously. The individual body should be
seen as the most immediate, the proximate terrain where social truths and social contradictions are played out.
—Nancy Scheper-Hughes and Margaret M. Lock, "The
Mindful Body"

The first Justice Harlan cautioned long ago that "it is the
duty of all courts of justice to take care, for the general good
of the community, that hard cases do not make bad law." . . .
Courts should observe similar caution with regard to easy
cases. . . . An easy case is especially likely to make bad law
when it is unnecessarily transformed into a hard case.
—Justice John Paul Stevens

A central assertion of this book is that racism—unjust and avoidable
discrimination based on race and ethnicity alone—is a fundamental
cause of destructive and even deadly health disparities in America.[1] The
question of whether the law should prohibit racism in health care would
seem to present an "easy" case for courts and legislators: Yes! In health
care, treating people unfairly based on their race or ethnicity should be
illegal. Because physical and mental health are the most basic requirements for any individual to compete fairly for all other resources and
benefits of life, the law should unquestionably preclude prejudices from
sabotaging an individual's lifelong endeavors. All Americans deserve an
equal opportunity to be healthy without regard to race, color, or ethnicity. Thus, one might expect to find an easy consensus on the importance
of legally regulating racial and ethnic discrimination in health care. But

no such consensus exists. In fact, nowhere has the relationship between law and medicine been more fraught with confusion than in the discourse about how to control racism in health care.

Throughout the pages of this book, I will show how the emergence of *unconscious* rather than overt racism has transformed the easy case for legally prohibiting racial and ethnic discrimination in health care into an unnecessarily difficult case for judges and legislators, as well as for scientists and doctors. Yet I will also show that because the law and health care delivery are inseparably interdependent, a legal approach to racism in health care is essential in order to significantly reduce health disparities. Tragically, the American legal system began during colonial times to sow the seeds of health inequality. The weak legal regime that currently regulates modern health care delivery continues to provide fertile ground for rampant health care discrimination today. Throughout most of our country's history, the rule of law has been perversely instrumental in enabling the racism—both conscious and unconscious—that has produced, and continues to exacerbate, the unjust distribution of health care, as well as other resources that permit people to live healthy lives, such as property, wealth, income, housing, food, employment, and education. To elucidate this dynamic, I identify four significant chronological periods in American history when law and health intersect.

First, during the colonial period, slave codes and land grants (which extinguished Native American rights) played a vicious role in causing injury to minority health because these laws equated the status of minorities to little more than livestock. Thus, even laws that had nothing directly to do with health or health care efficiently created disparate health outcomes merely by reflecting and reinforcing the hegemony that exposed minorities to inferior living and working conditions—conditions that ravaged their health and the health of their descendants. As America's economy and society became more complex, the legal constructs required to maintain racial subordination became increasingly explicit and virulent; laws that controlled access to housing, education, and food inequitably distributed these social determinants of health to whites and withheld them from blacks, Asians, Latinos, and Native Americans.

Second, during the first half of the twentieth century, racism in health care became expressly legal. Law that sanctioned appalling prejudices poured forth from the highest courts and chambers of Congress and from the offices of government in the tiniest American hamlets. Minority health fell victim to an environment of injustice that permeated the nation generally and the delivery of health care specifically. Next, the civil rights era represented a period when the relationship between the law and the state of minority health was positive and symbiotic. Title VI of the Civil Rights Act of 1964 became the weapon of choice in the fight to dismantle segregation in health care. But eventually, seminal civil rights victories gave way to only episodic progress, and then the nation's distaste for segregation in health care came to an end.

Today, we live in the fourth period, when American antidiscrimination law ironically performs an almost identical function to the role colonial law played in ensuring health disparities. Then, as now, law reflects the prevailing societal attitudes and conduct toward racial discrimination. Little more than legal indifference is needed for courts and legislatures to contribute to the destruction of minority health. Both the overt and explicit racism that harmed minority health during our colonial period and the subtle, implicit biases primarily responsible for producing health disparities today operate effectively to destroy minorities' health and lives because lawmakers virtually presume the correctness of the prevailing social order and its inequitable outcomes. This chapter traces chronologically the damage to justice, equality, and health that results from an infirm relationship between American law and medicine. The goal is to demonstrate how legal injustice maps onto minority physical and mental health outcomes and thus must be changed.

Because I am a lawyer married to a heart surgeon, I know that the task of finding common ground between doctors and lawyers can be perilous. In my litigation practice, I often encountered doctors who faced medical malpractice lawsuits, partnership battles, or challenges before peer review boards. These were not happy times. As a result, these physicians greatly distrusted the legal system that entangled them, and even distrusted me as one of its representatives. My physician clients often underscored their distrust of the legal system by referencing spectacular injustices they perceived from medical cases reported in the popular press: recovery for burns from hot coffee, a rapist's charge that a hospital failed to prevent his crime, multimillion dollar verdicts against a doctor for medical tragedies set in motion long before the physician and patient ever met. Still, the inescapable reality is that law and medicine have been symbiotic actors in creating health disparities since America began, and they remain inextricably linked to any meaningful solution to health inequality.

The Colonial Period: The Hegemonic Role of Law

At the dawn of our nation's history, neither Europeans nor their American descendants regarded non-whites as fully human. Thus, European law protected the health of minority persons in much the same way the law might control the health of cattle or yard dogs. For example, Thomas R. R. Cobb, a successful Southern lawyer, described English slavery legislation in his defense of slavery titled "An Inquiry of the Law of Negro Slavery." Cobb reported that an act of British Parliament restricted the number of slaves to be carried on a ship to "five for every three tons, up to 201 tons . . . and by the same act a well–qualified surgeon was required on every vessel" because "disease frequently made sad havoc among the poor creatures."[2] Generally, American law evolved to reflect a similar estimate of the humanity of non-whites. Early American law worked to facilitate the subordination of Native Americans, blacks, and other migrants in the service of the white settlers' emerging political economy.[3] The laws that affected minority health and health care during this period reflected the prevailing, culturally approved views that blacks were no more than "wretched creatures"[4] and in Thomas Jefferson's words, "as incapable as children."[5] Native Americans were deemed "fierce savages"[6] and in Andrew Jackson's words, lacked appreciation for "the causes of their inferiority."[7] The American legal system viewed people of minority descent as subhuman, and thus disregarded their health accordingly.

Early property laws provide an excellent example of the law's hegemonic role. Although they were aimed at governing land use, English and colonial property laws indirectly but dramatically affected Native Americans' health by facilitating racial hierarchy and domination by whites to the detriment of minority health and wellbeing. Thus, the legal right to claim land ownership was an early determinant of who might experience inferior or superior health in America. In 1609, King James I of England issued patent letters giving over titles of land he did not own to European settlers who claimed legal possession of land upon arrival to the world that was "New" to them. Later in 1823, the United States Supreme Court relied upon the "discovery" and forcible "conquest" of these lands to declare that this system of granting land titles from chartered colonies to English settlers had legally established the superior ownership of the white settlers as against the "savage tribes" that preceded them.[8] Colonists premised their property titles on claims of racial superiority in order to defeat any right or claim Native Americans might have had to the land they occupied and used before the whites arrived.[9] In *Johnson and Graham's Lessee v. William M'Intosh*, Chief Justice John Marshall cited a 1609 patent letter from the King of England to explain the necessity of expelling Indians from the land that had been their home, in order to transfer title to European settlers "by conquest," saying that

> the tribes of Indians inhabiting this country were fierce savages, whose occupation was war, and whose subsistence was drawn chiefly from the forest. To leave them in possession of their country, was to leave the country a wilderness; to govern them as a distinct people, was impossible because they were as brave and as high spirited as they were fierce.[10]

European settlers relied upon this legally sanctioned view to claim land ownership and build their farms, fences, and homes on lands previously settled by Native Americans. In this way, the laws that conferred private property rights to facilitate westward expansion, which history now reveals led to widespread dissemination of European-borne illnesses such as smallpox, measles, influenza, and other communicable diseases, also facilitated the decimation of millions of Native Americans who lacked immunological protection against foreign germs.[11] Certainly, the legal charters and land rights cannot be charged with directly causing the ill health and death that Indians suffered when whites began settling under the protection of English and American law. Nevertheless, the protections that the law provided to European settlers conflicted directly with the prior claims that Native Americans who preceded them had to the land, making it possible for colonists to settle among the indigenous people and introduce disease and destruction of entire populations. Some persuasively argue that these colonial plagues continue to manifest in health disparities today.[12]

Property laws also worked to the detriment of black people's health during the colonial period. When the European settlers brought African slaves to America, the courts enforced laws that deemed human beings to be mere property and thereby enabled whites to maintain their dominance over, and general cruelty toward, blacks. Judicial decisions such as the infamous *Dred Scott*[13] case provided protection to colonial slave owners, guaranteeing not only their financial ownership rights, but also their right to treat enslaved Africans inhumanely. Often this meant that blacks were deprived of health care and healthy living conditions. A legal regime prevailed that permitted slave owners to provide only the minimal food, shelter, and medical care necessary to protect their financial investment in humans as property and preserve income that flowed from the slaves' ability to work. Records document black slaves suffering and dying from maladies for which whites commonly received basic medical treatment.[14] Slave children playing in filth were regularly susceptible to worms. Adults working and living with little protection against the elements were frequently victims of dysentery, infection, and cold. Historians record slave accounts of their quarters where waste and sewage flowed in drinking water, parasitic worms proliferated, and people without adequate shelter regularly suffered frostbite, infection, and illnesses that could have been easily avoided.[15] Dr. Todd Savitt reports that slaveholders took into account the law that identified slaves as chattel to determine the treatment that medical problems received and to justify slaves' living and working conditions.[16]

Considered by law as property, ill slaves were often tended to by their owners, receiving medical treatment from a doctor only as a last resort and then in connection with the need to ensure their productive labor. The following letter from a Virginia slave owner, calling for a Fredericksburg physician, is one of many available examples in the historical record.

Doctr James Carmichael or Doctr Edwd H Carmichael
I send my Boy Israel down for youto examine him, I have examined
him, and find he has got the Pox, will you give him what medicine that
is necessary and write the directions very plain that it may be understood by any person—as I cannot be at home to attend to him myself . . .
and my overseer will have to do it. Please write very particularly, and let

him be cured as soon as possible for he is my best hand to the Plow and
I am about to seed Wheat, and am now loosing [sic]by his improvidence
I am Sir Yr Most Obt Sevt
F S Stoel
[unclear] Oct. 3rd 1820[17]

Remarkably, the author of this letter sent "Boy Israel" to a physician for care only after his own efforts failed; he sought the patient's recovery "as soon as possible" solely because he was needed to return to plowing and seeding. In the end of the letter, the author blamed the slave's "improvidence" for imposing financial loss on the master. The role of law in early American history functioned to preserve the power and privilege that allowed whites to remain oblivious to the health needs of blacks and Native Americans, except as those health needs impacted white interests.

The Seeds of Segregation: Legalized Racism

During the nineteenth-century industrial revolution, the American legal system operated to restrict minority access to the social determinants of good health. The law was instrumental in inequitably distributing resources such as clean housing, safe employment, and healthy food. As the growing American economy lured more foreign workers to our shores, housing, labor, and immigration laws figured prominently in creating segregated and unsanitary living arrangements. Ghettos densely packed with immigrant workers became vectors for the spread of disease among minority populations. These were made possible by laws such as the municipal ordinances enacted throughout the 1800s that encouraged Chinese laborers to migrate to work on America's railroads but prohibited them from becoming naturalized citizens.[18] As a result, these workers remained unwelcomed outside of their work venues. An 1890 ordinance prohibited Chinese immigrants from living or working anywhere in the city except in prescribed ghettos.[19] A court in 1901 spoke disparagingly of the Asian community's living conditions while imposing a criminal fine for "giving aid to the bringing of aliens to this country under contract." The district judge complained of the "evil" that West Coast states had been "overrun by the Chinese, until the traffic in coolies became a scandal." Referring to their overcrowded neighborhoods, the judge explained that Congress had enacted a law to limit Chinese immigration "partly because of their immoralities, but largely because from their methods of living they could underbid American workmen."[20]

Historian David LaVigne, who has studied recollections of immigrants to America, documents the health-harming impact of legally enforced residential segregation:

> Living conditions most starkly reflected the depths of immigrant poverty. Workers packed into shabbily built shanties or clustered into overcrowded and unsanitary tenement houses. Historian Peter Way notes that "canal 'contractors' often provided shelter for their hands as a means of keeping a stable of workers; and 'stable' is the right word, as the accommodations often did not differ significantly from those given the horses and oxen." It probably did not help that animals sometimes did share living quarters with humans. . . . In such impoverished conditions, disease and death flourished. Epidemics of tuberculosis, dysentery, typhoid, and cholera periodically spread through urban slums. . . . [A]n Irish immigrant wrote in a letter to County Cork that "it is a well-established fact . . . that the average length of life of the emigrant after landing here is six years; and many insist it is much less." The writer may have exaggerated, but the Irish did indeed suffer higher disease and infant mortality rates than any other sector of the population.[21]

De jure segregation ordinances isolated immigrants in squalid living quarters where communicable diseases flourished, but criminal laws also proved useful in keeping newly arrived workers separated from white neighborhoods and communities. Vagrancy laws passed under the guise of controlling the use of public spaces were often applied to keep minorities herded into ghettos where filth and disease flourished. In the South, vagrancy laws allowed police to arrest blacks for straying into white neighborhoods and to place them on prison work gangs.[22] In California, the legislature enacted an anti-vagrancy statute in 1855 that was commonly called "the Greaser Act." This odious law applied to "all persons who are commonly known as Greasers or the issue of Spanish and Indian blood . . . and who go armed and are not peaceable and quiet persons."[23] In addition to vagrancy laws, restrictive land covenants made segregation legally enforceable so that not only were desirable neighborhoods reserved for whites, but also unhealthy and hazardous locations were designated as sites for minority residences.[24] And once minority populations were segregated in unhealthy enclaves, zoning laws located garbage dumps, incinerators, and hazardous waste sites away from affluent neighborhoods and nearest to neighborhoods where minorities lived, disproportionately exposing these groups to further health hazards and risks.[25] At the same time, local land use regulation preserved the whiteness of healthy neighborhoods by ensuring these neighborhoods were beyond reach for minorities.[26] Beyond laws that produced residential segregation, legal regulations that governed employment and immigration also adversely affected minority health.

After the 1849 Mexican-American War, territory that formerly belonged to Mexico became American soil. Immigrants attracted to jobs in these regions could either accept deplorable working conditions or face the threat of jail or deportation for violating immigration provisions. Injury and death rates were highest in agriculture, where 80 percent of workers toiled outside and faced varying weather conditions, were frequently infected by bacteria, or were injured by animals. However, Mexican workers held other dangerous jobs, including mining and railroad work, where lax labor laws permitted low wages, long hours, and unhealthy working conditions.[27] Many southern states enacted another body of labor laws called the "black codes" to keep freed slaves subordinated immediately after the Civil War and to regulate all aspects of their lives, from voting rights, education, and jury service to marriage and religious assembly. The black codes are another example of nineteenth-century legal restrictions on employment that affected minority health. These laws required blacks to obtain permits to perform anything other than agricultural work and prohibited them from raising their own crops.[28] Travel permit requirements and limitations on labor options enforced food and job insecurity. Because southern white plantation owners no longer profited from a healthy black slave population during this antebellum period, physicians and hospitals simply refused to provide medical treatment to blacks. After slavery ended, blacks were largely denied any access to health care until Congress established the Freedmen's Bureau medical division.[29] Taking together the discriminatory property, housing, labor, and immigration laws that prevailed during our nation's early history, we can make a strong case that these inequitable restrictions on access to the most basic social determinants of health directly contributed to the inferior health status indicators that minorities continue to suffer today.[30] However, as the nation entered the twentieth century, legal restrictions extended beyond the social determinants of health, and the American legal system became directly and overtly hostile to minority health. Legalized racial discrimination in health care added to the derivative impact that more general laws had on minority health during the colonial and post–Civil War periods.

By the turn of the century, minority health and health care became the explicit subject of American law so that public health laws joined other bodies of law that ensured separation among the races. Public health law provisions expressly operationalized race-based stigmas and prejudices. In May 1900, the San Francisco Board of Health adopted a resolution requiring the city's 25,000 Chinese residents—and only its Chinese residents—to submit to inoculation with a dangerous serum called "Haffkine Prophylactic" or suffer quarantine, ostensibly to prevent the spread of bubonic plague. The resolution was later struck down as unconstitutional[31] when it was revealed that the serum was in fact harmful and the threat of plague conjecture.[32] In another American city, Mexican laborers working to build American railways became the victims of a typhus outbreak. In 1916, twenty-six people contracted typhus; twenty-two were Mexican. Moreover, all five victims who died from the disease were Mexican railroad workers. As a result, the Mexican community was declared "pathogenic" and became the target of intrusive hygiene inspections and an aggressive educational and sanitation campaign.[33] State-sponsored efforts to contain the typhus epidemic simply ignored the unsanitary living and unhealthy working conditions the workers endured, unmindful of the contribution these environmental conditions may have made to the typhus problem. The injustice of this discriminatory public health effort prompted one group of Mexican workers to write a letter objecting to the "offensive and humiliating" treatment they received at the hands of health inspectors. The letter protested against wages that were too low "for the nourishment of one person," the lack of adequate bathroom facilities, the location of overtaxed toilets near cooking and sleeping areas in their camps, and "many other details which compromise our good health and personal hygiene."[34]

Health care law also became a mechanism by which prejudice inflicted harm on racial minority populations. The law excluded minorities from receiving the same health care as the nation afforded to whites. Minority patients were relegated to less well staffed, equipped, and appointed facilities where they received an inferior quality of health care as compared to white patients.[35] In 1751, Benjamin Franklin and Dr. Thomas Bond founded the nation's first in-patient hospital, Pennsylvania Hospital, in Philadelphia; it was dedicated exclusively to the care of the poor and insane. Although this institution was called "Anglo-America's First Hospital," some records show that blacks and whites shared the same wards at first.[36] However, by 1825, the Pennsylvania Hospital's records provide evidence that hospitals began to admit black patients only into segregated wards. Shortly thereafter, by 1832, entirely separate hospitals began to appear to treat non-white patients. This segregationist policy was enforced by the rule of law when the Supreme Court infamously constitutionalized the "separate but equal" doctrine in *Plessy v. Ferguson*.[37] Throughout the nation, laws from federal pronouncements to local ordinances mandated segregation in private and public facilities including hospitals. For example, federal treaties with Native Americans allowed them to receive vaccinations to protect against diseases that European settlers introduced such as smallpox, but expressly stipulated that their care was not to be rendered in the same buildings or health care facilities as whites or blacks. Thus minorities received care in makeshift hospital wards located in basements or "cast-off" facilities vacated after whites moved to more modern ones. Often plumbing facilities as well as medical equipment were inadequate, and staffing reflected the availability of physicians who could attend to minority patients "after hours."

Following the Civil War, separate hospitals to treat newly freed African Americans sprung up in Washington, D.C. (1862), Philadelphia (1895), North Carolina (1901), and Michigan (1918) as minorities built institutions to address their own health needs. In 1852, Mt. Sinai Hospital opened in New York City to treat Jewish immigrants who were unwelcome in other hospitals. To the extent that hospitals admitted minority as well as white patients, these institutions maintained separate wards and floors for African American patients.[38] State legislatures passed laws to ensure unequal treatment. In Alabama, for example, white nurses were prohibited from even entering rooms where black men were patients. Several states, including Mississippi, enacted laws to require separate hospital entrances for "colored" patients and visitors.

Throughout the first half of the twentieth century, the laws that organized health care and public health formed a system that guaranteed inferior quality health care to minority patients. The result was devastating. Beginning in 1850, when life expectancy and infant mortality rates were first recorded for blacks in America, the indicators were grossly disproportionate: While whites enjoyed an average life expectancy of 39.5 years, 16.5 years longer than blacks, infant mortality was 57 percent greater for blacks than for whites, even though black birthrates were 35 percent higher. In 1900, when W. E. B. Du Bois recorded death rates for eleven cities during the period from 1725 to 1853, he concluded, "while the colored death rate greatly exceeds the white, the improvement is manifest in both races." However, Du Bois went further to analyze the structural causes of disparate mortality rates:

> How much is the Negro death rate affected by environment? One has only to compare the wretched Negro quarters of Charleston and New Orleans, with a death rate of over 40 per 1,000 with the far better although not ideal conditions in Atlanta and Louisville, with a death rate of 30 per 1,000. . . . When we remember that the highest death rate among occupations is for laborers and servants (20.2 per 1,000) we see here another contributing cause of high Negro mortality.[39]

The Du Bois study may be the earliest published study to highlight the important impact that social determinants have on health outcomes. His analysis connected racially disparate mortality rates to the inequitable conditions that prevailed where minorities lived, worked, and accessed health care.

In 1946, Congress codified the onerous separate-but-equal doctrine specifically for hospitals in the Hospital Survey and Construction Act, known popularly as the "Hill-Burton Act." Its purpose was to provide federal funding for hospital construction and modernization after World War II. Under the act, the U.S. government contributed over $4.2

billion in public funds to build and upgrade hospitals while at the same time protecting their segregationist policies. That is, although the act contained a nondiscrimination provision, an exception was made in cases where "separate hospital facilities are provided for separate population groups, if the plan makes equitable provision on the basis of need for facilities and services of like quality for each such group." Thus the Hill-Burton Act codified, and federal courts upheld, racist segregation in public and private hospitals through much of the twentieth century. In 1979, litigants in *Cook v. Ochsner Foundation Hospital et al.* challenged discriminatory hospital practices such as refusal to admit Medicaid patients and, as a result, Congress and the Department of Health and Human Services (DHHS) revised the law to eliminate the separate-but-equal provisions.

During the Jim Crow era, the equal protection provisions of the United States Constitution proved no match for America's legal commitment to racial segregation and discrimination. Litigation to make health providers comply with minority patients' constitutionally protected rights proved futile. In a 1955 Arkansas case, a state hospital for mentally impaired patients won a challenge to its segregation policy with the help of an Arkansas federal court willing to sidestep the constitutional issues. The hospital claimed that it denied admission to an eleven-year-old Negro boy because he was not mentally ill enough to be a patient at the hospital and because the hospital was full. Both defenses were questionable. Two days earlier, a sheriff had escorted the same child to the institution to admit him because an Arkansas probate court had issued an order of committal certifying that he suffered "from mental disease or psychosis as to need hospitalization." The evidence in the case showed that his IQ was "at the most only of 25," and his grandmother testified that he understood little or no English, was unable to distinguish hot from cold, and whenever he was outside his room, he had to be tied or chained to keep him from wandering away or injuring himself.[40] Yet, the court in *Johnson v. Crawfis*[41] found it "practically undisputed that the plaintiff [was] simply a mental deficient and without psychosis." Then, pointing out that other Negro patients were admitted to the hospital, the *Johnson* court concluded the state hospital properly exercised its discretion not to admit Negro patients beyond the number of beds assigned to them. The court avoided ruling on the fundamental injustice of the hospital's segregation practices and said that the constitutional equal protection question was "drawn into the case by a gratuitous argument on behalf of the defendant" but not properly raised by the plaintiff's complaint. This case is but one example of the way that the law winked at racial discrimination in American hospitals.

In 1958, privatization protected a once-public hospital in Wilmington, North Carolina, from a constitutional challenge to its practice of denying admission to black patients by refusing to grant admitting privileges to their black physicians.[42] In *Eaton v. James Walker Memorial Hospital*, three African American physicians sued the hospital, alleging that the hospital had denied them courtesy staff privileges solely on the basis of their race. The *Eaton* plaintiffs argued the hospital violated Sections 1981 and 1983 of the Civil Rights Acts of 1870 and 1871, and the Equal Protection Clause of the Constitution's Fourteenth Amendment. The antidiscrimination laws at the core of this case were a set of statutes called the "Reconstruction Statutes." These laws are generally known by their numeric sections, preceded by a "§" symbol, and they apply to all entities that receive federal funds. For example, the Reconstruction Statutes apply to health care providers such as hospitals that receive federal funding from Medicare and other public health insurance programs to pay for patient care.

These civil rights laws were designed to prevent discrimination by providing victims of discrimination an avenue to recover money damages against organizations that break the laws. When publicly funded organizations discriminate, individuals who claim their civil rights have been violated can sue the offender in federal court.[43] The first statute, 42 U.S.C. § 1981, prohibits discrimination based on race, color, or national origin in the making and enforcement of contracts; it ensures that all citizens have the "full and equal benefit of all laws and proceedings for the security of persons and property as is enjoyed by white citizens." The second statute, 42 U.S.C. § 1983, provides an opportunity for individuals to sue to enforce the rights guaranteed under the United States Constitution or other federal laws. Finally, 42 U.S.C. § 1985 prohibits conspiracies from interfering with civil rights and gives individuals an opportunity to collect money damages from coconspirators if they prevail in a private antidiscrimination lawsuit. Notwithstanding the unequivocal and indeed lofty antidiscrimination language of the Reconstruction Statutes, plaintiffs in the 1958 hospital discrimination case were unable to realize the law's promise of equality.

The plaintiffs suing in Wilmington, North Carolina, lost their case because the court concluded that, as a private entity, Walker Memorial Hospital was not subject to the Constitution's equal protection requirements. Although the hospital was chartered as a public institution in 1881, in 1901 the city and county conveyed the public land on which the hospital was located to a private board of managers. The board then charted the hospital as a private corporation because it was "desirable that the management of the hospital be removed as far as possible from the control of local municipal authorities, subject to changing political conditions."[44] Thus, using the legal maneuver of private conveyance, a publicly financed hospital transformed itself to avoid providing health care services to black patients and their doctors. Although the early twentieth-century legal challenges to segregated medical care were not successful, eventually repeated litigation inspired Congress to enact the Civil Rights Act of 1964, which at long last breathed life into the Constitution's promise of equal protection for all. The most important case that influenced Congress to enact the new civil rights law was a case that involved racial discrimination by a North Carolina hospital.

The Civil Rights Era: Legal Attacks on a Divided Health Care System

Simkins v. Moses H. Cone Memorial Hospital[45] is the watershed case that marked the beginning of a period of civil rights victories for plaintiffs mounting legal challenges to the practice of delivering inferior medical care to blacks solely because of their race. The *Simkins* case was brought by six African American physicians, three African American dentists, and two African American patients. The *Simkins* plaintiff group sued collectively to raise Fifth and Fourteenth Amendment challenges to the constitutionality of the two defendant hospitals' segregation policies, and also to challenge Congress's exercise of its spending power under the Hill-Burton Act. The plaintiffs prevailed, and the Fourth Circuit Court of Appeals held the separate-but-equal language of the Hill-Burton Act unconstitutional, declaring that "Racial discrimination by hospitals visits severe consequences upon Negro physicians and their patients." Following *Simkins*, civil rights plaintiffs argued and won antidiscrimination litigation in Virginia, Mississippi, and other states, further desegregating hospitals across the nation.

Moreover, when Congress debated the bill that became Title VI of the Civil Rights Act of 1964, many legislators cited the *Simkins* decision. The battle to enact federal legislation to end segregation in America gained potency because the *Simkins* plaintiffs based their constitutional challenges on the appropriate use of the federal government's spending power. Title VI provides that "No person in the United States shall, on the ground of race, color or national origin, be excluded from participation in, be denied the benefits of, or be subjected to discrimination under any program or activity receiving Federal financial assistance." Of course, virtually every health care organization in America receives some form of federal funding either in the form of health insurance reimbursements from Medicare, Medicaid, or the Children's Insurance Program, or as research grants from the National Institutes of Health, the National Institute of Minority Health and Health Disparities, or the Indian Health Program. Therefore, Title VI leverages the authority called the "spending power" that Congress has under the Constitution to control how federal funds are spent. Title VI prohibits discrimination or the denial of benefits by recipients of federal funding to any person on the ground of their race, color, or national origin by permitting two types of lawsuits.

The first action available under Title VI is called a "disparate impact" claim. In this type of case, the plaintiff alleges that an organization's policy, which appears to be racially neutral, actually has a disproportionately adverse effect on minorities in violation of the Title VI prohibition. The second cause of action permitted by Title VI is called a "disparate treatment" claim. To prevail in this case, the plaintiff must show proof that the defendant's discriminatory acts were intentional. Moreover, this second type of lawsuit is the only one that individual plaintiffs— patients, for example—can bring directly against a defendant such as a health care provider. The disparate treatment cases have ceased to be relevant in health care because few providers today treat patients with a demonstrable intent to discriminate.

In addition to constitutional provisions, state statutes, and federal statutes, there are other laws that prohibit discrimination in health care. These laws, called "regulations," are promulgated by administrative agencies that govern various aspects of health care delivery in the United States. In the case of health care organizations, the Department of Health and Human Services (DHHS) is the agency that has authority to enact regulations that govern health care delivery. The regulations found under Title 45 of the Code of Federal Regulations (CFR) were enacted "to effectuate the provisions of Title VI of the Civil Rights Act of 1964"[46] after the act was passed by Congress. They have been updated several times, and lawsuits to enforce Title VI and these accompanying regulations were instrumental in tearing down segregation in American health care organizations through the close of the twentieth century.

In 1969, a consolidated class action suit brought under Title VI ended the "separate and unequal services" policy practiced throughout all of Alabama's mental health system. The court in *Marable v. Alabama Mental Health Board*[47] was "clear to the conclusion that the segregation and discrimination based on race practiced by Alabama officials in the mental health system violate the rights of the plaintiff, Marable and his class under the Equal Protection Clause of the Fourteenth Amendment."[48] Several subsequent Title VI attacks on disparate health care also succeeded by alleging that exclusion or termination of minority physician privileges violated the Constitution. In one 1994 case, a patient successfully challenged a Title VI violation when she was denied medical care based on her African ethnicity and won the right to obtain fair access to HIV treatment.[49] In still another case brought by the Department of Health and Human Services, the federal government successfully defended its authority to inspect the credentialing and peer-review records of hospitals that received Medicare and Medicaid reimbursements in order to confirm their compliance with Title VI antidiscrimination provisions.[50]

From 1963 through the early 1990s, Title VI proved an effective weapon against the segregation and discrimination that minority patients and physicians had experienced in American health care since the colonial era. As late as 1995, a Title VI case brought in Tennessee effectively addressed a subtle but devastatingly discriminatory practice. The court in *Linton v. Commissioner* found the state's policy of certifying specific beds for Medicaid patients while opening all other beds for private paying patients violated Title VI and the Medicaid Act because the policy disproportionately excluded black and other minority patients from nursing-home care. The certification policy reserved superior facilities for whites while frail and elderly blacks were relegated to poorly funded, substandard boarding homes.[51] However, courts began to reject Title VI challenges to racial and ethnic discrimination in health care as the civil rights era came to a close. For example, in 1986, a Korean physician, alleging that he and the minority patients whom he served were harmed when his hospital privileges were wrongly terminated, lost his case when the court found he was not the intended beneficiary of the federal funds that reimbursed the medical care he provided.[52] Although Title VI effectively combated blatant racial segregation and discrimination for nearly two decades, by the end of the twentieth century, Title VI, and antidiscrimination law generally, became ineffective.

The Law of Post-Racial America: Intentionality, Causation, and Health Disparities

Following the civil rights era, courts uniformly rejected antidiscrimination efforts when minority communities tried to use Title VI to argue that the emerging pattern of hospital relocation away from urban centers to suburbia caused harm to minority communities' access to health care.[53] For example, in *Bryan v. Koch*,[54] a 1980 case challenging New York City's decision to close Sydenham Hospital, the court held that the plaintiff failed to show that the city had discriminatory intent to harm the predominately African American and Hispanic patients whom the closed hospital had served. During the same year, a federal district court in Delaware in *N.A.A.C.P. v. Wilmington Medical Center*[55] similarly rejected the Title VI claims brought by several civil rights groups. The plaintiff groups united the black, Hispanic, and disabled communities to argue that hospital mergers would disproportionately impact minority patients' access to care. They asserted that by relocating to an affluent, white suburb, the urban facility left behind would become "a 'ghetto' hospital serving the poor, the elderly, the handicapped, blacks, and Puerto Ricans." However, the court held the plaintiffs had "failed in all respects to show a violation of Title VI."

Although litigation based on the constitutional promises of equal protection and due process was successful in early health care desegregation cases, civil rights litigation became an ineffective weapon against health care disparities that originated from more subtle forms of prejudice by the end of the 1990s. Ironically, the geographic region of the nation that enacted some of the most racially oppressive black code laws also was most positively impacted by the civil rights era litigation. Today, southern Medicare hospitals are the most racially *de*-segregated hospitals in the country. However, racial segregation persists in hospitals nationally, especially in the Midwest and in northeast metropolitan areas.[56] This re-emergent pattern of segregated health care outside the South is directly related to the fact that cases brought under Title VI, the Reconstruction Statutes, and the Hill-Burton Act came to a screeching halt at the turn of the twenty-first century.

In 2001 the Supreme Court delivered the decisive blow to the efficacy of Title VI as a way to end segregation and discrimination in health care. The Court decided in *Alexander v. Sandoval* that while Title VI permits private individuals to challenge *intentional* discrimination by bringing disparate treatment claims, private parties may no longer bring disparate impact claims based on unintentional discrimination that have a statistically demonstrated discriminatory effect on minorities.[57] Since the *Sandoval* case, private plaintiffs such as the physicians, dentists, and patients who won pivotal civil-rights-era desegregation cases in courtrooms, instead must rely primarily upon agency enforcement to address modern forms of hospital segregation. Individuals may still obtain injunctive and declaratory relief under Title VI, but they may do so only by proving a defendant provider intentionally discriminated against a minority patient. In fact, proving intentional discrimination is nearly impossible when few Americans are careless enough to create an evidentiary record of outright bigotry. And while the Supreme Court has so far held that disparate impact actions under Title VI may be administratively enforced, the truth is that the governmental agencies charged with this task are underfunded and overextended and rarely pursue these claims. For all intents and purposes, through *Alexander v. Sandoval*, the Supreme Court has made Title VI into a dead letter with regard to fighting racial and ethnic discrimination in health care.[58] According to one legal expert, the "timid and ineffectual enforcement efforts of the government through the Office of Civil Rights (OCR) at the U.S. Department of Health and Human Services (DHHS) have fostered, rather than combated, the discrimination that continues to infect the nation's health care system."[59]

Most of the recent cases brought against health care providers allege discrimination against the disabled but few attack racial or ethnic inequality. OCR reports numerous settlement agreements with providers ranging from dialysis centers to nursing homes where the civil rights claim is brought to allege that the defendant violated the Americans with Disabilities Act (ADA) by failing to provide sign language interpreters for the hearing impaired. Other cases use antidiscrimination law to challenge hospital staff privilege decisions.[60] One recent OCR case indirectly addressed race and ethnicity health disparities. In *Madison-Hughes v. Shalala*,[61] the Sixth Circuit Court of Appeals affirmed dismissal of a lawsuit brought to allege that the DHHS was failing to comply with Title VI regulations that require health care organizations to collect race and ethnicity data. Nearly sixty years after the *Brown* decision and fifty years after Title VI was enacted, the pace of litigation to enforce antidiscrimination provisions under the law has slowed considerably, in large part because the laws that once provided potent offensive weaponry in the fight against segregation have been neutralized. This neutralization was accomplished partly through decisions handed down from the United States Supreme Court and partly by changes in the nature and complexity of discrimination itself. The current state of affairs is this: Antidiscrimination laws are largely unenforced[62] or unenforceable against health care entities, while an overwhelming body of empirical evidence makes clear that discriminatory practices in health care abound.

The Legal Legacy: A Persistent Gap between Minority and White Health and Health Care in America

The profoundly disturbing volume and consistency of data showing that African Americans, Latinos, Asians, and Native Americans receive inferior medical care and suffer worse health outcomes when compared with whites is the subject of future chapters.[63] This chapter posits that legal structures play a major role in creating this health inequality. Throughout American history, minorities have suffered higher morbidity and mortality than whites in virtually every disease and injury category since health records have been kept. The historical record shows how laws have directly and indirectly contributed to these disparities. Moreover, in the absence of legal redress, the problem of health inequality continues to worsen. In most measured categories, health disparities between minorities and whites are widening.[64] A large and important study designed by Dr. Kathleen Harris demonstrates why.

Dr. Harris followed an ethnically diverse cohort of more than 14,000 youths over an eight-year period, from adolescence to young adulthood. This longitudinal study showed that as people grow older, health risks increase, while health access decreases from teen to adult years for most racial and ethnic minorities when compared to whites in the United States.[65] Although no single racial or ethnic group consistently ranked as the best or worst for any of the twenty health indicators Dr. Harris studied, she observes that "the trend lines fan out, indicating increasing disparity in young adulthood, highest among black vs. white subjects. . . . The overall patterns of health disparities include significantly different trends for black relative to white female subjects across almost all domains. Among male subjects, the black-white disparity in trends was significant for more than half of the indicators. For both sexes, the white-Hispanic disparity in health trends was significant for 35% of the indicators."[66] It is important to note that in this study, no changes in ethnic and racial disparities resulted when the researchers controlled for disparate socioeconomic status among the youth. Dr. Harris's study shows, therefore, that in America, health gaps between minorities and whites generally widen as people age, notwithstanding their education, income, or ability to pay for health care.

Mental health care disparities are also worsening. A study by Dr. Carlos Blanco published in the journal *Medical Care* concluded that "from 1993 to 2002 there was an increase in mental health care disparities between Hispanics and non-Hispanics treated by office-based physicians."[67] This study examined the number of office visits, rates of diagnosis, and types of treatment mentally ill Hispanics and whites received for three time periods. Dr. Blanco's results showed that Hispanics received less mental health care than whites over time, and that when they did access care, their visits resulted in a diagnosis of mental disorder less frequently than for whites. Hispanics also received psychotropic medication prescriptions less often than whites. Lastly, psychotherapy visits declined over time for Hispanics while remaining constant for whites.

The researchers in this study concluded that mental health care disparities between Hispanic and non-Hispanic patients worsened between 1993 and 2002.[68] These widening health disparities deserve particular attention because they are unjust and avoidable. As the remainder of this book points out, it is important to clearly understand that the racial and ethnic discrimination that causes health disparities can and should be legally prohibited.

Figure 1.1 graphically isolates the racial and ethnic health disparities that are the focus of this book. The bar chart represents the differences in the quality of care that nonminority and minority patients receive. The boxes to the right explain the various sources of those differences. However, the point I wish to make from the diagram is that while justifiable "differences" in the quality of care that minority and nonminority patients receive can relate to clinical appropriateness or patient preferences, when differences are related solely to race and ethnicity, they become "disparities" and are unjustifiable. Throughout this book, I am not concerned with justifiable differences between white and minority health care and health outcomes. Rather, my attention is devoted to examining health care and health outcome disparities that arise from individual and institutional discrimination based on race, color, or national origin. These disparities are not just differences; they are fundamental inequalities, which are both unjustifiable and aptly described as unjust. Health inequality due to racial and ethnic discrimination represents exactly the type of injustice scores of state and federal antidiscrimination laws and the United States Constitution itself arguably are intended to prevent. However, subtle changes in the prevalent forms of discrimination have stymied legal remedies.

Americans now seldom espouse the overt racism, prejudice and bigotry that our laws prohibit. To be clear, direct and explicit racial bias still exists and operates to cause discrimination in health care delivery today, as it does elsewhere in America. For example, the ugly choice to believe that African Americans as a people group are inferior or uniformly uneducated when compared to whites or to assume a priori that Latinos do not deserve to benefit from American health care because they are "illegals" still motivates some physicians to give better medical care to their white patients than they do to their black or Hispanic patients.[69] However, this type of overt racial prejudice and racism has dramatically

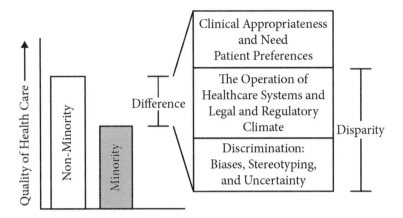

Figure 1.1. Isolating health inequality due to race and ethnicity. *Source*: Institute of Medicine Report, *Unequal Treatment: Confronting Racial and Ethnic Disparities in Health Care* (Washington, DC: National Academy of Sciences, 2003).

declined over the past half-century and is no longer the predominant mechanism by which health care discrimination occurs.[70] It is fair to say that today Americans share a collective belief that racial and ethnic discrimination is morally wrong. However, not surprisingly, we divide along racial lines on the question of whether, despite this belief, racial and ethnic discrimination does in fact continue to occur today and whether one's race or ethnicity matters in twenty-first-century America.

Americans who are members of minority groups—African, Hispanic, Native, and Asian Americans—all report to varying degrees that race still matters and that race discrimination, in their personal experience, is alive and well. Surveys show that few whites, on the other hand, believe that race is an important consideration in American life. Even fewer whites believe that discrimination continues to occur. A small 6 percent of white Americans polled say that they think about race at all, while over 95 percent of white Americans asked believe they are racially unbiased. In contrast, 35 percent of blacks and 20 percent of Hispanics say they have been discriminated against or treated unfairly because of their race in the past year.[71] This dichotomy plays out in health care as it does in the general population. Most physicians in this country are white. Therefore, most physicians believe as other white Americans do, that they are racially unbiased. In contrast, as with the general population, over half the black and Latino patients surveyed believe the health care system treats people unfairly based on their race or ethnicity.[72]

The explanation for these apparently mutually exclusive viewpoints is that both are correct from their respective perspectives. The bias and prejudice that patients of color perceive is real and accurate as a matter of their experience. However, their experiences occur as a result of behavior that is motivated by beliefs and biases that medical providers have no idea they hold. This phenomenon is called "unconscious racism" or "implicit bias," and it is responsible for the vast majority of racial and ethnic discrimination that persists in health care today. Physicians and other health providers contribute to disparate treatment of disease and sickness between majority and minority patients without even knowing they are doing so, and without any intention or awareness that they hold racially skewed viewpoints. Even patients contribute to disparate health outcomes without knowing they are behaving in accord with biases of which they are unaware. The contribution of unconscious racism to health disparity should not be ignored.

In this chapter, I have explored the relationship among law, discrimination, and health. I examined the many ways in which laws have historically contributed to health and health care inequality during America's transition from an overtly racist country to a presumptively post-racial society. This first chapter lays the foundation for the case in favor of using law to forbid unconscious racial and ethnic discrimination in health care. Indeed, at its core, the purpose of this book is to argue that the case for prohibiting all racism in health care is still an easy one and, as Justice Stevens admonished, must not be unnecessarily transformed into a hard case. In order to understand how and why unconscious racism might be legally regulated, however, I must first explain how these implicit attitudes operate to contribute to health disparities. The next chapter describes the "mechanics" of how implicit biases work to negatively impact patient health outcomes and cause health care disparities.

2

Implicit Bias and Health Disparities

I was surprised by the health care disparities. . . . I read a paper about a year ago about the disparities in adults using race
and ethnicity and it surprised me. . . . So I came back home
and had one of our residents use the kids' database, which is
a large, national administrative database, to look and see if
there were disparities at the same level in pediatric practice.
And it turned out to my surprise that there are. And we have
the same problem. We don't know why it is and there are a
lot of reasons why it might be. . . . I was surprised because I
thought pediatricians were more into their patients and into
their families. . . . But our results . . . were surprising to me.
—Professor of Pediatric Surgery, University Medical Center,
Southeastern United States

During my interviews with physicians, I was surprised to learn that
some are still unaware that health care disparities exist.[1] Among the
many more who were aware that racial and ethnic disparities are prevalent in America, most, like the doctor quoted above, did not believe
such disparities plagued their particular practices or specialties. And
almost none of the physicians I interviewed thought they contributed
personally to disparities among their patients or that they were personally influenced by implicit racial and ethnic biases. None accepted the
assertion that they might be guilty of unconscious racism. Because I
have been married to a physician for over thirty-three years, I know
from the large and representative cross-section of that community that
I have encountered that few doctors are, in fact, bigots; quite the contrary. Nevertheless, health inequality in America is not the result of what
doctors consciously think about race or minority patients. Instead, the
phenomenon of unconscious bias is the virulent driver of the thinking, behavior, and interactions that produce health disparities.[2] In this

chapter, I thus review the basic science of implicit bias, including how it is measured and the knowledge we have thus far about the neuroscience of the phenomenon. I end this chapter by distinguishing implicit bias in medicine from racism. My goal is to "clear the air" so that we can proceed in the remainder of this book with a forthright discussion of implicit bias, which is also properly described as *unconscious* racism.

Explaining a Blind Spot

Most Americans do not view their own behavior as racially biased. Few of the patients or providers I interviewed for this book readily admitted to holding biased attitudes or subscribing to racial stereotypes. Therefore, it is unremarkable that the physicians whom I interviewed denied that their treatment of patients might be racially and ethnically biased. Some were horrified at the suggestion. A few were even outraged by the assertion that their biased conduct contributed to racial and ethnic health disparities. In one sense, their disbelief is justified. When compared with other professionals, health providers express overwhelmingly altruistic, fair, and equitable motivations towards their work and the patients they serve. Doctors are well educated and therefore can be expected to be enlightened about equality matters. They are self-described as members of a "helping" and "healing profession," and throughout their training they adhere to a commitment to "first, do no harm" to patients. Many physicians are actively dedicated to achieving equity and distributive justice in health care,[3] often giving their time freely to serve needy populations at home and abroad. Physicians—like their counterparts in the health profession, including nurses, dentists, and pharmacists—belong to professional organizations that espouse unequivocally egalitarian values, requiring their members to treat all patients alike, regardless of race or ethnicity. When surveyed, most physicians report they entered their chosen fields motivated by the opportunity to benefit others. Many believe their objectivity and rationality insulate them from bias. Trained in the sciences, physicians regard themselves as impartial and even dispassionate, experts in making difficult decisions that require them to separate conflicting evidence from emotion. Physicians will tell you that it is their fairness and, at times, detachment that allows them to be truly compassionate. In fact, many physicians I interviewed flatly declared that apart from medical implications, to them, a patient's race and ethnicity "do not matter."

Physicians strive to limit their exercise of discretion to considering only the facts that are empirically supported and medically relevant. They take into account race or ethnicity in the course of a patient's care only when, and to the extent that, those factors are relevant to diagnosis and treatment. For example, racial cues can influence medical decisions appropriately where family history, disease etiology, epidemiological patterns, sociological influences, and anthropologic data are concerned. In those cases, race and ethnicity can have rational bearing on treatment.[4] Those cases are not the subject of this book. However, a vast body of social science research describes hundreds of experiments, in scores of medical journals, across virtually every major medical specialty that confirm that a patient's race and ethnicity continue to influence physicians' medical conduct and decision-making, well beyond the limits of what is clinically justifiable. The incongruence of these findings and the expressed race neutrality, education, scientific training, and ethical commitment of physicians is baffling.

Several explanations are possible. For reasons I have already described, I reject the possibility that the majority of health workers are dishonest people, who disguise their racism well. Another explanation is that the disparate treatment minority patients receive when compared to white patients is not due to racial or ethnic bias, but is a reflection of biological or behavioral differences among patients of different races that explain discriminatory treatment. These arguments take two forms. The weaker form, which represents an argument with readily conceivable solutions, blames minorities for generating health disparities by what they eat, how they exercise, and how they manage their health but fails to appreciate structural drivers of behavioral differences such as the inequitably distributed social determinants of health. Systemic inequity in housing, education, employment, access to healthy work places, food security, and health care contribute directly and substantially to these differences, but behavioral and biological theorists ignore these factors. The stronger form of their argument, which suggests a level of inevitability about disparities, asserts that minorities are genetically predisposed to diseases that do not affect whites or do not respond to drug therapies in the way that whites do.[5] This account relies upon unscientific descriptions of racial groups, mistakenly equates phenotype (observed traits) with genotype (heritable traits), and ignores the essential fact that genetic variability within people groups is far greater than the variability among people groups. In other words, this eugenic view falls flat in the face of scientific evidence that 99.9 percent of humans are genetically identical.[6]

The favored explanation for disparities employed by clinical and social science researchers today is that patient preferences and socioeconomic status are better explanations for disparate treatment than race and ethnic discrimination. In recent decades, physicians and social scientists have produced hundreds (and perhaps thousands) of studies that reveal associations between race and ethnicity, on the one hand, and inferior quality patient encounters, treatment decisions, and outcomes for minorities, on the other. Yet, authors of these studies have assiduously denied that providers themselves might contribute to these inequities and have instead pursued alternative explanations. They frequently cite patient preferences, clinical necessity, and socioeconomic status as key predictors of disparate health treatment or medical decision-making; that is, they prefer explanations that are outside providers' control. In chapter 6, I will discuss the difficulty of disentangling some of the confounding variables further, but for now it is sufficient to admit that although there are *other* factors that contribute to racial and ethnic health disparities, these do not eliminate the significant role that *this* factor—discrimination—plays in producing disparate health outcomes. While no study has precisely quantified the extent of demonstrated associations between race bias, inferior health care, and poor health outcomes, the scientific record is too well developed to ignore that there is more than a mere chance association between implicit bias and health disparities. Nonetheless, there are several reasons the medical community continually avoids concluding that unconscious racism causes health disparities.

American professionals are not generally rewarded for self-criticism and introspection. In preparing to provide patient care, physicians learn to manage objective data and subjective information about patients, but seldom are asked to include information about themselves in their analysis. Moreover, the scholarly and clinical discussion about disparities involves a complex tangle of overlapping determinants. This complexity has given researchers plenty to unravel without coming dangerously close to accusing physicians of bigotry and racism. Moreover, even when a preponderance of their studies point to causation, social scientists do not have the analytical tools to eliminate all competing explanations for health disparities. But while scientists cannot fairly be blamed for not reaching a conclusion that they cannot prove in a laboratory or field experiment, physicians, providers, policy-makers, and indeed lawyers cannot fairly be absolved from addressing the real-life, human tragedies that occur when doctors discriminate.

Another reason the discussion of implicit bias among physicians is difficult relates to the numerous thorny health care policy problems that already place blame and responsibility on physicians. For example, when policy-makers discuss health care cost containment, they target reductions in physician reimbursements rather than institutional facility fees. When the topic is a costly malpractice system, discussion centers on the cost of physicians' defensive medical practices rather than astronomical legal fees. Quality assurance legislation imposes peer review on physicians but is more generous toward institutional providers. And courts reserve vicarious liability based on medical error for physicians individually and collectively but do not hold accountable the third-party payers who constrain physicians' decision-making. Targeting physician practices to reduce racial and ethnic disparities may seem like piling on blame. The truth is that the data about health and health care disparities do point to the conclusion that physicians are major contributors, but doctors are certainly not the only contributors. The empirical record may be fairly criticized because the institutional effects of unconscious racism have not been well studied. Also, racial and ethnic biases held by health workers other than physicians have been ignored; nurses, physician extenders, technicians, and even medical staff workers such as receptionists, administrators, and insurers are also likely unconscious contributors to health disparities, but these actors have almost entirely escaped social scientists' gaze. All these reasons and evidentiary shortcomings notwithstanding, the empirical record that shows that physician bias contributes to shortening and diminishing the quality of minority lives in this country demands that those responsible be held accountable. This discriminatory conduct must be reversed because it causes disproportionate, fundamental, and unjust harm.

The effective approach to explaining the curious dissonance between physicians' good intentions and the copious record of disparate health care outcomes lies in uncovering and understanding the impact of physicians' *unintentional* attitudes and perceptions about minority patients. Most physicians' contributions to health care disparities arise from their subconscious, not their conscious, thought processes. They arise from the learned adaptive tendency to think by using categories—even stereotypes—in ways that allow all human beings to make sense of a complex world every day. Physicians, like everyone else, are capable of making automatic and unintentional judgments about race and ethnicity that serve as sorting mechanisms. An internal medicine attending physician at a university medical center in New England explains it this way:

> Our brains tend to store patterns because I realize that every new thing I encounter is absolute disorder. And every key we have is something that helps us sort patterns. Race is one of those things, ethnicity is one of those things. When I see somebody is wearing a turban, things are being triggered. So then I say, "Okay you are this," and that gives me a whole bunch of assumptions. In some respects it's functional, in terms of our being able to make sense of the world. But also because when I talk to you I have to make sense or else I won't know how to communicate. If you're nicely dressed, if you're wearing rags—it's going to change what level of language I use, what I refer to, the way I choose my words. I'll try to avoid saying something that's going to be offensive to you. . . . So I can't say I apologize for every generalization I make, or that people make, because you have to. The question is do you take it to a level of personal insight so you can check those things that are going to be destructive?
> —Cardiologist, New England University Medical Center

This physician gives a perfect summary of exactly how implicit biases work. Stored patterns turn into generalizations and assumptions that we use to sort out a complex world that he describes as being in "absolute disorder." But he also recognizes that the ways we "trigger" these sorting mechanisms can be destructive. Physicians are especially susceptible to allowing implicit biases to creep destructively into their practice because the core and very nature of what they do involves performing what this physician describes as "sorting patterns" in order to identify and solve medical problems. The diagnostic sorting process, called making a differential diagnosis, requires doctors to use familiar patterns and generalizations about people and their maladies to correctly identify, understand, and address illness. Certainly, considerations of race and ethnicity can be as relevant to this process as other categorizations such as age and weight. However, allowing implicit racial and ethnic bias to inform medical care goes beyond these clinically relevant considerations to cause unfair and harmful discrimination.

Understanding Implicit Bias

The empirical evidence that race and ethnicity influence physicians to make harmful distinctions in how they treat and interact with white patients versus patients of color is overwhelming. A preponderance of that evidence compels the conclusion that the vast majority of provider discrimination causing disparities is a product of implicit, not explicit, bias. Physicians' implicit biases lead to unintentional and in some cases, even unconscious discrimination. The resulting biased behavior may directly contradict the physician's sincerely held, explicit beliefs and intentions to provide excellent care to all patients regardless of their race or ethnicity.

People—all people—hold some implicit biases. A bias is a negative attitude held about one group of people relative to another group of people. However, the distinguishing feature of an *implicit* bias is that the negative association operates unintentionally or unconsciously. In contrast, an *explicit* bias is an evaluation about groups of people that operates at a level that includes awareness, choice, and conscious intentionality. Another important distinction between implicit and explicit biases is the extent to which each one influences behavior. Researchers have repeatedly shown that implicit bias more directly influences behavior than explicit or expressly held viewpoints. In other words, people act much more in accordance with their *implicit* or subconsciously held attitudes and beliefs and much less in accordance with what they say they believe and intend. This is true for all Americans, and it is true about a wide variety of personal characteristics. No matter how neutrally we may sincerely intend to behave, tests taken by hundreds of thousands of Americans demonstrate empirically that we are a nation of people who

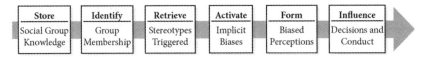

Store	Identify	Retrieve	Activate	Form	Influence
Social Group Knowledge	Group Membership	Stereotypes Triggered	Implicit Biases	Biased Perceptions	Decisions and Conduct

Figure 2.1. How implicit biases work in the subconscious mind.

hold strong implicit biases. Figure 2.1 is a schematic description of how implicit biases form and inform our perceptions, judgments, and conduct toward people from identifiable ethic and racial groups. Implicit biases operate whether the interaction is between two members of the same racial group or between members of different racial groups.

Figure 2.1 shows how implicit biases form and function without any conscious awareness whatsoever. The first step—storing social knowledge—is a process that occurs over a lifetime. We store social knowledge in memory from everything we see, feel, and experience in the world around us. Stored knowledge of social groups comes from all the messages, images, and signals we receive from our environment, including music, television, books, family members, friends, teachers, childhood experiences, stories shared by others, news media, movies, and so forth. The second step occurs the moment two people meet. Americans live in a race-conscious society and are conditioned to instinctively identify the group to which another person belongs. Once we identify the group, the process of responding to our implicit biases begins. At first, the simple function of identifying a person's racial or ethnic group is value-neutral—the identification is neither positive nor negative. But very quickly—scientists say within five hundred milliseconds from the moment of identification—we retrieve from our memory the most dominant associations we have stored with regard to that person's racial or ethnic group. These are the group stereotypes that have formed over time based on our social knowledge. Stereotypes can be based upon an ostensibly positive assertion ("Asians are good at math") or a patently negative one ("Asians are crafty"), but both are harmful to the extent that they devalue individual characteristics and reflect the assumption of power to label and judge another person inaccurately. The point is that unconscious stereotypes are pulled from storage to help sort out the new person or situation before us, regardless of their accuracy about or applicability to the individual in fact. This is where the stereotypes are accessed or "triggered" and become available to use in shaping our understanding of the situation at hand. Importantly, when we access stereotypes from memory, those stereotypes, built upon images stored for many years, dominate our understanding and experience. In other words, our stored stereotypes completely displace and supersede the new or even contradictory information we encounter as we meet and relate to new people and situations. After we access our stored stereotypes, we form implicit biases, which are unconscious attitudes that we apply to our perceptions of the specific person or situation we face. In turn, these biased perceptions inform the overt judgments that ultimately direct how we engage and interact with the outside world. This is how implicit biases influence the way we perceive, judge, and relate to people of different racial and ethnic groups. Implicit biases operate at an unconscious level; we are not even aware of their influence. And yet, implicit biases have a dominant impact on how we think about, and act toward, members of other racial groups.

Implicit Bias and the Brain

Research confirms that most Americans hold implicit anti-black and pro-white biases. Over the past twenty-five years, implicit biases against blacks and in favor of whites have been well documented among the general American population, despite the correlative evidence that explicit racial bias against minorities has dramatically declined during the same period.[7] Moreover, the empirical evidence confirms that implicit race biases are as prevalent among professionals in the health care industry as they are among the American public generally. Because it is clear that implicit biases can operate to produce the same pernicious harm as intentional or discriminatory bias, it is imperative to understand and address how implicit biases operate in health care. Beginning with the physiological evidence for how the brain processes implicit biases will help underscore the ubiquity of the unconscious and automatic nature of the stereotyping that produces implicit biases. Next, in reviewing the cognitive processes that lead to implicit bias, we can see how implicit bias unconsciously and unintentionally affects decisions and conduct. Finally, understanding the ways in which social scientists have been able to measure the extent of implicit bias will offer a methodology for concretely assessing the likely pathways or mechanisms by which implicit bias influences health care providers and their patients. The aim is to use this evidence to take the sting associated with charges of overt racism out of forthrightly addressing the problems presented by implicit bias in the health care context.

Implicit biases are attitudes, preferences, and beliefs about social groups that operate outside of human awareness or control. Neuroscientists believe there are three regions of the brain that relate to the automatic activation of implicit attitudes. First, the amygdala, a small group of nuclei located in both the left and right hemispheres of the brain, has been linked to implicit attitudes in numerous studies.[8] The amygdala is believed to control memory, attention, and automatic responses to stimuli. It plays a role in our ability to evaluate members of other social groups. MRI studies show that elevated blood-oxygen level responses in the amygdala region of the human brain correlate to a person's implicit attitudes, but are suppressed in the presence of explicit stimuli in the form of faces of a person from a different racial background.[9]

Activity in two other regions of the brain appears to work in a correlated fashion with the amygdala in order to keep implicit racial associations responses below the threshold of conscious awareness. Studies show that the dorsolateral prefrontal cortex (diPFC) and the anterior cingulate cortex (ACC) have both been correlated with the attenuated responses of the amygdala. In lay terms, a three-part neural model exists in which the amygdala generates automatic responses to racial stimuli, while the diPFC and ACC work to maintain those responses at an unconscious level.[10] While neuroscientists have measured and studied the physical activity of the brain that generates implicit attitudes, social psychologists have studied the cognitive processes that produce them.

Implicit bias is a form of automatic thought. According to the classic, dual processing model of human cognition, thought generally occurs on two levels. On the one hand, explicit or *conscious* thought occurs by processes that are intentional and deliberate. Automatic thought, on the other hand, is a system of information processing that occurs without any intentionality. There are four basic processes of automatic thought. First, a person acquires and stores social knowledge in a way that is *accessible* from memory when triggers or cues stir up the associations that make up social knowledge. Social knowledge is the information generally available to members of a community by virtue of the messages chronically reinforced and adopted about people or things. Stereotypes, for example, are a particular form of social knowledge in which attributes or traits are assigned to a group of people. Second, a person's ability to retrieve social knowledge from memory is the next process of automatic thought, and social psychologists call this function "accessibility." When cues or triggers from familiar contextual settings allow a person to "activate" social knowledge so that it is ready to direct conduct or judgments without deliberate or conscious decision-making, the second process of automatic thought is enacted. The third and fourth processes involve automatic application of social knowledge to a current situation because of the apparent fit between knowledge stored in memory and the situation at hand. However, the remarkable discovery about these processes is that stereotyping and prejudices can occur unintentionally, at an implicit or *unconscious* level. This means that a person can apply negative group attributes or traits, presumed from memory of social knowledge, to an individual who is a member of the group, despite the lack of evidentiary support to confirm the truth of the presumed attribute or trait, without or even *against* that person's intentional will. In short, the evidence shows that implicit biases can operate automatically, unintentionally, and unconsciously.

Where race and ethnicity are concerned, Americans gather their social group knowledge from the environment. From the abundance of images of minorities on television and in the print media, to commentary by political leaders, lyrics in popular music, discussions among friends, entertainment outlets, chance encounters, and interracial relationships or experiences—the subconsciously gathered information that unconsciously becomes stored group knowledge is as pervasive as it is powerful. Consider this example. It is a statistical fact that white Americans receive the greatest share of public entitlement assistance, or "welfare." Nevertheless, the social group knowledge many gathered from the 2012 presidential campaign was that it is minorities who predominantly receive welfare. One politician attempted to capitalize on the social group knowledge that presumed a poor work ethic among blacks by labeling President Barack Obama a "food stamp president,"[11] while another candidate sought to distinguish himself from the president by promising that he will not "make black people's lives better by giving

them somebody else's money."[12] Neither of these campaign pitches accurately reflected the fact that whites are the predominant recipients
of welfare funds, Medicaid support, and food stamps, but references
to these programs were deemed useful in the campaign against Barack
Obama because they matched the subconscious impressions some voters have of blacks, even if they contradicted the truth. Let's look at the
facts: In reality, African Americans do not constitute the majority of welfare recipients. The DHHS reports that in 2012, Temporary Assistance
for Needy Families (TANF), the cash assistance program to families in
need, helped 1.8 million families; 30.1 percent of those families were
white, 31.5 percent were black, and 31.1 percent were Hispanic.[13] Indeed,
DHHS also reports that "the percentage of African-American TANF
families has slowly decreased since 2001."[14] The Centers for Medicare
and Medicaid (CMS) report that in 2013, Medicaid enrolled a monthly
average of 57.4 million people; 41.1 percent were white, 21.6 percent were
black, and 24.7 percent were Hispanic.[15] In 2013, a total of 22.8 million
households used food stamps—the supplemental nutrition assistance
program called "SNAP." The United States Department of Agriculture
reports that 40.2 percent of households receiving SNAP had white heads
of households; blacks headed 25.7 percent of SNAP households; and 10.3
percent were headed by a Hispanic.[16] Clearly, despite the political claims
that captured the airways, blacks are not, in fact, the primary recipients
of "welfare." Whether the source is a political campaign advertisement,
television news channel, sports and music personalities profiled in su-
permarket tabloids, Hollywood box office hits, or lessons taught in high
school history classes—the negative imagery of minority Americans that
is readily available in our culture tends to override reality and dominate
the stored social group knowledge most whites have about people of
color in this country. Social scientists have reported study after study
that confirms the power of negative imagery of African Americans and
Latinos which associates them with criminality, animals, and socially
undesirable behavior such as drug abuse and hypersexuality.[17] These are
the associations that create stereotypes that inform implicit biases. Doctors, nurses, pharmacists, dentists, and others in the health care industry
are not insulated from this negative social group knowledge. These same
types of biases influence decision-makers within the health industry as
well. Thanks to the work of social scientists over the past thirty years,

tools have been developed to measure implicit bias. We are now able to quantify reliably the extent to which stored social group knowledge produces implicit racial and ethnic bias.

Measuring Implicit Bias

The tool of choice that both neuroscientists and social psychologists use to measure unconscious attitudes is called the Implicit Association Test (IAT).[18] The IAT is a computer-based test that works on the straightforward premise that when people are asked to associate photographs with words that are consistent with their implicitly held beliefs about those pictures, they will make those associations quickly. But when people are asked to connect photographs with words they would not naturally or automatically associate with those photographs, their response times will be too slow to allow them to override their automatic instincts. The IAT measures the time a person takes to associate selected pairs of positive and negative words with selected pictures.

The IAT has been used extensively to measure implicit attitudes about race. The Race Attitude IAT measures the time a person takes to quickly sort photographs of African American and European American faces and combinations of those facial shots with positive and negative adjectives. The closer a subject's IAT score is to zero, the more neutral are their preferences for blacks or whites. A high positive IAT score signals strong, automatic, implicit biases in favor of whites over blacks—a "pro-white" or "anti-black" bias. A very low, more negative IAT score denotes a strong bias in favor of blacks over whites—a "pro-black" or "anti-white" bias. Between January 2004 and May 2006, 404,277 visitors to the public demonstration website known as "Project Implicit" have taken the Race Attitude Implicit Association Test.[19] More recently, IATs have been developed to measure bias against Hispanics, but similar tests to measure biases against other ethnic minorities are not yet available. Also, IATs currently measure relative biases between two racial groups, but not among several racial or ethnic categorizations.

Harvard's Project Implicit researchers reported that they found "a strong implicit preference for white Americans over black Americans among all test takers" They also reported substantially the same findings for physician test-takers who identified as white, Asian, and Hispanic, though not for African American MDs.[20] All female test-takers generally showed a weaker preference for whites over blacks, and female physicians who took the IAT showed a "weaker but still substantial" bias in favor of whites. Importantly, the research confirms that people who are explicitly race-neutral can still hold strongly negative implicit biases. The implicit bias measures that test-takers scored showed only a modest relationship to the measures of explicit attitudes about race. This weak relationship supports the conclusion that "one may explicitly hold egalitarian beliefs while simultaneously holding implicit attitudes that favor Whites relative to Blacks." Furthermore, applying these results to the health care context, "It is plausible that during medical decision-making, even among those with egalitarian values, implicit social attitudes and stereotypes stored in memory may be retrieved automatically without awareness and may influence medical care, albeit unintentionally."[21]

The IAT specifically, and implicit cognitive psychology generally, have been criticized by some as failing to "satisfy key scientific tests of validity—internally, statistically, and externally."[22] However, these claims have been unpacked and shown to rest principally on the critics' normative view that antidiscrimination law should not concern itself with bias that is unconscious and unintentional.[23] I will defer a detailed discussion of my disagreement with this normative view for later chapters. Here, I will only assert that if unintentional discrimination leads to the substantial harms caused by disparate health outcomes, this discrimination should not go unaddressed merely because it is unintentional. At the same time, the differences between intentionally discriminatory conduct and unintentional discrimination should not be overlooked either. In 1998, two professors—one in psychology and one in law—introduced the idea that antidiscrimination law should be reformed to reflect scientific information about people's unconscious behavior and to treat that behavior differently than intentional discrimination. They made this assertion because the IAT had proved reliable as a scientific measure of unconscious mental processes and thus provided sufficient basis to alert discriminators of their conduct and give them the information needed to change. [24] Moreover, as discussed later, in chapter 7, a school of legal analysis called "behavioral realists" has persuasively asserted that antidiscrimination law should and must regulate conduct that results in harmful inequality of opportunity among members of the American community because law should correlate with the most recent and accurate knowledge about the human behavior that is being controlled.

The process of automatic thought called "implicit bias" was discovered over thirty years ago.[25] Over the years, the IAT has not been the only method used for measuring implicit bias.[26] Using the IAT and other measures of unconscious bias, researchers have demonstrated some rather startling observations *outside* the health industry. For example, high implicit bias scores have been associated with biased conduct and decision-making when government attorneys decide whom to prosecute in the criminal justice system,[27] when lawyers participate in jury selection,[28] when corporate managers make hiring or promotion decisions in employment settings,[29] and when teachers and administrators decide which misbehaving students to discipline in schools.[30] Police officers with higher IAT scores have shown a tendency to shoot unarmed blacks more readily than unarmed whites during video-game simulations.[31] Researchers have used the IAT to show that jurors' hold unconscious biases related to whether they value black or white defendants' lives differently when deciding who should receive the death penalty.[32] A study that has implications for the most ordinary daily interactions found that when photos depicting the onset and disappearance of anger in black and white faces were shown to whites who had pro-white IAT scores, they were quicker to judge a black (but not a white) face as angry and slower to judge a black (but not white) face as no longer angry.[33] In another study, white college students who scored strong pro-white biases on the IAT also made fewer positive comments, smiled less readily, and were visibly less comfortable in the presence of black peers when videotaped.[34] A surprising finding was that some African Americans have shown anti-black discriminatory biases just as strong as those held by whites.[35] African Americans who scored pro-white biases on the IAT were more likely to choose white over black partners for intellectually challenging tasks.

The implicit association test and the existence of implicit bias in general retain a small cadre of critics.[36] These researchers continue to insist that the IAT is not measuring bias at all. It is not altogether clear what they believe tests such as the IAT are measuring. However, they put forth the possibility that implicit bias does not exist, is not measurable, or should not be acted upon by lawmakers even if implicit bias represents a quantifiable phenomenon. The majority of social scientists have discredited this view, likening these criticisms to "an island of dissent within a sea of consensus."[37] Moreover, some scientists have expressed preference for other tests as better measures of implicit bias. While no single measure of implicit bias is perfect, the research in this book relies principally on findings using the implicit association test because that test has become what one social scientist describes as "solid empirical bedrock for understanding the occurrence of implicit bias." Using the IAT, researchers have confirmed that the primary actors in American health care—physicians and patients—both carry strong implicit biases.

Physician Implicit Bias

If a white, male family-practice physician with a largely white patient population walks into a new patient's room and encounters an elderly African American woman, immediately and automatically the physician begins to retrieve information from his memory to help him navigate this unfamiliar scene. Even before speaking his first words, the physician will subconsciously recall images stored in memory to help him interact with his new patient. Those images–his "social group knowledge"— may be from television news stories about blacks in poverty, African American incarceration rates, or the war on drugs in black and Hispanic neighborhoods. The physician may be well-read and familiar with studies reported in the *Wall Street Journal* or the *Los Angeles* or *New York Times* about the rate at which African Americans graduate from college, drop out of high school, or lag in their standardized test performances. This doctor is not likely to have been spared images from television advertisements played throughout a recent election cycle in which politicians made claims about "welfare queens" while flashing pictures of black women; or from pictures of black women enjoying "southern style" fried chicken in fast food commercials. The physician may have stored memories of song lyrics or MTV videos featuring African Americans played by his teenage children; or he may recall clips from an Oscar-nominated film about a crack mother or black household maids. Some of the stored information about African Americans may come from his medical training or positive interactions he had with an older black woman who befriended him or worked for his family. Taken together, all of these images "trigger" stereotypes in the subconscious mind.

If the physician is relatively young, he may have received cultural competency training that will remind him to be respectful and sensitive in his communication. Yet these reminders from his medical school class will compete with the minimal number of opportunities he has had to encounter black classmates in high school and college, in his neighborhood and social circles, and certainly in his elite medical school training. The point is that a wealth of images and background knowledge, inaccessible to his conscious thinking, but entirely accessible to his subconscious mind, will automatically dominate, and form into implicit biases concerning the individual patient. Studies show that these implicit biases, whether accurate or inaccurate, will powerfully inform how the physician behaves with this new patient from the very first moment that they meet.

If asked, the physician would truthfully admit to harboring no ill will toward African Americans generally or toward this African American patient specifically. Yet, without consciously thinking about it, the physician is likely to have made some implicit assumptions about his patient even before meeting her. With some justification drawn from his past limited experiences, the doctor may assume this patient has limited means, less education than himself, and has had few opportunities to take care to eat well, exercise, or rest over the course of her lifetime. Most likely, the physician will not even be aware that his judgments about the patient have been reached subconsciously, and certainly without any actual information about the individual woman who sits before him. But the fact that this physician's assumptions and stereotypes—his implicit biases—are neither irrational nor consciously chosen, does not mean that the discrimination that arises from them will not be extremely harmful to his new patient's health. Indeed, her health and health care are quite likely to be adversely affected by these biases from the moment the clinical encounter with her doctor begins. Even in those instances when physicians' react with sympathetic compassion in response to the negative stereotypes triggered in their subconscious, the evidence is that the treatment choices they make as a result, such as withholding complex information or deferring expensive treatments, are more likely to harm rather than improve a minority patient's health.

Implicit biases affect behavior. From the data collected and reviewed in depth in the chapters that follow, we can surmise how this physician-patient encounter will be affected by implicit bias. Therefore, we can expect that the doctor's biases will impact everything about his conduct toward his new patient. The physician's decision as to where to sit in the examination room, how closely he will listen when this new patient speaks, how much credence he will ascribe to her account of her health condition, whether and for how long he makes eye contact, reaches out to touch her shoulder, or answers her questions directly and patiently, may all be influenced by his implicit biases concerning African Americans. On one hand, this physician may be a self-aware fellow who conscientiously attends to making adjustments in communication that will be appropriate to this new patient and her expressed cultural background. But much more likely, studies show, the physician will be uncomfortable communicating with his African American patient, misinterpret her meaning, and send signals that cause her to know she is being treated poorly. She may even perceive she is being treated differently than she would be if she were white.[38] In return, the elderly black patient is also likely to respond negatively. Her conduct and communication with the doctor, as well as her trust, adherence, compliance, and satisfaction will be affected, all to the detriment of her health outcomes following the visit. Moreover, because of the powerful influence of his implicit biases, this doctor is most likely going to rely upon the cumulative background probabilistic data—both social and clinical—to fill in the gaps due to his inexperience with African Americans, as he seeks to reach reasoned and efficient medical decisions about her care. Thus, the physician is likely to rely upon his stored background knowledge to tell him what he does not know about this patient, and does not feel he has time to learn, given the constraints and realities of his busy medical practice. Unintentionally, this doctor is likely to make statistical judgments about the medical data he receives about this black patient that are different than the judgments and conclusions he would reach based on the same data about a white patient. For this African American patient, this doctor will likely make treatment decisions that are different from those he would make if she were white. And because he will make them with less consultation and shared interaction with the black patient, she in turn will not have the same view towards follow-up and compliance with the treatment plan that a white patient would have. And if this physician's implicit biases have a deleterious impact on his communication, interpretations, diagnosis, treatment, trust relationship and ultimate follow-up with this patient, how can these same implicit biases not have a deleterious effect on her health outcomes? Indeed they will. I will show in the chapters that follow how physicians' implicit biases affect disparate health outcomes because they affect disparate health care.

Patients Have Implicit Biases, Too

Doctors are not the only ones to harbor implicit racial and ethnic biases. Landlords have been shown to unfairly decide not to rent property based on implicit biases. Undecided voters have been shown to make election choices based solely on their implicit biases. Employers have been demonstrably influenced in their decisions to hire, fire, and promote employees due to implicit biases. Lawyers' implicit biases have been shown to influence how they evaluate judges' performance. And tragically, implicit biases figure prominently in the decisions law enforcement officers make when arresting, charging, or even taking aim and firing a deadly shot at presumed suspects. Implicit biases do not operate only to the detriment of those who are racial or ethnic minorities. Some hold implicit biases against those who are overweight. Others hold biases that cause them to prefer young people to the elderly, women to men, or Christians to Jews and Moslems. Because implicit biases are so ubiquitous, any model of implicit bias in the healthcare setting must include all actors—even the patients who seek medical treatment and care. Patients have implicit biases, too. While it is easier to see how physicians' implicit biases can work to the detriment of patients, consider the ways in which a hypothetical patient may hold implicit biases against his or her physician.

According to the model in figure 2.2, when a patient meets a physician—even one of his or her own race—that patient brings a store of social knowledge about physicians generally and about the physician's racial or ethnic group, specifically. Patients may also retrieve and access assumptions about the physician's intellectual stature based on where the doctor trained: Was it in the United States or abroad? Was the medical school prominent and well known or small and unfamiliar?

Generalizations and stereotypes may be triggered by the affiliations a physician has: Is the physician part of a nationally known medical center, or a staff-member at a community clinic? Institutional affiliation with a health plan or hospital may trigger biases. Information from the Internet or from direct-to-consumer advertising may bias a patient's regard for a physician, or patients might completely disregard the doctor's professional status and training, and instead focus on his or her race, gender, age, or appearance in order to summon stereotypes and form implicit biases—all at an unconscious level.

One of my favorite stories comes from my husband's time as a resident "moonlighting" to make extra money in the emergency room of a small, southern town's community hospital. My husband is black, and the patient in this story was white. He had suffered a gunshot wound to the chest and was pretty badly wounded, but not unconscious when he first encountered my husband. I am told that the patient had been rushed into the ER, and that my husband entered the examination room to begin gathering information rather urgently. But before Thomas—my husband—could begin speaking, the patient looked up and said, "You must be the ghetto doctor! I don't want you treating me!" "Well," Thomas said, "I'm the only doctor you've got tonight so welcome to the ghetto!" and off they both went into surgery. This patient's implicit biases prompted him to conclude, based only on Thomas's skin color, that he was poor, poorly trained, and would be the source of poor medical care. In this instance, the patient's implicit biases informed his overtly racist pronouncements. Unconscious bias does not often reveal itself in such frank expressions. But I recount this story, both troubling and amusing, to make an important point about how implicit biases operate on both sides of the physician-patient relationship in a reciprocal, almost circular manner. A multiplier effect of this cycle is responsible for an enormous impact on health care and health outcome disparities that has been grossly underestimated to date. Figure 2.2 presents a graphic depiction of what I will call the physician-patient, implicit bias "feedback loop."

When a patient arrives in the hospital, clinic, or doctor's private office for a check-up, all of the patient's experiences and expectations arrive, too. Whatever the physician does will be filtered through those experiences, and the patient's implicit biases will influence his perceptions, decisions, and conduct. In turn, the doctor, having stored her own ste-

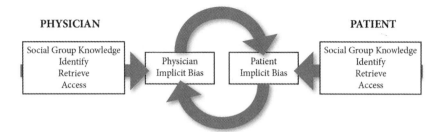

Figure 2.2. Reciprocal implicit biases between physician and patient.

reotypes as well, may "read" the patient's behavior through the lens of her unconsciously held stereotypes. The reciprocity is not only circular but duplicative. I discuss this research describing this implicit bias feedback loop later, but because of its powerful influence in the physician-patient dynamic, implicit bias reciprocity is important to understand at the outset. Both physicians and patients have implicit biases; both may be guilty of either conscious or unconscious racism. However, the distinctions are important.

Is Implicit Bias Racism?

"Racism" is a dirty word in American culture. Racists are generally despised characters, and their practice of assigning negative attributes to racial and ethnic groups and then acting in accord with those negative assumptions is almost universally disdained. Therefore, it is very important to understand the connection between implicit bias and purely malicious racism. To be sure, implicit bias is distinguishable from overt expressions and acts of prejudice because implicit bias is unintentional. Yet, if we simply look at how racial implicit biases function, it is clear that people who act on their implicit biases reach negative judgments and conclusions based on what they know and think about members of a race rather than what they know and think about an individual person. Implicit biases, however, cause them do so at a subconscious and therefore unintentional level. Is that not racism? Yes, I argue, it is.

Racism generally refers both to the state of mind belonging to one who holds negative prejudices and stereotypes about the intrinsic value, relative importance, and appropriate social roles for members of a given racial group, based solely on their membership in that group. Racism further describes the discriminatory actions undertaken as a result of these negative beliefs, thus making those who adopt these beliefs and actions, "racists." Racists treat people disparagingly and unfavorably because they are from a particular racial or ethnic group. Moreover, racism engages the historically supported and institutionalized power structures between races and nationalities deemed "superior" and those that have been dominated and oppressed as though "inferior." Importantly, the historical power differential that underlies the perpetuation of racial and ethnic inequality in America fundamentally informs both intentional and unconscious racism. The overt racist engages in racism deliberately, intentionally, and with awareness that historic, social, and economic institutions support his or her choices and actions. In contrast, an unconscious racist unintentionally operationalizes historically and socially reinforced negative perceptions, judgments and behavior toward those from disfavored racial or ethnic groups through their implicit biases. Implicit bias is pervasive; we *all* carry some forms of implicit bias because we have all gathered social group knowledge from our environment and culture. And yet everyone with implicit biases is not a racist. With regard to overt racism, not everyone makes the choice to be a bigot. However, where unconscious racism is concerned, despite the distinctions from overt racism, several similarities must command our attention. Certainly where health and health care are concerned, even when implicit biases are based on seemingly benign distinctions, or supported by apparently rational or widely held observations, these biases can cause grave individual, group, and societal harm that is commensurate to and even exceeds the harm caused by outright racism. Implicit biases can operate to reinforce the same inequalities that blatant racism perpetuates and continue the tradition of generally allocating societal resources disproportionately to the historically dominant and powerful racial groups at the expense of historically oppressed groups. But while overt racism is subject to nearly universal derision, unconscious racism due to implicit bias is hidden, tolerated, and even excused despite its destructiveness. While implicit bias is not *overt* racism or bigotry, the injustice and inequality that flow from both conscious and unconscious racism are equally egregious. As the next chapter shows, these harms are especially lethal in the health care context.

3

Physicians' Unconscious Racism

I was raised in a certain way that wasn't completely free of bias and my wife was raised in a way that wasn't free of bias but she has changed. I think it definitely can be overcome and I think if people can see the right thing to do . . . it's absolutely your responsibility to make your behavior reflect what you believe. . . . I try very hard to avoid bias with my patients and I'm sure I'm not completely free of it and that's why I'm anxious to find out how I can be better myself.
—Attending Cardiac Surgeon, University Medical Center, Northeastern United States

Annually, unconscious racism harms patient health, cuts short patient lives, increases health care costs, and diminishes health care quality. This chapter reviews the damage that unconscious racism causes in the medical context to understand exactly what is at stake for tens of thousands of patients. To begin, recall the hypothetical encounter between one physician and a single patient introduced in chapter 2. There, a white male physician and his new, elderly African American patient meet for their first office visit. At the outset of the visit, the physician's intentions were to deliver impartial, high quality care to his patient. The patient's objectives were to receive the same. But surreptitiously, implicit bias invaded the clinical encounter. In this chapter, the focus is on the physician's unconscious racism and the harm it causes. The doctor's implicit biases may cause discrimination in a variety of ways. For example, he may decide not to refer this patient to a specialist to treat her coronary heart disease symptoms and choose instead to recommend that she receive only a conservative course of medical treatment, though a white patient in the same condition would have been referred for an interventional procedure. If this is the case, the black patient would not be a victim of overt discrimination; however, the covert disparity in treatment may ultimately decrease the quality of her health and longevity of her life just as if the doctor had hung a "Whites Only" sign on his door and refused her admission to his examination room.

Yet physician's implicit bias discrimination does not rise to the level of a legally significant offense. Notwithstanding a national consensus that racism is wrong and a plethora of antidiscrimination statutes and regulations currently on the books, the existing law takes virtually no notice of discrimination that is the result of unintentional beliefs or conduct. In general, the United States Constitution as well as federal and state statutory laws strongly prohibit only *intentional* discrimination based on race, national origin, gender, age, disability, or the fact that a person is an immigrant to this country. When the discrimination against members of these protected classes of people is unintentional, the legal remedies available are few and difficult to access. And so this quandary exists: On the one hand, the health care industry has seen little enforcement of federal or state antidiscrimination law largely because few cases involve the outright, odious, intentional discrimination that we typically associate with racism. On the other hand, absolutely no accountability—legal or otherwise—seems to exist in health care to control the harmful effects of racial and ethnic discrimination that arises from implicit biases.

The legal record reflects this dichotomy. Several recently reported cases penalize medical providers who violated the law by engaging in discriminatory employment practices. However, these cases uniformly involve intentional, not implicit discrimination. For example, in 2008, when a nursing home complied with a patient's demand for "white only health care providers," a federal court held that the provider violated federal antidiscrimination law. In another case, when a health care staffing agency refused to hire "Blacks or Jews" in Oregon and the provider cited Klu Klux Klan activity to justify its practices, the court held the provider violated federal law. A pharmacy chain settled a class action claim that it systematically discriminated against black retail pharmacists in 2007. Clearly, courts are intolerant of explicit discrimination against minority health care workers. However, modern legal records contain no cases that punish health care providers for racial discrimination against patients. For example, the legal record contains no cases alleging that a physician withheld the most effective treatment from a patient based on the patient's race while prescribing that same treatment to a similarly situated white patient. Is this because such discrimination against minority patients does not occur? Surely not—indeed, examples of discriminatory health treatment abound in the medical literature. Despite the absence of any legal cases alleging this type of clinical discrimination, the empirical and medical evidence illustrates that a virulent form of unconscious discrimination regularly and ubiquitously occurs against minority patients.

The Health Impact of Physician Bias

The 2003 Institute of Medicine report titled *Unequal Treatment* provided the first comprehensive and systematic proof that health disparities are associated with the fact that minorities in this country receive unequal health care from medical providers. The report collected and broadly disseminated empirical evidence based on over one hundred studies that were described as representing only a fraction of the empirical record. Yet, the data overwhelmingly showed that compared to whites, minority patients are less likely to receive appropriate medical treatment for cardiovascular disease, cancer, cerebrovascular disease, renal disease, HIV/AIDs, asthma, diabetes, or pain. Moreover, minorities are also more likely to receive inferior rehabilitative, maternal, pediatric, mental health, and hospital-based medical services than their white counterparts.[1] Since the IOM report, the evidence of profound inequality in our health care system has continued to mount. The evidence of racial discrimination in the treatment of heart disease, end-stage renal disease, and cancer, three of the leading causes of death nationally, provides a compelling sample of the published data on disparities.

African Americans are three times as likely as whites to develop cardiovascular disease[2] and are twice as likely to die from it.[3] Yet, notwithstanding controls for genetic differences, socioeconomic status, health behaviors, and unequal access to care, research shows that race and ethnicity powerfully determine that blacks are less likely than whites to receive the treatments of choice for cardiac illness. Doctors provide inferior preventative care for blacks when compared to whites. Studies show physicians are less aggressive about urging black patients to modify risk factors for heart disease such as smoking cessation,[4] diet modification, and increased exercise.[5] In a large longitudinal study of racial differences in heart disease care, researchers assessed the use of aspirin and beta-blockers, statins and other lipid-lowering therapies, as well as ACE-inhibitors (drugs used to treat hypertension). These researchers found that black women experienced less aggressive risk factor control and preventive therapy and therefore suffered worse outcomes than white women after adjusting for disease severity, socioeconomic status, and access to care.[6] However, another study of four hundred U.S. hospitals showed that black heart patients are more likely to receive older conservative coronary treatments than newer or more expensive therapies; by the same token, they are less likely to receive many evidence-based treatments that are newer, more costly, and more readily available to whites.[7] For example, African Americans who are appropriate candidates for surgery are less likely than whites to be admitted for coronary artery bypass operations.[8] When admitted to hospitals, black coronary patients are more likely to receive poor quality care than white patients. One study based on a cross-sectional sample of 10,000 Medicare patients discharged from 297 hospitals in five states showed that African Americans were less ready for discharge than other coronary heart disease patients.[9] Over a dozen studies have demonstrated persistent underuse of invasive procedures that are effective in treating coronary disease, such as angiography and bypass graft surgery, in African Americans as compared with white patients.[10]

In addition to clinical disparities, providers show bias in their social judgments and expectations about treating black and white patients with coronary complaints, even before the clinical encounter begins. Physicians' perceptions of patients' race, education, and physical activity significantly predicted the quality of medical recommendations for male coronary patients.[11] Whether the providers studied were medical students in training, private doctors, or public hospital physicians, researchers found that providers bring negative prior beliefs about blacks' intelligence, proclivity to engage in risky behavior, and likelihood of medical cooperativeness or adherence to prescribed regimens to influence their treatment recommendations. The decision to diagnose, treat, and follow a patient's coronary illness medically depends not only on the technical assessment of objective data, but also on physician a priori assumptions about racial groups' nonmedical, social information.[12]

Black Americans represent a disproportionate number of patients with end-stage renal disease (ESRD).[13] For patients with ESRD, there are only two treatment possibilities: dialysis therapy or kidney transplant. Transplants are the treatment of choice, offering longer life expectancy, especially if the transplant occurs before dialysis. Younger patients live even longer, though older adults—as old as seventy-five—gain an average of four or more years of longevity than if they remained on dialysis. Therefore, the extensive documentation of race and ethnicity disparities in the evaluation for transplants and in the rate of transplants between blacks and whites is disturbing. Researchers have found that blacks are less likely than whites to be informed about transplant treatment, referred for transplant evaluation, or placed on transplant waiting lists.[14] Disparate treatment for renal patients runs through the entire scope of their clinical experience. Epidemiologist Michelle van Ryn reported in a widely cited white paper that black dialysis patients "were less likely than their clinically similar white counterparts to report that they had been told about transplantation before undergoing dialysis."[15] Studies of patients and families who desire transplants demonstrate that patient preferences do not explain these differences.[16]

Predictably, blacks are far less likely to undergo kidney transplantation, even after adjusting for patient preferences, expectations, treatment facility, socioeconomic status, health status, and comorbidities.[17] Although U.S. physicians regularly point to worse graft function and shorter graft survival in African American kidney transplant recipients to explain this disparity,[18] curiously, even after adjusting for patient preferences and expectations, graft outcomes between black and white Canadian renal transplant patients are similar.[19]

A large National Cancer Institute study convincingly showed that when black and white patients receive similar treatments for similar stages of cancer, they enjoy similar survival rates.[20] However black and white cancer patients in this country do not receive similar treatment. Doctors afford vastly different diagnostic services for white and minority cancer patients.[21] Minority patients are generally diagnosed at later stages of cancer's progression. African American women, for example, are less likely to receive diagnostic progesterone receptors or radiation therapy in connection with a mastectomy to treat breast cancer than are white women.[22] Once seen by a surgeon, blacks were still significantly less likely to receive surgical resection. The resulting disparities between minority and white cancer patient survival rates are broad and broadly reported.[23] But when data were adjusted for surgical resection, racial disparities in long-term cancer survival disappeared.

Dr. Peter Bach conducted a study to examine the conjecture that such survival disparities are due to biological differences between minority and white patients.[24] Bach's research team sought to determine whether the racial disparities in survival between blacks and whites persisted when the patients all received the same treatments for similar stages of cancer, regardless of their race. In their systematic review of the literature, Bach's research team evaluated eighty-nine cohorts of blacks and whites who received comparable treatment for similar stage cancers. Across the eight-nine cohorts, which included analysis of survival rates for over 32,000 black patients and 189,000 white patients, Bach found, after adjusting for differences in population mortality, that the survival rate of blacks who received comparable treatment for similar stage cancers was merely 1.07 percent of the risk of death for white patients. Moreover, for three of the four most common cancers—lung, colorectal, prostate—there was *no* evidence of excess cancer mortality in blacks. Bach concluded that differences in cancer biology between racial groups are unlikely to be responsible for a substantial portion of survival disparities. Instead, disparities are more likely the result of differences in cancer treatment. Bach's conclusion not only replicates numerous studies that have demonstrated that blacks are less likely to receive optimal care for cancer than whites, but also provides a basis for the conclusion that differences in treatment by race result in differences in survival rates among white and non-white cancer patients.

Black women have been shown to be less likely than whites to receive rehabilitation support following a mastectomy for breast cancer.[25] Black men are less likely than white men to undergo prostatectomies to treat prostate cancer,[26] and studies show that all African American cancer patients are less likely to receive post-treatment surveillance care.[27] The results are deadly. Indeed, not only are African Americans less likely than white patients to undergo surgery for lung cancer, but researchers have also used survival analysis to estimate that a non-trivial number of black patient deaths over white patient deaths could have been avoided. Dr. Bach's study, which included 10,984 patients, concluded that if blacks had received surgical treatment at the same rate as white patients, 303 more black patients would have been alive five years after surgery. In other words, the disparity between black and white patients' five-year survival rate would have been cut in half from the 7.7 percent difference black patients actually experienced to 3.3 percent, had nondiscriminatory surgical intervention been utilized for both black and white cancer patients.[28]

Beyond the three examples from heart disease, renal disease, and cancer data summarized here, racial disparities in treatment of disease and injury in the United States are pervasive across a wide variety of facility types, age groups, and treatment modalities.[29] In long-term care facilities like nursing homes, whites are more regularly treated for pain than blacks.[30] In emergency rooms, black children are treated differently than whites.[31] Similar inequities characterize treatment of childhood infirmities. For example, African American children have higher hospitalization rates and lower access to preventative care for asthma than white children.[32] Some researchers have found that black children also receive the poorest disease management[33] and have the least access to specialists and mental health care.[34] In 2003 the IOM reported unequivocally that African Americans, Hispanics, and Native Americans experience a much higher burden of illness and mortality due to diabetes than white Americans, and yet the disease appears to be more poorly managed among minority patients; they are less likely to undergo glycosylated hemoglobin or lipid testing, participate in ophthalmologic visits, and receive influenza vaccinations than whites.[35] Sadly, there are some treatments that minority patients receive more readily than whites, but these are not treatments of choice. I call these "reverse disparities." For example, African Americans with bipolar disorder receive more antipsychotic medication than whites despite the danger of long-term damage from these drugs and a lack of evidence that antipsychotics are effective.[36] Another troubling example of a reverse disparity is the finding that minority patients are more likely to be the recipients of amputations than white patients, even after controlling for prior hospitalizations, geography, or co-morbid diseases such as diabetes.[37]

Despite the wealth of available disparities data, two observations from this evidence bear mention. First, health disparities do not affect all minority communities uniformly. Though the data showing differ-

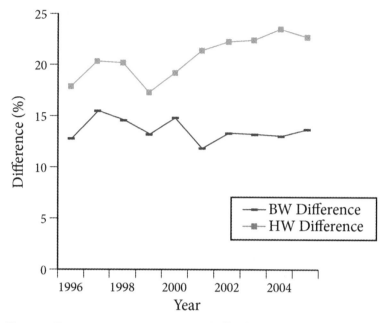

Figure 3.1. Disparate access to outpatient and office-based medical care. *Source*: Benjamin Le Cook et al., "Measuring Trends in Racial/Ethnic Health Care Disparities," *Medical Care Research and Review* 66, no. 1 (February 2009): 23–48.

ences in health and health care between black and white patients is well developed, data on other racial groups is lacking. We know, for example, that blacks and Hispanics access health care differently from whites and from each other. Using data from 1996 to 2005, researchers noted a sharp difference in black-white and Hispanic-white total medical expenditures over the nine-year period.[38] "From 1996 to 2005, the Hispanic-white disparity increased steadily over time whereas the black-white disparity remained relatively stable during that time period."[39] Figure 3.1 depicts the changes in disparate access to outpatient or office visits by blacks, Hispanics, and whites. The top line shows that differences in the rates of access between Hispanics and whites are greater than differences between blacks and whites, and that differences between Hispanics and whites have been increasing over time, while those between blacks and whites have remained relatively stable over time. This data shows that the differences between and among minority patient groups are salient. Yet, Latino and Native and Asian American health and health care disparities do not receive adequate research attention. As a consequence, the nuances and unique features of the inequality these communities suffer are not well understood.

Second, socioeconomic differences among minority and majority patients influence racial and ethnic health disparities but should not be misunderstood to explain them away. Studies that control for differences in wealth, ability to pay, and socioeconomic status confirm that health inequities remain and are associated solely with race and ethnicity.[40] Figure 3.2 describes health care access for black, white, and Hispanic patients and isolates the measure of disparate access that reflects changes in socioeconomic status (SES) rather than racial and ethnic differences. Figure 3.2 shows that even when controlling for socioeconomic status, disparities in access to care between blacks and whites and between Hispanics and whites worsened over time. Disparities in health spending (HS) shrunk by a wider margin for blacks ($260) than for Hispanics ($179) when SES factors were controlled. This means that blacks got a bigger boost in health expenditures from improved SES over time than did Hispanics. Nevertheless, health disparities due to race and ethnicity alone were both significant and growing over the nine years studied.[41]

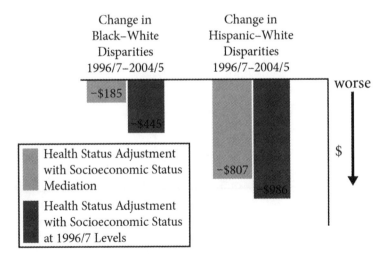

Figure 3.2. Isolating the effect of socioeconomic status on trends in medical expenditure disparities, 1996/7–2004/5. *Source*: Benjamin Le Cook et al., "Measuring Trends in Racial/Ethnic Health Care Disparities," *Medical Care Research and Review* 66, no. 1 (February 2009): 23–48.

Certainly, there is little evidence in either the medical record or the case law to suggest that bigotry and explicit prejudice are the primary sources of the racial and ethnic discrimination that produces these broadly disparate outcomes. But the fact that these differences are not due to overt "racism" is very much beside the most important point. Where patients from minority racial and ethnic backgrounds are discriminated against in health care, and where the outcome of this discrimination is poorer health than that enjoyed by whites in almost every category; something must be done to eradicate this as well as *all* forms of discrimination in health care. This racial and ethnic discrimination is not due to clinical differences among minorities and other patients; nor is the discrimination explained by minority patients' preferences for inferior medical treatment. What then remains to explain the abundant evidence that health care providers do *regularly* discriminate against minority patients and that their discrimination causes disparities in the quality and duration of minority patients' lives? I believe the answer lies in the fact that the discrimination physicians practice is not intentional but *unintentional*. The scientific record convincingly confirms that medical providers' decisions contribute to the relative inferiority of the patient care minorities receive. The studies that link disparate treatment to providers' implicit bias involve physicians who provide cardiac, pediatric, and general medicine care.

Implicit Bias and Physicians' Treatment of Heart Disease

In 1999, Dr. Kevin Schulman reported the first path-breaking study of how patients' race and gender influenced physicians' treatment and decision-making for cardiovascular disease. Schulman studied 720 primary care physicians, using a computerized survey to show the doctors videotaped vignettes of hypothetical patient interviews. The patients were actually scripted actors who were selected to appear similar in age and affect. The eight actors—two white women, two white men, two black women, and two black men—presented identical scripts and diagnostic data. Therefore, in each vignette, the patients differed only by race and gender. After reviewing the vignettes and patient data, the physicians were asked to make treatment recommendations based on this information. Schulman analyzed the physician responses by using a multivariate regression model and found that the patients' race and gender independently influenced how physicians managed chest pain.

Schulman first reported that his data showed white male patients were 40 percent more likely to receive a recommendation for cardiac catheterization than black and female patients. However, responding to criticism of his methodology, Schulman later reduced the ratios that described the relative odds of obtaining interventional catheterization as 13 percent lower for black female patients as compared to white males, and 7 percent lower for black males than their white counterparts. While the final treatment disparity between blacks and whites and between men and women was lower than initially reported, the differences remained disturbingly significant. Schulman concluded, "We doubt that lower utilization rates observed consistently among black patients reflect an effort to provide more appropriate care to these patients."[42] The doctors tested provided black and female patients with different and inferior medical treatment than they provided to white and male patients, and the evidence suggests that the differences were *solely* because of their race and gender. However, although Dr. Schulman's study linked considerations of race and gender to physicians' treatment decisions, the study did not attribute those considerations to the physicians' implicitly held biases.

That further step was taken by Dr. Alexander Green, whose 2007 landmark study explained how well-intentioned, egalitarian providers might unintentionally make racially and ethnically biased medical decisions. Green and his researchers at Harvard University's Massachusetts General Hospital used the Implicit Association Test (IAT) to measure unconscious bias. The result demonstrated that white physicians hold implicit racial biases against African Americans, associating their black patients with negative attributes such as being generally uncooperative and medically noncompliant.[43] Moreover, these researchers showed that the clinical decisions the physician participants made in diagnosing and treating patients with chest pain were informed by their implicit racial biases against blacks generally. Importantly, however, Green's study confirmed that the physicians' racially skewed decisions were inconsistent with the physicians' explicit statements and beliefs about their neutrality with regard to whether patients were black or white patients.

The Harvard research team tested physicians' level of implicit race bias by asking them to complete two IATs. The physicians' explicit racial preferences were assessed using a questionnaire. Next, they were asked to watch an online clinical vignette of patients who described their chest pain and medical history. The doctors were randomly assigned to view a video in which either black or white actors played the part of a patient with coronary artery disease (CAD). Then, the doctors were asked to rate the likelihood that the patient's chest pain was due to coronary artery disease and to state whether they would prescribe thrombolysis for the patient. Treating CAD with thrombolysis is a way to introduce clot-dissolving medication through a catheter in order to prevent blood clots from lodging in the brain and causing strokes or near the heart and causing heart attacks. The Green study findings were remarkable.

First, the researchers found that physicians demonstrated anti-black implicit biases at approximately the same level as the general American population. Next, the researchers showed a statistical interaction between the physicians' willingness to prescribe thrombolysis and their implicit biases against blacks and against black patients.[44] In lay terms, the researchers found that as physicians' level of anti-black, implicit bias increased, the frequency with which physicians prescribed thrombolysis to treat black CAD patients decreased. Conversely, as the physicians' IAT scores increased, revealing greater anti-black implicit biases, the likelihood these physicians would treat white patients with thrombolysis also increased. Said another way, more *unconscious* race bias on the part of physicians meant less treatment for black patients and more treatment for whites. Notably, the physicians in this study expressed absolutely no racial bias on questionnaires seeking their explicit preferences between black and white patients. In fact, for all 287 physician participants, this study showed no *explicit* bias in favor of white patients whatsoever. This is important. The physicians' responses confirmed their racial neutrality and good intentions to treat patients of all races equally. Yet, the Green study revealed that what physicians believe *unconsciously* is a more significant determinant of the quality of patient care they give than what they say about race or ethnicity explicitly.[45] Finally, Dr. Green and his researchers struck a crucial and hopeful note for policy-makers when they separately tested sixty-seven of the physicians who were told at the outset that the study's purpose was to evaluate racial bias in medical decision-making.

Those physicians who were aware that the study sought to determine the impact of implicit bias on treatment decisions made completely different treatment recommendations than those who were unaware. Physicians who were aware of the study's purpose showed an increased willingness to prescribe thrombolysis to blacks even as their IAT scores evincing anti-black implicit bias increased. Social scientists call this phenomenon a "novelty effect"; in this context, the effect involved study participants self-correcting their biases to improve their outcomes once made aware of the study's focus. However, I propose an alternate view of the difference between physicians who knew Dr. Green's purpose and those who did not. These results reasonably suggest that physicians can recognize, modulate, and even counteract the effect of their implicit race bias on treatment decisions, at least when they are being studied. Therefore, it is also reasonable to view this self-correction as positive and hopeful evidence that physicians in real medical settings generally are willing and able to reverse the impact of their unconscious racial biases if they are made aware that they have them.

The view that physician bias contributes to health disparities is supported by yet another helpful result from Dr. Green's study. The majority of physicians in that study candidly admitted the likelihood that implicit bias may affect their medical decisions. Indeed, 71.6 percent of the physicians who were aware of the study's purpose agreed with the statement that "Subconscious biases about patients based on their race may affect the way I make decisions about their care without my realizing it"; 60.5 percent of those unaware of the study's purpose also concurred. This evidence of physicians' ability and willingness to self-evaluate *and* self-correct is further confirmation that any suggestion that implicit race bias makes one a racist, a bigot, or evil is just plain false. In fact, all that we know about implicit bias from social and neuroscientists suggests the exact opposite. Implicit racial and ethnic biases often operate in complete contradiction to one's actual and sincerely held racial views and preferences. But like the physician quoted at the beginning of this chapter, doctors, according to this study, are willing and able to change.

The Green study is not without critics. Some have alleged that because the physicians who showed lower IAT scores treated black and white patients differently, while physicians with higher IAT scores treated black and white patients similarly, Green should have concluded the IAT does not measure true racial bias.[46] This criticism misses the point of the Green findings entirely. The Green study findings are remarkable because of the interactive *relationship* between the level of implicit bias and treatment choices *within* each racial group, not as compared *between* the two racial groups. Indeed, the *directions* of the physician choices are exactly opposite for black and white patients; a physician's likelihood of recommending treatment for black patients is *inversely* related to the IAT score but *positively* related to IAT scores for white patients. The salient finding is that there is a predictive relationship between increasing physician bias and treatment decisions. Physicians with high anti-black bias gave whites more treatment, and those with lower anti-black bias gave white patients less treatment. The converse was also true for physicians treating black patients. High anti-black bias was associated with less treatment for blacks, while low anti-black bias is associated with more treatment for black patients. Thus, Green's findings are remarkable not so much for the lack of correlation between physicians' neutral explicit racial preferences and their treatment decisions, as for their indicating a direct relationship between doctors' implicit racial biases and their treatment judgments.

Implicit Bias and Pediatricians' Treatment Decisions

A pair of studies reported by Dr. Janice Sabin refines knowledge about the association between implicit bias and physicians' treatment decisions by focusing specifically on pediatricians. Using case vignettes written for this research study, Sabin asked pediatricians from a large urban research university to make treatment recommendations for four commonly occurring pediatric conditions: urinary tract infections (UTIs), attention deficit hyperactivity disorder (ADHD), asthma, and post-surgical pain.[47] Two patients, one black and one white, represented each condition, and each physician participant was randomly assigned a vignette from each disease category. The results from these studies help to explore the different ways in which implicit bias operates depending upon the type of patient and practice each physician has. Generally, Sabin found that pediatricians showed lower implicit preferences for whites over blacks when compared with most IAT test-takers and with the physicians among that population. However, even these lower implicit bias measures were not associated with the doctors' treatment recommendations for patients with UTIs, ADHD, or asthma. Sabin's study was the first to demonstrate that physicians with more pro-white implicit bias were more ready to prescribe pain medication to white patients than to African American patients. This finding is consistent with the often-reported erroneous physician perception that blacks misuse prescribed pain drugs more than whites. This assumption is untrue. But Sabin reasoned that the clinical uncertainty presented by a pediatric patient's claim to pain introduces the cognitive stress that often leads to clinical bias.

Together, the Schulman, Green, and Sabin studies lay a strong foundation for a new understanding of how providers' implicit racial biases lead to disparate medical treatment and outcomes. Schulman identified race and gender as driving influences on physicians' treatment decisions, while Green provided the evidence that doctors could unconsciously allow race to bias their medical decisions, leading to disparate treatment of otherwise similarly situated black and white patients. Sabin's study refined our understanding of how implicit biases affect physicians from different specialties who treat patients with different illnesses. In addition, the social science record further confirms what many physicians will admit: that they and their colleagues unconsciously allow learned, negative instincts about minority patients to influence their medical decision-making.

Implicit Bias and Physicians' Diagnostic Decisions

Dr. Gordon Moskowitz published a study in 2012 that demonstrates how unconsciously triggered group stereotypes can inform a physician's diagnosis.[48] Moskowitz tested a physician's ability to identify medical terms quickly from a group of randomly generated words appearing on a computer screen. However, immediately before the selected words appeared, physicians were subliminally "primed" with a photograph of either an African or a European American face. The photograph flashed quickly in the physician's peripheral field of vision so that it could not be consciously perceived. The researchers found that physicians were fastest at identifying medical words for diseases stereotypically associated with African Americans after subliminally seeing a black face, but slower identifying *the same* medical words after being primed with a white face. Moreover, physicians responded fastest to terms for conditions that were perceived as arising from behavioral choices, such as HIV, drug abuse, and obesity. In contrast, physicians were slower to identify terms for medical conditions that were genetic in origin, such as hypertension, stroke, sickle cell anemia, and coronary artery disease, even though the study showed these diseases are also stereotypically identified with blacks. Thus, Moskowitz's study showed not only that physicians unconsciously associated certain diseases with African Americans without being aware they were doing so, but also that they were quick to unconsciously associate diseases arising from antisocial behavior with African Americans.

> According to Dr. Moskowitz, "This is important because (1) it occurred without the doctors realizing they were invoking stereotypes (or even that they were thinking about African Americans), suggesting that stereotypes influenced them in ways and at times they did not consciously intend, and (2) these implicit associations were apparent for both conditions associated with lifestyle choices and diseases associated with genetic predisposition. Implicit stereotypical beliefs about African Americans may be accurate and medically justifiable, and they may equally have no basis in medical evidence. Our aim was to examine whether implicit stereotyping exists among medical doctors, because it may bias diagnosis of and treatment recommended to African American patients even in the absence of intent or awareness by the practitioner.[49]

By showing the subconscious operation of the disease associations, Moskowitz has pointed to a serious concern: A physician's recollection of stereotyped information she or he associates with a patient's racial or ethnic group may *crowd out* the physician's unbiased assessment and treatment decisions about the individual minority patient she or he is treating. Moskowitz explains the danger to minority patients and their health:

> Implicit stereotyping among health care providers presents 2 dangers: (1) inaccurate components of a stereotype may be used in diagnosis and treatment without conscious knowledge of this influence, [and] (2) even an accurate stereotype may unduly influence diagnosis and treatment.[50]

As the Moskowitz study clearly shows, the erroneous judgments that may result from the implicit associations can compromise the quality of care a minority patient receives and contribute to the disparity gap between white and minority patients' health outcomes.

Implicit Bias and Other Health Professionals

A group led by Dr. Adil Haider published a study involving first-year medical students at Johns Hopkins Medical School.[51] Predictably, Haider found that the majority of doctors-in-training hold similar implicit preferences for whites over blacks as their more senior physician colleagues. However, unpredictably, Dr. Haider also found no association between the medical students' IAT scores and their clinical assessments based on patient vignettes. Approximately 200 of the total 241 first-year students volunteered to participate in the study. They were shown patient vignettes and then given a multiple-choice question to test their medical judgment across four scenarios. The scenarios required a pain assessment, a determination of the appropriateness of informed consent, and assessments of patient reliability and trust. The vignettes were selected to randomly show students patients of different races—black and white—and patients of different socioeconomic class and occupations. The results showed a marked contrast between implicit biases held by incoming medical students and their medical judgments, on the one hand, and the implicit biases and decisions made by more senior practitioners, on the other. In this study, only one vignette—informed consent—showed that student-physicians' responses correlated and varied with the patient's race. In all other scenarios, the students' responses did not vary with the patient's race or socioeconomic status. In other words, notwithstanding the evidence that these students held implicit biases similar to more experienced physicians and residents in other studies, the students' biases did not affect their clinical determinations. This one study is not generalizable to the entire incoming medical school population training to become physicians in the United States. However, the Haider study does raise important questions about when, why, and how in the course of their medical training physicians' implicit biases begin to influence their medical decisions.

Hypertension and Other Counterfactuals

Dr. Irene Blair recently reported the results of a study that failed to find an association between physician unconscious bias and hypertension-related outcomes in 4,794 black, Latino, and white patients.[52] The study included 138 primary care physicians from two Colorado health systems. Blair used the IAT to measure physician bias, and then examined the association between physician bias and treatment intensification, medication adherence, and patients' hypertension control using a multilevel regression model. While 70 percent of the physicians tested showed some implicit bias against blacks or Latinos, and nearly 40 percent showed moderate to strong levels of bias, the researchers found physician implicit bias was not associated with less treatment intensification, worse adherence, or worse blood pressure control for black or Latino patients when compared to whites. The researchers cited the fact that physicians in their study were experienced primary care practitioners as a possible explanation for their outcomes, and they observed that the nature of primary care practice may account for strong working relationships that result in standardized care across racial and ethnic groups. One commentator suggested that imperfect outcome measures and individualized patient coping mechanisms may, in part, account for the lack of relationship between outcomes and bias.[53] In fact, many other factors, including the infrequency of patient visits with physicians in the three-year study and its focus on a single disease outcome, hypertension, require further examination of these results. Dr. Blair points to factors such as the general awareness that patients have concerning hypertension control, the integrated nature of the health systems studied, and the fact that primary care physicians develop strong working relationships over a long period of time that may mitigate the impact of physician bias on hypertensive patients' health outcomes. Providers and policy-makers certainly must take note of the possibility that the features of a primary care delivery-system that Blair identifies have a mitigating impact on physician implicit bias.

However, another feature of the delivery systems studied by Dr. Blair may provide less hopeful explanations for the hypertension study results. For example, patient interviews that I conducted for this book strongly suggest that minority patients who experience discriminatory health care simply switch providers or cease to access medical care altogether. These patients who "drop out" of care systems and are likely to experience adverse health outcomes that are associated with provider discrimination may not be accounted for in this study. Therefore, the lack of health care alternatives available to patients in the health systems Blair studied, along with the possibility that the study did not capture the minority patients who stopped going to high-IAT physicians, suggest that further research is required to understand fully how this study influences our understanding of physician bias and health outcomes.

In addition to the questions that Blair's hypertension study raises, researchers have found that there is important variation in the general findings as well. Researchers have shown that the nature of implicit bias itself, as well as the ways in which it affects real-life medical decision-making outside the confines of the research setting, is likely to be complex, nuanced, and not yet fully understood by the current scientific studies. Patients, for example, do not ever fit the demographic pigeonholes often tested in reported research. Few studies have been performed to consider the effect of implicit biases on minority groups other than blacks and whites. And besides the simplistic black and white categories tested, patient characteristics overlap outside and within those categories. Studies do not reflect that white patients may be poor, wealthy, or somewhere in between, while black patients may have light or dark complexions, even though all these variations have been shown to impact implicit bias levels. All patients possess overlapping characteristics. Their gender, age, geographic origin, and countless other characteristics are also prone to trigger physicians' implicit biases and stereotypes, but few other traits have been tested independently or as they overlap with one another. It is also the case that taken alone, these few studies cannot be read as conclusive proof that implicit bias affects medical decision-making in a way that causes providers to contribute to health disparities. However, the social science research reviewed throughout the next three chapters shows that these studies that associate physician implicit biases and medical decision-making are only the tip of the empirical iceberg.

In 2003, when the Institute of Medicine's *Unequal Treatment* report suggested that physicians' implicit biases and resulting stereotypes or prejudices against minority patients might be a cause of racial and ethnic health disparities, the IOM concluded that the scientific community lacked a full understanding of "the degree to which these attitudes might affect the outcome of patient care."[54] At the time of the report, the IOM also confessed that the scientific community knew little about the pathways by which these attitudes, biases, and stereotypes may result in differences in clinical treatment. Over a decade later, the medical and scientific communities have made only modest progress towards understanding, and virtually no progress in addressing, the role that physicians' unconscious biases play in causing the disparate treatment and health outcomes that racial and ethnic minorities suffer. The next chapter introduces a new conceptual model to explain the connection between biases and disparities.

4

From Impressions to Inequity

Connecting the Empirical Dots

With few exceptions, the literature on racial disparities in medical care is reluctant to admit and address racial bias among providers as a critical causal factor. . . . It is unlikely that personal discrimination on the part of providers is the sole cause of disparities in health care. In any area of societal evaluation, the causes of racial differences are complex and multi-dimensional, with discrimination being only one of them. Moreover, institutional discrimination is often at least as important as individual discrimination. . . . However . . . recent research . . . suggests that discrimination remains as a central plausible explanation.
—David R. Williams and Toni D. Rucker

This chapter introduces a conceptual model to address unanswered questions about the mechanisms that link implicit bias to health disparities, which the Institute of Medicine (IOM) posed in its compelling 2003 report. After reviewing the copious data on health disparities, the IOM confessed that current scientific knowledge does not "elucidate the mechanisms by which these attitudes, biases, and stereotypes may result in differences in clinical treatment, or the degree to which these attitudes might affect the outcome of patient care."[1] In this chapter, I propose a new conceptual model to provide the elucidation the IOM called for, and to identify target areas where future researchers and policy-makers might quantify and reduce the effects of implicit bias.

The Biased Care Model identifies six mechanisms by which physician and patient implicit biases operate to produce disparate health outcomes. I offer the model to synthesize the complex empirical literature on health disparities. My objective is to provide a set of general principles that will help predict the interactions that are the most likely source of increasing health disparities. These principles will help inform future applications of the accumulated research record on health disparities. Social and clinical scientists have generated a veritable mountain of data examining the problem for a variety of patient populations, clinical settings, and illnesses. However, this vast literature lacks a theoretical framework to turn these data into a practical approach to addressing the egregious inequity problem. Providers and policy-makers are stalled, suffering from what appears to be collective cognitive dissonance. On the one hand, the scientific community annually produces copious new and damning knowledge about the death and destruction that health disparities cause. Yet, on the other hand, the volume of information is so overwhelming that it produces either a series of ineffective pronouncements about cultural competence, astonishing attempts to blame patients for their behavior and genetic characteristics, or indifference. I have constructed the Biased Care Model to help make sense of the research record.[2] The Biased Care Model is designed to guide policy-making by providing both an explanatory theory and a change theory of implicit bias in medicine. First, this model will answer the IOM's call to "elucidate the mechanisms" that link biased attitudes to disparate health outcomes. Once identified, the model's mechanisms will inform the development and implementation of intervention strategies to change the way that implicit biases operate in health care. The explanatory power of any model must not only find support in social science literature, but must also fit descriptions of "real life." Therefore, this chapter supports the Biased Care Model with quantitative data and qualitative interviews. Patient and provider narratives accompany discussion of each of the model's six mechanisms. While the social science findings document an association between each mechanism and disparate health outcomes, interviews provide the words and voices of patients and physicians as evidence of the causal connection between implicit bias and health inequality.

The model also explains how prevailing medical practices exacerbate the journey that unconscious biases make from memory to influencing health outcomes. These conditions include the fact that providers function under enormous time and financial pressure and carry large patient loads. The inherent uncertainty of medical decision-making is made more difficult by the political and legal uncertainty that major health reform legislation introduces. Ours is a health care system undergoing a structural transformation. The result is that modern health care providers carry a sizeable cognitive load related to the change they are experiencing. Patients similarly face uncertainty that compounds their relative lack of medical information and control. In these conditions, all parties to the clinical encounter rely more heavily on the implicit biases they hold, and these attitudes have even greater influence on the quality of care and resultant health outcomes that patients experience. Implicit biases can compound cumulatively without following any sequential pattern or chronological timing. The Biased Care Model demonstrates this complexity and yet offers a framework to simplify and sort out the network of biased-tainted exchanges between physicians and patients.

The Biased Care Model

The six mechanisms of the Biased Care Model operate in three roughly chronological domains, affecting physician and patient interactions before, during, and after the clinical encounter. Therefore I describe the six mechanisms in pairs. The first pair—Mechanisms #1 and #2—impacts health outcomes before doctors and patients meet in person. The first mechanism explains how physicians' biased perceptions about the minority group to which a patient belongs influence their expectations of patients they have yet to encounter. The second mechanism involves physicians' erroneous statistical interpretations and use of data about a patient's racial or ethnic group, whether or not the data turns out to actually apply to the individual patient. The second pair of mechanisms serves as a conduit of implicit racial bias during the clinical encounter. Mechanisms #3 and #4 interact reciprocally to influence physician and patient communication. Finally, after the clinical encounter, physicians make treatment and diagnostic decisions, and patients make decisions about compliance, adherence, and follow-up. These post-encounter decisions are the Biased Care Model's fifth and sixth mechanisms.

Figure 4.1 lays out a schematic diagram to show how all the six mechanisms of the Biased Care Model interact to impact minority patients' health.[3] The diagram provides a graphic summary of the categories into

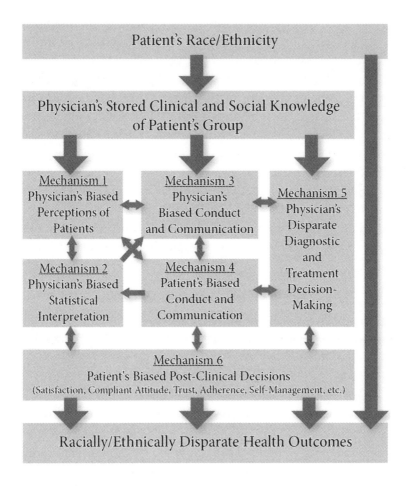

Figure 4.1. The Biased Care Model: Six mechanisms by which providers' racial and ethnic biases contribute to disparate health outcomes.

which empirical findings about implicit biases and health disparities can be sorted. Shown visually, the model drives home my assertion that the six mechanisms, through which implicit biases operate to cause health disparities, are far more significant contributors to unequal health outcomes than biomedical or behavioral causes. Moreover, the model provides a picture of the mechanisms that precede and influence many of the patient preferences and behaviors that some have erroneously identified as major causes of disparities. The schematic diagram prioritizes the powerful ways that racial and ethnic bias produce health disparities, while visually placing other explanations for health inequity into perspective.

The Biased Care Model is built upon the theory that racial discrimination is a fundamental cause of health disparities.[4] Thus, at the top of the model's diagram, two rectangular boxes show that a patients' apparent race and ethnicity automatically trigger retrieval of the negative social group knowledge that causes discrimination. Between the top two causal rectangular boxes, and the bottom rectangle that pictures the resulting outcome, six mechanism boxes provide pathways through which implicit bias travels before, during, and after the physician-patient interaction. The bidirectional arrows between boxes represent the fact that many of these mechanisms mutually influence one another. For example, physicians hold biased perceptions that influence the way they interpret statistical data, and these biased interpretations in turn reinforce their perceptions. Some arrows point in only one direction to show, for example, that while patients' conduct and communication may influence the way physicians interpret statistical data, these interpretations are invisible to patients and do not directly influence their conduct. In other words, the chronological timeline that I use in the model helps to organize the literature and data that supports each mechanism, but in reality implicit bias attitudes are not orderly or sequential. With this overview in place, in this and subsequent chapters I will walk through each mechanism of the model to set forth the principles, literature, and real-life experiences that they reflect.

Bias before the Clinical Encounter

Mechanism #1: Physicians' Biased Perceptions Negatively Impact Minority Patient Health Outcomes

The portal through which implicit biases enter health care interactions forms long before the patient-provider relationship begins. Physicians bring a wealth of knowledge and expectations about their patients into the examination room, operating theater, or hospital bedside. As discussed in chapter 2, psychologists call this information "stored social knowledge." Thus, when provider and patient meet, many subconscious expectations and judgments will automatically be triggered. These a priori assumptions, in turn, will shape the ensuing interactions, especially when physicians are unused to interacting with people from a patient's racial or ethnic group. For example, a number of studies show physicians prefer and interact most comfortably with patients whom they describe as "likeable"—that is, those who are not excessively demanding, and are instead cooperative and good communicators.[5] Tests show that all people generally respond to the level of "warmth" and "competence" they sense from the person with whom they are interacting.[6] However, basing their responses on race or ethnicity alone, physicians will ascribe these characteristics to patients they do not know because of their prior assumptions.

Anyone who has spent any time with doctors in clinical or scholarly settings knows that these subjective categorizations often show up when a patient is being presented on rounds or in a conference: "A pleasant 51 year old white woman presented with back pain . . ." or "This nice gentleman came to the office with a chief complaint of . . ." Words that describe a patient as "nice" or "pleasant" curiously find their way in among the very first, and presumably most important, sentences when doctors explain the relevant facts and medical data about a patient. In contrast, when these kind words are absent, physicians may be communicating negative perceptions of the patients they discuss. Studies show that physicians generally find patients who are abrasive, angry, lacking in language proficiency, or having poor personal hygiene undesirable. Race and ethnicity differences between provider and patient are likely to introduce automatic stereotypes that will overlay these preferences and dislikes and influence the quality of care.

Consider the following narrative by an experienced emergency physician. This doctor willingly admits her implicit biases, but despite her obvious commitment to egalitarian principles, it is doubtful that she fully appreciates the extent of her biases:

> Yes, I think there are implicit racial disparities and I think there's a fair body of evidence for that. But I know for instance in my own experience, I think that I probably have implicit [biases]. I would bend over backwards to say that it's not explicit in my case but the more I say that the more I think it's probably implicit. And it comes out in peculiar ways: The surprise when it turns out that a patient who's African American turns out to be the son of a prominent official in the government. And I would

not start from the basis that I could be surprised if that person were Caucasian, I suspect. Ok, so it's starting from a different base and then going "Oh! Ok, so you're the son of . . ." kind of thing.
—Emergency Physician, Midwestern University Hospital

Note this physician's reference to the "surprise" of finding that her black patient belonged to a prominent family. Note further that she would not have been surprised at the affiliation if that patient were white. And finally note the ever-so-subtle admission that her disposition toward her black patient changed once she realized his connections. This physician is more than just "well-intentioned" as her willingness to "bend over backwards" confirms: She is committed to fairness and is an outspoken advocate for the underserved. Yet even this physician reserves one approach for black patients who fit her expectation that African Americans are not prominent or well connected, but shifts her demeanor if she encounters an individual who defies this expectation. These are not behavior choices she attaches automatically to white patients, and so it is clear these are expectations about race and not class.

Few recognize the far-reaching consequences of the biases they hold. The following statements, however, exemplify one doctor's awareness of the impact that physician bias can have on entire populations of affected patients:

I think it [implicit bias] is pervasive. . . . Let me give you what I think is a concrete example. This is the one that I actually remember being discussed during my training: Older, Hispanic women, who present with whatever complaints and I don't remember exactly how this was described—but to paraphrase it, [the message was that] they tend to be more somatic, often feeling like they have to bring some things forward when they're talking with a physician so you will get a kind of medicalized view. They will feel like they are wasting your time if they aren't complaining about something, and describing those complaints, and describing them physically because you're a doctor. Yet the underlying problem is that they're nervous about their kids and things like that. So that is or at least was a pervasive view and something that was overtly discussed. So what that's going to do is that's going to bias the way that somebody interprets those symptoms, so a patient of that demographic

description who comes in complaining of chest pain . . . the person bearing that bias is going to be less likely to consider that a cardiac source, and we already know they are less likely to order diagnostic testing for women in general, they're going to be less likely to order diagnostic testing for older Latinas specifically for that reason, which then is going to affect the diagnosis and ultimately affect the treatment and I think wherever you enter that diagnostic and treatment chain, those sorts of things happen.
—Attending Physician, Internal Medicine, Southwestern University Medical Center

This doctor rightly characterizes the negative perceptions that form based on preclinical stereotyping as "pervasive" with the potential, in this example, to taint every Hispanic patient's care. Moreover, this physician's statement reveals that the biased attitudes he described were communicated during medical training, thus impacting students' perceptions about the Hispanic female patients whom they would encounter for years to come.

In contrast to this physician, most caregivers whom I interviewed viewed their implicit biases as "helping" minority patients. For example, when I asked one nurse about his experiences with implicit biases, he responded:

I'm not sure I view it completely as a negative . . . for example if it was a clinical setting, because of your preconceived judgment [about a person's resources] you may be trying to cater to and help someone [find cheaper care solutions].
—Cardiac Care Nurse, New England University Medical Center

This nurse mistakenly thinks his stereotypes serve as useful cognitive short-cuts to assist him in personalizing patient care and achieving better health outcomes. However, racial and ethnic stereotypes are not the same as clinically relevant categorizations physicians and other health workers are trained to use when making a differential diagnosis. Generalizations about athletes may help diagnose leg pain, and commonalities shared by members of a similar profession may help narrow treatment alternatives for patients with respiratory illness. These are nonracial stereotypes, and doctors use them all the time to diagnose and devise effective treatments. Admittedly, neutral information about a patient's race can be helpful in providing good care. However, when physicians use derogatory and factually unfounded racial and ethnic stereotypes to form perceptions about patients prematurely, the results are harmful. That a doctor may be overworked, fatigued, or under significant time pressure does not justify the harms. Instead, circumstances of uncertainty make a physician's use of negative biases more likely to cause disproportionate injury to minority patients.

The problem, as one researcher has put it, is not with the use of classification and heuristics that are common and helpful in medicine, but with "fixed, untrue stereotypes resistant to modification [that] threaten the accuracy of decision-making."[7] Physicians have been shown to allow stereotypes about minority patients to override the medical facts, their own good intentions, and even their medical training.

UNTRUE, NEGATIVE PERCEPTIONS CAN TRUMP THE FACTS
When a physician has had a negative experience with one minority patient in the past or has even encountered negative generalizations about the racial group to which a patient belongs, the memory of that negative experience or preconception can confirm a negative stereotype even though the *current* clinical encounter does not. For example, physicians who are consumers of popular culture may subconsciously view black women as promiscuous, reproductively irresponsible, or even deceptive. All three stereotypes are evident in the experience an African American woman recounts from her interaction with an internal medicine physician in the southwestern United States:

> My husband and I are hoping to get pregnant. Recently, my African American physician removed scar tissue following my myomectomy. After the surgery, my surgeon reported that he wasn't prepared for what he saw; my large intestines and small intestines had been connected by scar tissue. Knowing that we are trying to have children, my surgeon consulted an internist to help put organs into their proper location.

From the outset, this woman's story makes plain that she is married, interested in becoming pregnant, and consulting a specialist to help correct an anatomical problem so that she might be able to have children.

She expressed no interest in sterilization. Continuing her story, the patient reflected on the internal medicine resident's recommendation:

> The resident on my case, however, advocated that instead of this time-consuming procedure, "why don't we just give her a radical hysterectomy?" which is . . . nine times out of ten what they propose to have done on black women.

Without a doubt, this patient sees the resident's decision to recommend a radical hysterectomy to be all about her race. The patient came for help getting pregnant, so that she could have and raise children, but instead the resident proposed to sterilize her! Because she neither wanted nor needed a hysterectomy, this patient considered the resident to have proposed the procedure solely on account of her being black, in the belief that black women should not reproduce. History supports this patient's suspicion of racism. The nineteenth-century pseudosciences of phrenology, craniometry, and anthropometry gave rise to proponents of the eugenics movement and social Darwinists who advocated sterilizing the "unfit," by whom they meant Chinese, Mexican, Japanese, Jewish, and black migrants. Moreover, as this patient's story reveals, the horrors of the Tuskegee experiments, and the copious evidence of the thousands of abusive sterilizations performed on prisoners, members of the military, and minority women is part of the collective memory and discourse of most African American patients.[8]

The patient continued her story:

> The same resident came into my room the next day. She said that my level of scarring suggested to her that I must have had a previous STD [sexually transmitted disease]. This, she said, without asking me any questions and in front of my husband who is Caucasian. I don't believe she would have said this if I was white.

To complete the patient's perceived insult, the resident announced the presumption that she must have been sexually active before her marriage (contrary to her report) and that she must have been active with a diseased partner. And just in case her husband did not know this nefarious secret about the patient, the resident physician violates every imaginable standard for ethical and professional conduct to report the suspicion of promiscuity in front of this patient's family.

> I felt resentment at her remarks and interpreted them as an effort to hint to my husband that he didn't know my entire medical history. She did not know me or care about my deep interest in childbearing. In fact, I was married a virgin. That was not her assumption, however, based solely on my race. Both my husband and my surgeon forbade this resident from any further interaction with me and I felt fortunate they were there to protect me.

Sadly, this patient's story is not exceptional. Indeed the woman who recounted this experience shared her narrative openly while we were sitting in a black hair salon. The women around us shared a collective disapprobation for the doctor's behavior, but also nodded knowingly as we all identified with the experience of being a victim of a similar form of racial bias. The resident internist in this narrative is now likely a practicing physician who has carried these stereotypes and attitudes into practice without knowing the impact she is having on black women's health to this day.

In a study conducted by Drs. Michelle van Ryn and Jane Burke, physicians rated their perceptions of patients' intelligence, education, self-control, pleasantness, rationality, independence, and responsibility. The physicians also rated patients on their feelings of affiliation with them and in terms of their perceptions of patient behavior, such as how likely they were to lack social support, over-report discomfort, fail to comply with medical advice, abuse drugs, or try to manipulate physicians. The results showed an important and statistically significant correlation between patient race, socioeconomic status (SES), and physician perceptions. Physicians in this study were less likely to have positive perceptions of black patients in numerous categories. Black patients were rated as less intelligent and less educated than white patients, even when the education and income levels of patients in the study were adjusted and controlled. Physicians studied were more likely to rate blacks as being at risk for substance abuse, being noncompliant, and being unlikely to participate in cardiac rehabilitation if prescribed. In fact, the stereotypes about the prevalence of drug abuse among blacks are untrue. In 2007, the Substance Abuse and Mental Health Services Administration reported that blacks are less likely than whites to have injected heroin, cocaine, stimulants or methamphetamines. Moreover, blacks and whites show no statistical differences in their rates of illicit drug use overall, with 8.3 percent of whites and 8.7 percent of blacks reporting such abuse.[9] Nevertheless, van Ryn and Burke have demonstrated that negative cultural perceptions can more powerfully influence a physician's impressions of a patient than actual, factual information even before the clinical encounter.

Researchers have further found that patient SES has a broad effect on physician perception, even beyond the effect of race alone. Thus, when included in the lowest 33 percent of the SES distributions, blacks were overwhelmingly perceived to be less pleasant, less likely to be self-controlled, and less rational than whites. Race, of course, is highly correlated with SES in America and therefore compounds the negative impact of perceptions mediated by both variables in the health care context. Moreover, because these negative perceptions persisted even in the face of disconfirming individual information presented to physicians in this study, van Ryn and Burke concluded that the doctors' stereotypic expectations were biasing the way they interpreted information; unconsciously, physicians may fail to distinguish between "content accuracy (the accuracy of a generalized belief about a group of people) and application accuracy" with regard to the individual patient sitting before them in the examination room. The danger is, of course, that this failure may have a deleterious effect on the medical treatment that some patients receive. One doctor explained the tenacity of biased perceptions this way:

> It's interesting that no matter how much schooling you go through, you can't get away from your home training and your home biases that you actually grow up with. So, in residency training, in medical school training, and even now, there are clearly people who feel more comfortable with certain types of patients than they do with others. And you can't get away from being human. I mean, even though you're supposed to be this dispassionate, consummate professional who's unemotional, it turns out that that probably only works out in the movies with Dr. Marcus Welby and all the rest of those.
> —Attending Physician, Pulmonology, Southwestern University Medical Center

Once they understand the dynamic of unconscious bias, most physicians will honestly and transparently confirm the power that negative stereotypes have over their medical judgments in numerous settings. Surgeons interviewed have reported that their decisions not to offer transplantation as an option to minority patients were based upon their past experience with minority patients who did not have sufficient resources, family support, and work flexibility to allow them to adhere to the difficult and time-consuming medical follow-up required to remain healthy, even in the absence of evidence that the particular patient currently being treated lacked the means to adhere to a treatment regimen. In another example, physicians tested assumed incorrectly that the African American patient participants were uneducated and less intelligent than white patients, based on their past experiences, regardless of the patients' true educational background.[10] Studies involving pain treatment have shown that physicians are more reluctant to prescribe opioids for minority patients due to their background expectations of the propensity toward drug abuse each group may have. Although the fact is that white patients are equally as likely to abuse or divert narcotics as minority patients, researchers believe physicians' reluctance may be due to the erroneous belief in the stereotype that drug abuse is more common among racial and ethnic minority patients than it is among white patients.[11] Another commentator has observed that physician fears are fueled by media imagery of the black drug dealer or violent criminal; for more than sixty years, social scientists have been documenting that white Americans commonly hold both these stereotypes.[12] There is no reason to believe that white health care providers hold fewer or different stereotypes of their minority patients than whites hold generally. In fact, the evidence is to the contrary. Most physicians exhibit the same implicit bias patterns as the general population. Moreover, most physicians also exhibit the patterns of implicit and explicit bias that researchers have called "aversive racism"—that is, a combination of low levels of explicit bias, together with high measures of implicit bias. This is important because evidence confirms that in physician-patient interactions, when physicians display such aversive racism, minority patients have a particularly negative reaction that is detrimental to their relationship with their physicians and their ability to communicate with them, which, in turn impact the medical decisions made with their physicians.

Consider this black male patient's response to my question about physicians whom he perceives as biased:

> Q: When you have a conversation with someone who may not be a racist overtly, or explicitly, are there any signals that you can read or that affect you to tell you that they may be unconsciously racist?
>
> A: Oh yes. And the first one is presumptions about knowledge—you know that "well you never heard of this, have you?" And they use a term and they'll look at you and if they don't see a reaction they'll just presume that you don't understand what they said. You know? I'm sure you've encountered that too.

The aversive racist is more offensive to minority patients than the explicit racist; in fact, this same African American patient easily separated derogatory language from a physician's well-intentioned motives, despite the plainly inappropriately derogatory expression "boy" used in addressing an adult, black male patient: .

> He was the one that said, in his Louisiana accent after I had had the [minor heart attack] . . . [imitating southern accent], "This thing here is gonna blow, boy!" It was in a very southern kind of way. And I totally understood he was coming from a position of caring. And somebody might have thought he was being just a peckerwood, you know, but it was clear to me that he was—because of his eye contact, and the way he looked at you. You know he looks at you straight in the eye . . . so you know that he's sincere and it has nothing to do with his bias . . . you know . . . that kind of thing. But the external way he was saying, you know, it's fair to say you had to first get a hold of yourself, and say, "Wait a minute here, who's this talking to me?"
> —African American Patient, Midwestern City

The aversion minorities have to aversive racists explains why this patient recoiled less at being called "boy" by one doctor, than he did when another physician implicitly presumed his ignorance.

UNTRUE, NEGATIVE PERCEPTIONS CAN TRUMP
GOOD INTENTIONS

In chapter 3, we reviewed Dr. Janice Sabin's 2012 study of how implicit bias affects pediatricians' treatment recommendations. In 2008, Dr. Sabin conducted the first study to compare measures of implicit and explicit racial attitudes held by a large group of physicians with the attitudes of the general population.[13] The Sabin study analyzed data from hundreds of thousands of voluntary visitors to Harvard University's Project Implicit website. After reviewing the race attitude IATs taken by over 2,500 physician volunteer participants on the interactive website, Sabin compared the results to the same tests taken by approximately 404,000 overall test-takers during a twenty-eight-month period. Then the researchers administered a questionnaire to the physicians in order to determine and compare their explicit race preferences. Sabin found that the American physicians tested held implicit and explicit attitudes about race that are the same as the general pattern seen in the population at large. White male physicians showed the strongest pro-white associations, while female physicians, like other female test-takers, showed weaker pro-white preferences. While Hispanic physician test-takers reported little express preference between blacks and whites, their IAT scores showed they strongly favored white Americans. African American physicians presented a more complicated picture. As a group overall, they showed no implicit preferences for blacks or whites; their average IAT scores were nearly zero. However, the data also revealed a wide standard deviation from the mean for this group, suggesting that some individual black physicians showed a strong preference for whites over blacks, while others showed a strong preference for blacks over whites. While this is not data that many discuss, even minority patients are aware that some minority physicians hold antiminority biases. One African American patient explains her experience not only with a black physician, but also with a black physician's assistant this way:

> This brings me back to an experience that happened to me a few years ago. The very interesting thing about implicit bias . . . it made me think of a time that I went to the doctor about six years ago and it was the exact same situation where a PA had come in and I told the PA that I wanted to see the doctor. And she was visibly pissed at me for wanting

to do that. . . . This PA was pissed. And I even overheard her saying, "She wants to talk to you" as if "the nerve of her wanting to talk to you—she's double checking me." And this was not necessarily the plan that we laid out. Maybe they had laid out who was going to see who but at the end of the day if my insurance is paying for me to see a physician, then I want to see a physician. But bringing this back full circle to when I was talking about *Pedagogy of the Oppressed*, this particular physician and physicians' assistant were African American. So . . . when you look at implicit bias in the context of law and in the context of law enforcement specifically, it has been shown that African Americans have just as much bias towards African Americans as white Americans have towards black Americans.

This patient's reference to Paulo Freire's classic book about how those who have been oppressed themselves become oppressors summarizes her assessment that the power dynamic between herself, as the patient, and her health care providers was as racially charged with unconsciously held perceptions as any interaction she may have had with white providers! She continues by directly naming implicit bias as the culprit:

And so that was the full circle, because actually, even though I feel like . . . if I had not asked I probably would not have seen [the physician], I did not get the attitude or the "how dare you" that I got with the African American physician. And obviously I'm not saying that would be the treatment that I would be getting all the time but . . . it did happen. And I think if we look at implicit bias we also have to look at the fact that there is implicit bias that comes from people of color toward people of color. And that is something I can definitely say has . . . happened to me. . . . I think that could be multifaceted. I think it could be African Americans to African Americans.

With poignant honesty, this woman concludes by sharing the fact that providers of color, both American and foreign-born, may be biased against minority American patients because of the social cues they receive from American culture. In this patient's view, this discrimination can be most hurtful of all.

There are large amounts of ER doctors who do not come from this country. One of the challenges that my grand aunt has had, there is a barrier because she's in inner-city Detroit and there are some people who don't understand her and she does not understand them. And I think that the bias can be bigger . . . when it comes from people of color because when you're talking about doctors you're talking about this whole international element. And so it can be like multifaceted the whole implicit bias thing.
—African American Female Patient, Northeastern United States

Not all physicians studied displayed high levels of anti-black bias on IATs, and not every physician who displayed implicit bias made inferior treatment decisions for the minority patients they treated. In one study involving primarily foreign-trained, non-white physicians, the providers displayed slightly *pro*-African American preferences on their IAT tests. In another study, academic pediatricians showed a much lower tendency to harbor implicit race bias than other physicians tested, even when their IATs showed moderate implicit preferences towards whites. The pediatricians tested tended to provide preferred treatment recommendations for African Americans more often than they did for white patients.[14] Both these outcomes were contrary to the researchers' expectations, which were based on findings in other physician populations studied. They also demonstrate that there is much to learn about how physicians' implicit biases operate.

One of the most important findings of the Sabin study was the "disconnect" between explicit bias and measures of implicit bias. In other words, physicians self-reported that they had relatively weak explicit preferences for white Americans over black Americans, but their IAT scores showed strong pro-white implicit preferences. As a group, physicians' IAT scores revealed that their implicit pro-white attitudes were about twice as strong as their self-reported explicit attitudes. These findings are consistent with the "dual-process" theory of human cognition, which concerns how people gain knowledge and can help describe how and why people can have two different responses to a patient's race simultaneously. Most importantly, this evidence helps to explain how genuinely well-intentioned, egalitarian-minded physicians may still hold unconscious or implicit attitudes that favor whites over members of minority groups. In other words, the discrepancy in explicit and implicit measures explains why what people say about their biases can be different than what they subconsciously think. In Sabin's words, "this weak relationship substantiates the supposition that one may explicitly hold egalitarian beliefs while simultaneously holding implicit attitudes that favor Whites relative to Blacks."[15]

Sabin's research can be criticized because it did not test a random sample of physicians and because it relied heavily on participants to self-report their explicit race preferences. Moreover, in an earlier study of pediatricians, mentioned above, Sabin found that these doctors showed less implicit preference for whites over blacks than the majority of physicians and other participants who have taken the IAT. In other words, all providers do not uniformly display identical levels of implicit bias or respond identically to the biases they possess.[16] The test data Sabin used was limited to physicians, and evaluated preferences only for whites and blacks, not any other racial or ethnic minorities. Nevertheless, it is certainly reasonable to conclude that if Sabin has shown that a large group of physicians, who voluntarily took an interest in self-testing and then self-reporting on their own racial preferences, have pro-white preferences, other physicians who did not seek out information about implicit biases, may also be surprised to find that they, too, harbor unconscious attitudes about the patients they treat. The empirical and qualitative evidence confirms that these pro-white, and anti-minority, perceptions that physicians hold due to their implicit biases have a grave impact on the quality of care patients receive. Again, the observations of an emergency department physician quoted earlier prove insightful:

> I think that part of what I do know explicitly is that I would assume economic barriers that are associated with race. And I think that actually as a society that we're more comfortable talking about racial disparities than about the economic disparities, and they go hand-in-hand . . . . We use one as a surrogate for the other. . . . I've struggled my whole life with how to parse out the difference between those two. . . . In this city one of the refreshing things is there is a good middle- and upper-class African American community. And so, I think it's actually loosened me up over the last 20 or 30 years to realize that. . . . And I think we all resonate with

patients who are more like us than not, and that includes economically, educationally, as well as racially.
—Emergency Medicine Physician, Southwestern University Medical Center

Recall the study by van Ryn and Burke mentioned earlier in this chapter, which demonstrated the connection between biased perceptions and quality of care by testing physician perceptions of patients based on their race and their socioeconomic status (SES).[17] Their study reviewed medical records for patients with coronary artery disease (CAD) and surveyed physicians from eight New York hospitals. First, these researchers evaluated patients' appropriateness for aggressive cardiac treatment and then compared that evaluation with the actual treatment patients received. Patients' SES was evaluated based on their education and income data, while their race—either white or black—was determined, also from the medical record. The race and SES data were correlated with physician answers to questionnaires that surveyed their perceptions.

Beyond simply relating the physicians' perceptions to patient characteristics, the data from this study further confirmed that the physicians' stereotypical expectancies affected their behavior. For example, the average "encounter length" physicians reported for their clinical meetings with patients was significantly shorter for black CAD patients than for white CAD patients. After studying over six hundred encounters with physicians treating cardiac patients, van Ryn and Burke concluded, "There is substantial reason to be concerned about physicians' likelihood of perceiving African American and lower SES patients more negatively than White or upper SES patients. . . . Physician attitudes, perceptions, and beliefs about patients have been shown to influence physician behavior in medical care encounters."[18]

UNTRUE, NEGATIVE PERCEPTIONS CAN TRUMP
CLINICAL TRAINING
There is some empirical evidence that younger physicians learn to hold damaging implicit biases that taint their initial perceptions of patients and that they develop these biases early in their medical careers. The evidence suggests that early in their training, first-year medical students

are less likely to permit their perceptions of race or social class to influence their clinical assessments,[19] but later in their training they become increasingly more susceptible to the influences of their implicit biases.

Dr. Shelley White-Means studied implicit and explicit race and skin-tone bias among preprofessional medical, nursing, and pharmacy students training at a university located in the south.[20] This longitudinal study followed three hundred health services students over three years[21] to examine their perceived levels of cultural competency and changes in their implicit bias scores. White-Means used two IAT's—one measuring racial preferences, and the other measuring skin-tone preferences—to test students in their first, third, and fourth years of training. After the first year, the White-Means study results were remarkable for several findings. First, the pre-professional students tested exhibited significantly higher levels of implicit pro-white bias than test-takers in the nation as a whole. Virtually all Hispanic students tested, as well as the vast majority of white (94 percent) and Asian (76 percent) students tested, revealed a statistically significant unconscious preference for whites over blacks. Remarkably, even a large majority of black students tested (64 percent) revealed the same unconscious pro-white bias. The fact that the study involved students from a university in the Mississippi Delta region of the United States may help explain these results. But the students themselves were not exclusively from the south, even though the school they attended and the White-Means study were located there.

Second, the IAT results from this study were also remarkable because the students' implicit bias measures were negatively correlated with their self-reported levels of cultural competency. Self-reported levels of cultural competency, defined by the DHHS as "a set of congruent behaviors, attitudes, and policies that come together in a system . . . [to enable] effective work in cross-cultural situations,"[22] were predictably high as students training for the health professions perceived themselves as highly capable of interacting with patients of diverse backgrounds. Students ranked their confidence in areas such as using interpreters to interview patients and their ability to elicit diverse patients' perspectives of illness during interviews. Ironically, among the highest measured mean values were the scores students gave themselves for their ability to accurately explain the difference between a stereotype and an assumption. Students also favorably assessed their ability to identify the influence stereotypes have on their thoughts, feelings, and behaviors towards different groups of people while providing patient care. Black and Hispanic students scored themselves significantly higher on cultural competency measures than white students. However, all students' contrasting IAT results seriously call these rosy self-assessments into question.

A third notable finding relates to the differences in bias measures over time. The medical students' cultural competency scores got worse as their training progressed, while pharmacy students scored higher in cultural competency by the time they matriculated. One senior medical student describes the changes she observed during training as a "transformation":

> Ironically, at least within my medical training at this point, still being a student at this point, there have been efforts at the level of medical education to have conversations about this [medical students' declining cultural competency during medical training] as much of the research has shown the extent that these biases come into play. Probably the first week of medical school we had this course called "Introduction to the Profession," where we were simply not only getting adjusted to the curriculum and what we'd expect for the next four to five years, but also reading a lot of texts and literature in which we discussed biases and watched excerpts in terms of patient care and clinical examples. . . . It's funny because I remember feeling as though we were spending far too much time discussing these things in the context of that first week, to the point where all of it seemed obvious. Well clearly at some point if I felt that way, and I felt like my fellow colleagues felt that way, somehow down the line, that wasn't the case, and a transformation occurred.

Unfortunately, White-Means did not report changes in the IAT measures for the same students in their first and third years of training, but compared only different students in their first and third years. Thus, the results, rather than revealing changed attitudes that evolved over time, could simply reflect differences between the two classes of different students. Nevertheless, the White-Means finding provides an intriguing set of data to examine in order to determine whether physicians develop discriminatory patterns as a result of their medical education. Recall the study of first-year medical students' biases conducted by Dr. Adil

Haider discussed in chapter 3; Dr. Haider's results add to the concern that medical school itself may contribute to the discrimination problem in health care.[23] In that study, researchers examined only first-year medical students in the entering classes at Johns Hopkins School of Medicine. There, the majority of the 211 students studied also showed a preference toward whites and toward those in the upper socioeconomic strata. However, these first-year students, at the beginning of their medical training, did not change their responses to or treatment assessments of patient vignettes when the patients' race was randomly changed.[24] Again, the same senior medical student's observations are salient:

> There's an ongoing conversation that I've had with some of my mentors at the medical school asking when the transformation occurs. And largely people say it starts your third year of medical school when you're fully immersed in the clinical environment. I think you have to end up checking yourself a lot. Because in that context, you are a student to learn, to be evaluated, and to also fit in—fit in with the team, fit in with the culture, fit in with how you examine a patient, your knowledge base, and how you interact with everyone who is really your superior in terms of knowledge, in terms of evaluation, some of the power dynamics that happen. And you conform. And even if you temporarily or say you will temporarily conform to a way of doing things for this rotation, invariably you've been doing it for years. You then do it for another year in the context of applying to some training program. And you go through a training program, and before you know it you're perpetuating the same thing.

The student's observations suggest that the changes in attitudes occur imperceptibly. Her comments also suggest that the changes are the product of immersion in a culture where more senior physicians exhibit the biased behavior she describes.

> There's something that happens. Even when they enable points of reflection in the course of the third year, to discuss this, it still doesn't change the reality of how training happens. And so I think the most you can do is try to remain conscious of it as an individual, or if you realize, "Wait a second—why am I acting this way?" and kind of push yourself in terms of the environment. Because once you get familiar and comfortable, it's

done. But when you're new in this environment, you don't know what [is what] and you're also more acutely aware of yourself as this entity in something new, and then who you're interacting with and to do so I think enables you to feel some of your biases, wherever they are, and then to acknowledge them and work with them versus when you're comfortable and you fall into a routine, whatever that routine is.

—Fourth-Year Medical Student, New England University Medical School

White-Means's study, as well as this medical student's observations, raise important questions about the role of medical education in the acculturation process that may reinforce implicit biases among providers, notwithstanding the considerable attention and resources that American medical schools have directed at cultural competency training.

Not all students in the White-Means study demonstrated the same level of implicit bias; students from other health professions tested differently than medical students. Nonetheless, researchers found a correlation between the nursing, pharmacy, and medical students' socioeconomic status and their levels of bias. The study found that race bias is significantly higher when economic deprivation was a reported part of the students' history. The discussion in this study appropriately acknowledged the research limitations presented by correlations that are only barely statistically significant. Thus, the researchers assert that their main contribution was to show that IAT measures are good ways to quantify bias in health care providers.

However, I submit that the White-Means study makes a far more meaningful contribution to the discussion about the role of medical education. Clearly, medical educators have a responsibility to address the detrimental influence that unconscious bias has on the quality of patient care for racial and ethnic minorities. However, it is very possible that institutions' egalitarian, educational objectives inside the classroom are at war with the indirect, clinical education that young pre-professionals receive when they begin interacting with patients and observing their practicing role models. Most medical schools include cultural competency training in their curricula. However, the negative perceptions modeled by seasoned physicians, and possibly other health professionals as well, do not disappear simply because of medical school training in cultural competence. The evidence suggests that cultural competency curricula can indeed impact explicit biases and that they are a necessary component to combating health disparities. But the evidence also suggests that cultural competency training has little impact on the transfer of implicit biases from senior practitioners to their medical students. In short, cultural competency training is far from a sufficient solution.

Mechanism #2: Physicians' Implicit Biases Can Lead to Discriminatory Statistical Interpretation

> Probably for a good eight years of my life I struggled with monstrous fibroids. And all of the doctors I was going to—I was being passed from gynecologist to gynecologist—none of them thought my condition was serious enough to warrant surgery, even though the condition was putting me out of work, out of school, three or four days of the month. I absolutely was not able to do anything because of the pain. I was being given pain medication. In fact, maybe a year before I got surgery, I began to be prescribed serious pain medications like Percocet. I shudder when I think back on it. I was taking Percocet for period pains! They ascribed it to fibroids but they always, almost invariably, each gynecologist I went to would say, "Yeah, you know, fibroids are really, really common amongst African American women or women of African descent, and aside from the little bit of discomfort they are causing you, they really don't cause any other problems. If in the future you are trying to have a child, and maybe you have problems with fertility, then we can look into surgery." So I guess if I had never seriously expressed a desire to have children, I would to this day, have fibroids.
> —African Female Patient, Managed Care Program, Midwest United States

The story of statistical discrimination is best told through the eyes of a patient, like this woman, whose experience reveals that for many years, she was treated as a member of a data set rather than as an individual. Statistical discrimination occurs when providers respond to the inherent uncertainty of the diagnostic and treatment processes by interpreting the data and information relevant to a minority patient differently from the way they do with white patients. The irony of statistical discrimination is the fact that it most often occurs in the context of physicians' use of *accurate* information. Statistical discrimination involves a physician misusing and misapplying factually accurate information to reach an *inaccurate* conclusion concerning the specific patient. It is my hypothesis that these inaccurate conclusions are informed by stereotypes a physician holds about the racial or ethnic group to which a patient belongs. In short, due to implicitly biased attitudes the physician holds, racial and ethnic stereotypes supersede the clinical information available about a minority patient and cause the physician to make inaccurate medical judgments about the statistical information he or she has. Statistical discrimination is most likely to occur when physicians are under pressure to conduct short exams, process numerous patients, and reach an actionable conclusion in order to satisfy quality control and other standards of modern medical practice.

The experience of the woman quoted above during various emergency room visits continues to be illustrative:

> I think that a woman who walks in the amount of pain that I'd walked with into different doctors' offices, or the emergency room, multiple times—a woman walking in with that kind of pain, I think would get a much more serious response if she were not black, because it would be less common. I think it's not intentional, I think the bias is just a categorization of women, by their race, into what kind of pain is common. And we can just mask it over with painkillers and they're fine. And they think it doesn't cause any serious long-term effects. So you're in pain for four days out of the month, so what—it's no big deal. But if you're the person who is missing work, that often, who's missing class as often as I did, it's not good. And, it turns out that there actually are a lot of problems. There's a huge connection between fibroids and infertility amongst African American women.

Lest there be any doubt about the harm that follows this misapplication of objective, scientific information, consider the impact the correct treatment—which was always readily available—had on this patient:

> So women who are not able to finally make that break, and come across a doctor who finally takes them seriously and finally leads them into

surgery and takes out an enormous fibroid or a terrible fibroid that was causing all that pain, a woman who doesn't get that lucky break could potentially become infertile. . . . So my lucky break was when I blacked out, and was taken by ambulance to the emergency room. . . . I happened to have individual health insurance. . . . So while I was there, [I was seen by a] gynecologist. . . . He came in and he did the usual thing. He did the ultrasound. And while he was doing this thing I blacked out again. The gynecologist said, "I don't know what to do with this anymore. A friend of mine happens to be in town. He's a reproductive endocrinologist, and maybe he's had more experience with these cases. I don't know what to do with your case." And so [the endocrinologist was called in . . . and he ordered his own set of ultrasounds. And when he saw the size of the tumor that I had, his response was, "I have no idea how you've been under the care of gynecologists and they've allowed this to grow to this size." It was a six pound fibroid when they took it out. Six pounds! It was the size of a full term baby—and I'd been walking around with that thing for a long time, for the longest time ever. After surgery, it was amazing! It was like I had a whole new body! It was really amazing.

In concluding her narrative, this patient points out what I found in several interviews I conducted: Physician-neglected fibroid pain is a common experience shared by many black women in America. Moreover, this experience is exemplary of the implicit bias that operates through the mechanism of statistical discrimination and affects the health outcomes of many women. Physicians' assumptions about the experience of black women as a group—their threshold for pain, their goals for family planning, or even the ordinariness of the problem they suffer—can prevent them from treating a specific black woman as a distinct individual. As a patient observed in an interview,

> I was so sick of hearing that sentence, that statement coming out of their mouth: "This is very common." And I'm sitting there writhing in pain saying, I don't care how many millions of women have this. I want you to look at me. And I want you to give me an answer. And I want you to take this pain away.
> —African Female Patient, Western United States

To understand how otherwise caring doctors can be unimpressed by a black women's complaining of pain, first recall that whenever a physician initially encounters a new patient or a new patient complaint, that physician's task is to sort and order various pieces of information—whether from diagnostic tests, the patient's own descriptions, observations shared by family and friends, the physician's first-hand observations, consultations with a colleague, or research into a medical text or article—into a medical story that is consistent with the reported information, resolves the uncertainty, and identifies a course of action that will address the patient's problem. This task is called making a "differential diagnosis." This is a sorting exercise that involves placing all of the newly presented external evidence into the context of the prior information available to the physician. It is in the use of prior information that implicit bias may infect differential diagnosis.

The rational and efficient physician compares the patient's current report with prior information that could pertain to that patient in order to make sense out of nonsense, bring rational order to the chaos of all the reported data. The physician retrieves information collected from past experiences and brings it forward to inform the analysis of the patient as a way to introduce some measure of certainty into the realm of complete uncertainty that prevailed when the patient first presents a complaint. As a physician faces the uncertainty of a new patient problem, in order to make a differential diagnosis, the physician must access the knowledge he or she possesses from experiences that happened before encountering the new patient or new problem. This prior stored knowledge includes information learned during the physician's medical school training, clinical experience, journal readings and conferences, and past conversations with colleagues. Accessing this stored social knowledge is essential to provide context for the patient's reported symptoms and information. However, the prior information the physician accesses can also include the physician's stored social knowledge about patients and the groups to which they belong; it can include implicitly biased attitudes, as well as negative, fixed, and untrue stereotypes. When the physician imperceptibly and unintentionally accesses prior information tainted by bias and stereotypes, the physician may mistakenly interpret a minority patient's data in ways that would not occur when interpreting a white patient's data. According to researchers, this "statistical discrimination" can occur in at least two different ways.[25]

In the first instance, a physician may correctly recognize the prevalence of a disease that does, in fact, occur disparately in minority populations and white populations, but in the face of uncertainty, may substitute the statistical probability, or "base rate," of a disease occurring in the population group, for the actual, individualized probability of the disease occurring based on the information the patient presents, in order to make a treatment or diagnostic decision. Essentially, because of implicit biases and stereotypes the physician holds about the patient's people group, his or her prior knowledge about prevalence crowds out more accurate information about the individual minority patient. For example, a family physician whose black patient walks into the examination room and reports, "Doctor, in the last two weeks I have felt sad, blue, depressed, and lost all interest and pleasure in the things I usually care about and enjoy," will correctly consider major depression as a part of the differential diagnosis for this patient's condition. The physician knows from prior experience and education that the prevalence of major depression is 10.4 percent for whites, as compared with only 6.2 percent for blacks. Moreover, the physician may be aware that the symptom the black patient has reported—two very lousy weeks—is a more sensitive indicator of major depression among black patients than among white patients, but a more specific signal of depression for whites than for blacks. However, beyond the data and reported symptoms, the physician may also hold implicitly biased attitudes about blacks and their susceptibility to mental illness, which can cause the physician to unintentionally discriminate against an African American with this patient's symptoms. Therefore, the physician may *incorrectly* decide not to collect any further information about depression on this patient because the lower prevalence of major depression in the black population combines with the physician's social expectations that to suggest that this black patient does not suffer from this infirmity. Similarly, a physician may decide to discount a black patient's complaints of pain because the doctor incorrectly presumes all women who are black have a high pain tolerance because they are perceived as being "tougher" and needing less care or relief. This is statistical discrimination. In fact, the "right" response would be to infer that there is a 14.1 percent chance that this particular patient has major depression, whereas a white patient with the same test result has a 24.5 percent chance, and continue to gather information until the conclusive diagnosis is made.[26] But, succumbing to implicit biases, the physician allows perceptions of data pertaining to the patient's racial group to overwhelm the information the individual patient has presented.

The second form of statistical discrimination occurs when a physician hears diagnostic information with "more noise" from members of minority groups than from white patients, and then incorrectly either presumes or overlooks the probability of a disease based on the physician's miscommunication with the patient. This type of error occurs when physicians meet with patients from ethnic or racial groups who speak a different language or dialect or communicate with unfamiliar cultural patterns. In these cases, the physicians' diagnostic and treatment decisions applied to minority patients vary from the decisions the provider would make were the patient white. Of course, a variety of factors such as the country where a patient was born, the patient's education, or the dialect or accent that characterizes the speech of a patient from a certain geographic region can interfere with physician-patient communication. Statistical discrimination could theoretically affect these interactions to some degree as well. Nevertheless, the stereotypes most regularly tested by health care researchers involve the racial and ethnic minorities who have historically experienced prolonged and systematic discrimination in the United States, and about whom negative social imagery is pervasive and influential in forming implicit biases.

Sociologist Ana Balsa and health economists Thomas McGuire and Lisa Meredith have tested for and demonstrated the first form of statistical discrimination, which they describe as "Bayesian" assessment, in a study that showed strong evidence of statistical discrimination against minority patients in physicians' diagnosis of hypertension and diabetes. In the same study, researchers found evidence of statistical discrimination through miscommunication when physicians diagnosed depression. By beginning with the assumption that fair allocation of the benefits from medical treatment do not depend on race, Balsa, McGuire, and Meredith demonstrated that physicians' diagnostic decisions for treating hypertension, diabetes, and depression were distorted by statistical information the physician held about a patient's race and other demographic characteristics prior to and in spite of the clinical encounter.[27] Some researchers have argued that statistical discrimination is neither the sole nor primary cause of disparities in health care,[28] while others have described its effect as "potent."[29] Even without a precise or quantifiable measure of exactly how quantitatively *large* a problem statistical discrimination is, we do have evidence that statistical discrimination is a *serious and pervasive* problem that contributes to disparities.

Dr. Diana Burgess has shown the extent to which medical providers' unconscious use of stereotypes can drive diagnostic discrepancies.[30] In addition to the substantial evidence that race, ethnicity, gender, socio-economic status, and other patient categories influence providers' beliefs and expectations, researchers have also shown that providers will use stereotypes to fill in gaps relating to patient groups when they are under time pressure—as, indeed, clinicians frequently are. For example, providers may misapply population statistics, such as rates of college graduation or average income, to establish an "evidentiary basis" to conclude something that is true about a majority of members belonging to an ethnic group is also true about the individual patient even when the statistic neither applies based on the information communicated by the individual patient, nor finds any support in the patient's medical record. In epidemiology, the over-application of statistics to individual patients is called an "ecological fallacy." When health providers make the same error, they are using what is called a "base rate." Because modern medical practice places physicians under extreme time and productivity pressure, we can reasonably conclude that base rate errors occur frequently in all racially discordant interactions, including clinical encounters. This may be the first form of statistical discrimination, not the second.

Research also shows that when the provider and patient are from different racial groups, the human tendency to generalize "out-group" members may lead clinical providers to view all minority patients as homogeneous, without making the distinctions that would set, for example, a Latino patient apart from the base rate data for all non-white Hispanics, but by contrast regularly individualize white patients who are members of their own "in-group." Researchers have documented in-group biases that motivate members of the same racial or ethnic group to favor one another, giving the benefit of the doubt in questionable situations or going "the extra mile" to help. Given that the overwhelming majority of physicians in America are white and male, we can safely assume that to the extent that in-group biases operate, they do so to the detriment of minority patient care. The evidence summarized here contradicts the assertion that including stereotype and biased perceptions in the definition of statistical discrimination equates the theory with bias and renders it meaningless.[31] In Balsa, McGuire, and Meredith's words:

> Discrimination stemming from prejudice is of a very different character than discrimination stemming from application of rules of conditional probability. . . . But statistical reasons for discrimination may also be unfair. A finding in the case of depression that miscommunication is the explanation for a race effect does not ameliorate the disparity in services or outcomes that results, in spite of not stemming from doctors' ill will. Minorities still fare worse than whites in the clinical encounter and attempts to bridge this gap through policies that improve doctor-patient communication should be encouraged. Better communication between doctors and patients will improve doctors [sic] understanding of patients' condition, reduce reliance on population averages in clinical decisions, and thereby improve the match between treatment and the health needs of the patient."[32]

In short, these researchers correctly point out the importance of matching health policy solutions to an accurate understanding of the source of the inequalities in health care and health outcomes. Additionally, health policy addressed at statistical discrimination in particular must take into account the influence that physicians' prior implicit biases have on their statistical interpretations.

In fact, physicians may engage in statistical discrimination at any time. But this chapter reviews the phenomenon together with biased physician perceptions because both of these first two mechanisms can transmit implicit bias into adverse patient outcomes even before the physician and patient meet. In contrast, Mechanisms #3 and #4 arise only during the time a physician and patient are interacting in person during the clinical encounter.

5

Implicit Bias during the Clinical Encounter

Now, my gut instincts, and what I've known based on my experience would say that it [bias] is not uncommon either. That you have these biases and they go into the room of every patient. And particularly people who are immigrants, and particularly people who [represent] ethnic and racial diversity. Certainly . . . you can't convince me that there isn't somewhere, right now, at this very moment, a doctor walking into someone's room, who they're surprised to see that there's this person sitting across from them, and who is not getting ideal care. That's a fact. I think it's happening somewhere all the time.
—Pulmonologist, University Medical Center, Southwest
United States

The clinical encounter between provider and patient is infused with implicit attitudes. Bias affects how both parties hear, see, and respond to one another. This chapter explains how implicit biases that impact conduct and communication during the clinical encounter contribute to health disparities. I begin by describing the impact bias has on physician communication and conduct—Mechanism #3—and conclude by reviewing data that demonstrates the influence that bias has on patients—Mechanism #4. The third and fourth mechanisms interact to form a feedback loop that adversely impacts minority health. In short, this chapter demonstrates that clinical communication can be toxic. Figure 5.1 isolates the mechanisms by which implicit biases link to health disparities during the clinical encounter. These are the communication mechanisms in the Biased Care Model.

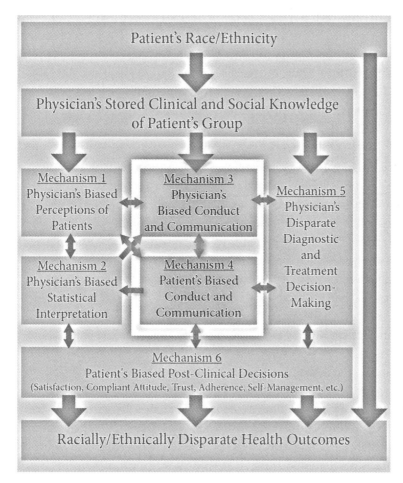

Figure 5.1. Physician and patient communication mechanisms.

Mechanism #3: Physicians' Implicit Biases Influence Their Conduct and Communication

There is ample evidence that physicians' physical clinical conduct, influenced by automatic racial prejudices and stereotypes, affects the quality of their verbal and nonverbal communication with patients. Moreover, studies reveal that the way that doctors behave and communicate has an impact on patient health outcomes. Implicit biases affect doctors' nonverbal and verbal signals. Some of the best evidence confirming this comes from medical students. Student physicians make keen observers because their objective is to learn from the example set by their physician instructors. Thus, in the clinical setting, medical students stand shoulder to shoulder with physicians at a patient's bedside, watching both the physicians and the patients interact. Here is one fourth-year medical student's reflection on the experience:

> Especially, I think, as a student, you are privy to a lot of observation. You're at that interface, and you're acutely aware of your status. . . . When you're forced to observe, you'll see things as simple as how quickly physicians will interrupt their patients, time [they spend], the speed in which they basically set the tone and the pace of the conversation. And I think that if you encounter a patient who is not coming from the same perspective, for example whether it's language, culture, level of education as well, that will quickly turn into yes/no questions, very little eye contact, you see changes in body language, you see the people are no longer physically open, they kind of turn away, and you know something is going on.

This student saw that a physician's conversational pace and tone was different when the patient was from a minority background and that the physician's body language changed perceptibly as well. Indeed, numerous studies confirm these observations. Research has shown that the differences include the length of time doctors spend with minority patients as compared to whites; the level of verbal exchange and shared decision-making in which they engage; their body language, verbal tone, and eye contact; and their willingness to credit and respond to information provided.[1] Some physicians with higher implicit bias ratings also appear to spend more time with white patients than with minority patients.[2] Nevertheless, this medical student also understood that the individual physicians who exhibited these changes were often compassionate caregivers who were wholly unaware that their conduct changed.

> And I think it [unconscious discrimination] often comes from, the times when I've seen it happen, you know even with excellent, kind, caring clinicians it's when I feel like they've been pressured by a system to get things done so they go into a routine, and what is familiar. And what's

familiar are the closest biases that we're born with, you know, our context, our reality, our own biography. And it's just interesting to watch. It's very interesting.
—Fourth-Year Medical Student, New England University Medical School

The student identifies the time and financial pressures of a "system" and "routine" that force providers to resort to "what is familiar." Correctly, this student points out that under these clinical circumstances, physicians resort to the "closest biases that we're born with" to inform their conduct and communication. Simply put, this is precisely how unconscious racist biases infiltrate the clinical encounter, to result in discriminatory care. While the evidence confirms that the differences in physician communication and conduct with minority patients are not intentional, neither are they benign. The social science literature abounds with confirmation of the detrimental impact that physicians' biased communication and conduct can have on patient health outcomes.[3]

Differences in Style of Physician Communication

A large body of research documents the extent to which non-prejudiced whites often display heightened levels of anxiety, arousal, and even hostility when interacting with members of minority groups.[4] These general observations translate into specific behaviors during the clinical encounter. For example, a classic study by Dr. Elizabeth Hooper demonstrated that physician behaviors with patients—interviewing, nonverbal attention, courtesy, information giving, and empathy—varied with the sex, age, appearance, and ethnicity of the *patients* studied.[5] In the Hooper study, researchers used two-way video to observe fifteen medical residents in their weekly outpatient clinics. The researchers observed a total of 150 patient interactions. The ethnicity of patients studied was described as either "Anglo-American" or "Spanish American." Hooper and her team found that physicians' interviewing skills, such as the use of open-ended questions, eliciting details, and allowing patients the opportunity to ask questions, were significantly lower with Hispanic patients than with whites.[6] Similarly, physician empathy, defined as the physician's ability to acknowledge the patient's prominent feelings, assess the patient's mood, or acknowledge the patient's emotional needs, was significantly lower with Hispanic patients than with whites.

These kinds of differences manifest in the way that physicians express themselves verbally with minority patients. Some minority patients describe the communication difference as "being talked down to":

> So in the past I've actually gone with my parents or grandparents to physicians when they're having an appointment so I can explain to them what was going on. . . . I actually start a conversation generally with "I am a biomedical engineer, I've worked in a hospital for ten years, please don't talk down to me!"—not saying it exactly in those words, but basically saying I can understand what you're saying and if I don't understand a particular word I can ask you and you can explain it to me in a way that I will understand it. So generally I start that way because it tends to cut down on—pardon the expression—the crap. And then when there's an explanation that I think is incomplete, I'll just ask, what are the side effects, what are the negatives, what are the positives of what you're proposing?
> —African American Male, Southwestern United States

By audiotaping clinical encounters between sixty-one physicians and 458 African American and white patients, Dr. Rachel Johnson was able to observe examples of the communication styles this patient refers to in his frustration as "the crap."[7] While Dr. Johnson found no significant differences in the duration or speed of speech in medical visits with African American and white patients, she did find that physicians were more verbally dominant with African American patients than with white ones, speaking more than they did with white patients. Also, using the widely accepted RIAS coding system, Johnson's team found medical visits with white patients were more patient-centered than with black patients. This measure considered partnership building, counseling, emotional and psychosocial exchanges that were open ended, and patient as well as physician talk aimed at conveying biomedical information. The importance, then, of Mechanism #3 of the Biased Care Model is that it connects the distinctive communication styles physicians used when interacting with minority, as compared to white, patients with disparate and inferior minority health outcomes.

Researchers have determined that patient-centered communication directly influences patients' health status. Dr. Moria Stewart, for example, audiotaped thirty-nine family physicians and 315 of their patients and determined that those patients' perceptions and health status after a patient-centered visit improved substantially.[8] Patients who felt their problems had received a full discussion and who had, in their opinion, achieved common ground with their providers concerning future treatment required fewer subsequent referrals and fewer follow-up tests. Additionally, two months later, these patients exhibited better recovery from their discomfort, better emotional health, and a reduction in their chief concerns. Overall, the Stewart research team found higher positive affective tone in physicians and patients when visits were with white patients than with blacks. Together, the Stewart and Johnson findings are significant because, as Johnson concludes, "Patient-centered communication, including greater patient input into the medical dialogue, has been associated with better patient recall of information, treatment adherence, satisfaction with care, and health outcomes."[9]

Differences in Content of Physician Communication

Beyond experiencing different styles of communication, minority patients also routinely receive less information from their providers about their health and health choices than white patients. These disparities in the content of the messages that physicians provide to minorities also appear to be related to unconsciously biased perceptions of the racial and ethnic groups to which these patients belong, rather than to individualized judgments about the knowledge and circumstances that dictate what is appropriate to share with each patient. Some physicians filter the information they communicate based on their biased expectation that minority patients cannot afford to pay for excellent health care or will not understand complex treatment regimens. The following excerpt is exemplary of what I heard from several black males about the way they believed white physicians perceived them.

> But there's also the other side of the coin, where they don't think you can afford it, or they don't think you're knowledgeable. And consequently, they really don't tell you all the issues, complications, side effects, what-

ever, that a treatment can impose. And that's where it's important to have at least some knowledge of whatever the condition is. Fortunately, from the Internet, people can gain more knowledge than they should gain probably about certain conditions. But it helps to be educated, bottom line, and if you're poor, it doesn't matter whether you're black, white, Hispanic, Indian, whatever—you're not aware of the treatment options or you don't understand the side effects of particular treatments and that could lead to trouble.

—African American Male, Southwestern United States

Another patient explained that not all white doctors are equally culpable of filtering the content of their communication with minority patients. Some have less experience with minority patients and the issues that affect their health.

In the next narrative, a minority patient cites a physician's insecurity and the social climate as two reasons for his not getting adequate information. The patient distinguishes two physicians, A, the unsuccessful communicator, and B, the white physician with whom he related well:

The bottom line between A and B is that A did not expect a level of knowledge or intelligence or problem solving that was comparable to what B did even though B was infinitely more trained and more knowledgeable than the second guy [A] because the second guy [not only] had a M.D. from Harvard and a Ph.D. from Yale [but] was also certified in naturopathy. So that was the real difference between someone who had the knowledge, was secure enough to say ok—to really engage in the dialogue around this issue versus someone who was not as secure and perhaps trepidatious [sic] about their whole lack of knowledge. So I think that that could very well have been a part of the picture. . . . Well in both cases they were both physicians who were white.

This patient points out that more than knowledge and intellectual training are required to communicate equitably with minority and white patients alike. The physician's intangible characteristics of being "secure" instead of "trepidatious" influenced the quality of interaction with this black patient. The patient dismisses the Ivy League credentials, and instead identifies the naturopathy certification as the training that really distinguished Physician B. Moreover, this patient goes on to explain that the larger social context in which each physician practiced, and the environment surrounding racial issues also played a part in defining the quality of communication between this patient and his providers.

> I don't think either one of them had large numbers of black patients either. But I do think that there probably was a difference in terms of the general social state of practice that they were in. One was in an Ohio town which was very conservative and very role definitive in terms of how people related to one another, and Dr. B was in [liberal city]. So go figure that one.
> —African American Male Patient, Midwestern United States

Drs. Warren Ferguson and Lucy Candib conducted a literature review to assess the evidence for racial and ethnic disparities in physician-patient communication.[10] They found consistent evidence that effective communication can improve health outcomes, patient satisfaction, and patient adherence. Yet, they also found that race, ethnicity, and language all have a negative effect on the quality of the physician-patient relationship. Minority patients, especially those for whom English is not a first language, are less likely to receive sufficient information from physicians and are less likely, therefore, to participate in shared medical decision-making. As a result, these patients are also less likely to experience satisfaction from their clinical encounters, less likely to comply with physician recommendations, and less likely to experience health outcomes as positive as their English-speaking counterparts.

Studies have shown that physician behavior is very important to eliciting participation from patients. For example, Dr. Klea Bertakis followed the practice styles of physicians for one year, as they interacted with over five hundred patients, and then compared patients' health status and satisfaction with physician practice styles. Bertakis identified specific behaviors that successful providers used to build interactive relationships with patients. This study demonstrated that physicians who provide a highly technical, noninteractive style of care do not generally encourage patient discussion or interaction. The study showed that patients with less education and income—groups in which minority patients are overrepresented—often receive less information and less effective communication behavior from their physicians. In contrast, those physicians who structure the clinical interaction by discussing what is to be accomplished in the visit, providing feedback about lab work or examination results, asking questions about the patients' beliefs about health and disease, seeking information about changes in the patient's behavior, asking questions about nutrition and exercise, and discussing the patient's interpersonal relations or the current emotional state of the patient and the patient's family are more likely to elicit increased patient participation during the clinical encounter. Perhaps most importantly, this study showed how communication matters to health outcomes. Patient health outcomes were significantly related to the style of the physician-patient interaction during the clinical encounter. Not only did physicians who encouraged patients to participate in their medical treatment decisions have patients with a high level of satisfaction, but also these patients showed the greatest improvement in their health status scores over the year.

Discounting Minority Patient Narratives and Complaints

Interviews with minority female patients pointed to an additional feature of physician conduct and communication that reflects unconscious racism. Several women reported that their narratives were discounted, disbelieved, or simply ignored by physicians who seemed committed to a stereotype of minority women patients. A commonly repeated narrative was the experience of being told "you are fine" despite evidence of debilitating pain. The patient below felt this as discrimination first because her pain was not taken seriously even in the presence of physical evidence that she was very ill. While this narrative is longer, the story that unfolds is tragically representative.

> Yes, I have been discriminated against twice. . . . I should also add the night that I was admitted to the hospital, I also had a clear difference . . . so that's the third time . . . I felt I was treated unequally. The first time was on . . . September 9th. I came to the emergency room with excruciating pain. . . . They took a CAT scan and they'd seen that I had two cysts. He indicated they were the size of a grapefruit and I could live with it and go home. . . .

I suffered with this excruciating pain for seven days, and then it subsided. . . . And I did call around to see if I could make an appointment with some of the doctors here in [western city] but a lot of the doctors don't take Medicaid. And I personally do not like to use Medicaid because I know and I'm so aware that they only are paid a small percentage—I understand totally why they don't accept it because of the small payment that they receive. So that's why I make sure that I try my best to eat right, and to exercise, and get the right food and do whatever I can to stay healthy.

This patient's story first points to discrimination based on her class. Even more disturbingly, as this patient went on to explain, she suspected that her claims of extreme pain were ignored because providers feared she was seeking drugs, assuming, based on her race, that she was likely to abuse any drugs prescribed to her. Note that this patient reports that inaccurate stereotypes even made it into her written medical record.

So the second time when I went to the ER the doctor said he checked me out, he said, "You have a clean bill of health—you're fine!" and I'm like— "Oh these people must think I'm crazy. Because I really have these pains." And I know people come to the hospital and pretend like they have pain just to get pain medicine. But I told them, I said, "You know I can hardly even stand up it's just so bad." But he said, "I'm sorry, I can't find anything wrong with you." He said he could give me some morphine while I'm at the hospital. But I said, "No I have to go pick up kids in the next hour." So that was the second time I left the hospital. . . . I just feel so discouraged. They are trying to make me look like I'm a bad person. They're saying I had six kids and I had two abortions. I never had an abortion! . . . Well I do have six children—that is true. . . . I read the whole report. And then it also says, "African American, she's a very healthy person," which is right, because I am 54. And she said, "She has six grown kids, and two abortions. . . . I didn't have that and I never said that! I never had any abortions! There are a lot of things in here that I just didn't understand! Why would they say that?

This patient reports she was finally admitted to the hospital and had surgery to remove two large dermatoid cysts, each well over twelve centimeters in diameters. She was admitted on her third visit to the emergency room, but only after virtually begging to be admitted when she was told she could "live with" her pain:

> I sat in the wheelchair. I couldn't even sign the papers—that they use to admit you. I couldn't even stand up. I told them I had to go to the restroom. I went to the restroom and I threw up again. I came back and she told me to have a seat. I said, "Really?" I said, "I really need to go see what's wrong with me now." I was in so much pain—the worst I had ever experienced, to the point that I couldn't even sit down. I had to lay on the floor in the ER! That's how bad it was. . . . It felt like I waited like thirty minutes because I was so sick, but think it was more like ten minutes that I laid on that floor before they came out. . . .
>
> Again the lady came out—she was a Chinese doctor. . . . And she said, "You know what, we can't find anything wrong with you." And I said, "Do you think these cysts have anything to do with it?"—because I was kind of perturbed by this time. And she said, "Well you can live with those dermatoid cysts. We don't think it's that." So I said, "Oh my word, God what am I gonna do?" I just started praying. [Weeping] I said, "I'm not going home until we find out what's wrong. I can't come back and I can't live like this." So she went and got the OB/GYN surgeon. They came and did an ultrasound. And she noted that there was no flow to the fallopian tubes. And at that time she said, "You know what, I think we should take those cysts out." She said that . . . something has really gone wrong— stopping her up.

This African American woman's story recounts feelings of being disbe- lieved, discounted, and disrespected, not only by physicians, but also by hospital staff. Ultimately, the question she asked earlier—"Why would they say that?"—proves to be rhetorical. She provides the sad answer at the close of her narrative. She believes that because she is black, because she is a woman, and because she is poor, the health care providers she encountered simply did not care about her as a person.

> I think they just do not value African Americans. I think they have a stereotypical view of African Americans and they're keeping that. They're keeping that view, they don't want to let go of it. They feel that they are

better in the world, or they just don't have any compassion. Or to me, they just don't care. They feel they are superior. Then on top of that I'm in that poverty class. So not only am I a female, and African American, but it's class too. I'm considered in the ranks of poverty using my Medicaid card. So all three of those went against me when I went to the hospital.
—African American Female Patient, Southwestern United States

The empirical literature convincingly shows that minority patients are less likely to arouse empathy in their physicians than white patients and less likely to establish rapport with their physicians. White patients, in contrast, generally experience positive non-verbal and verbal expressions such as active listening and questioning from their providers. In the following narrative, a black woman speaks for many who have shared her experience of not being heard:

And the sad thing about it that makes me want to share my story with you . . . is that there are so many women like me out there. . . . I actually joined several blogs and newsletters for women with fibroids all over the world. The stories that they shared were the same. It sounded to me that there were a lot of black women saying, "Nobody seems to listen to me. Nobody seems to understand how much pain I'm in." When I was reading posts of women of other races, particularly white women, there didn't seem to be that kind of just being ignored . . . whereas with black women it's quite common.
—African Female Patient, Western United States

This patient's narrative suggests that physicians receive better information from their white patients because they do not discount their complaints. Thus, when providers receive better information from patients and achieve a better understanding of white patients' perspectives on symptoms, those patients are likely to be more forthcoming with medically relevant information and feel more comfortable asking questions. As a result, providers more often create a successful clinical encounter, and indeed a collaborative partnership, that encourages these patients to trust their provider and comply with recommendations and instructions. It is no surprise, therefore, that the literature confirms that the better quality communication white patients experience during the clinical encounter is closely associated with their improved health outcomes. Conversely, researchers have found that minority patients' poor health outcomes are significantly related to the style of physician-patient interaction that they experience.[11]

Clinical Encounters Reduce Minorities' Trust in Physicians

Dr. Howard Gordon conducted a study of black and white lung cancer patients in a large, southern Veterans' Affairs hospital. His research focused on the common disparities in levels of trust that black patients and white patients, respectively, have in their physicians. Consistent with many studies on physician-patient communication and race, the findings of Gordon's researchers were that after their initial visits, black patients judged their physicians' communication styles to be less informative, less supportive, and less partnering than white patients did.[12] Though these results are not uncommon, physicians are generally unaware that their conduct with white and minority patients is different. However, minority patients are acutely aware of these differences, as this study showed. Gordon's second finding provides an especially poignant explanation of why Mechanism #3 is important. Before their initial visits, black and white patients in this study had statistically similar levels of trust in their physicians. In other words, they approached their clinical encounters with roughly the same expectations, and presumably for similar purposes. However, their post-visit levels of trust diverged, and as Gordon observed, the impact of disparate physician communication styles on patients' perceptions was associated with patients' adherence to medical advice and future use of medical services. Thus, Gordon also identified *patient responses* to physicians' communication and conduct during the clinical encounter as a mechanism by which racial health disparities can arise.[13] The direct association between these disparities and disparate patient satisfaction and health status is undeniable. Therefore, understanding the way patients respond to physician practice styles provides further insight into how providers' implicit biases impact health disparities.

Mechanism #4: Patients' Implicit Biases Influence Their Conduct and Communication with Physicians

The tragic message of Mechanism #4 is that during the clinical encounter, patients react to physician bias with biased communication and conduct of their own to the detriment of their health outcomes. Perhaps the single most telling data point is that African Americans and Latinos use health services at lower rates than their white counterparts, even after differences in their initial access to care, diagnosis, and illness severity are controlled.[14] That bears repeating. Health outcome and health care disparities do not appear to arise solely because minorities have disparate *access* to health care. Even when black and Latino patients have the same access to health care as their white counterparts, the minority patients do not use the health care they have as frequently as whites do. The evidence strongly suggests this utilization disparity is due at least in part to something that occurs *during* the clinical encounter.

Of course, some argue utilization differences may simply be explained by differences in patient preferences. They theorize that white patients rely upon medical services to a greater extent, while minority patients generally choose to place less reliance on health care providers. Some theorists mistakenly point to minorities' preference for superstitious "folk remedies" over effective medical treatment, or they describe minority patients' attitudes as "fatalistic" or "magical" to account for utilization disparities, rather than admitting that throughout history and today, some minorities have resorted to self-care not out of preference but because medical treatment was withheld from them by whites.[15] In fact, we have empirical evidence to show that racial and ethnic differences in patient preferences alone are not large enough to explain the enormous differences in treatment that arise following clinical encounters.[16] Instead, it appears that minority patients *initially* seek out and rely upon medical services to the same degree as white patients do. However, events and interactions that arise during the clinical encounter change the relative rates at which minority and white patients continue to access the health care system. That is to say, some racial and ethnic disparities in health care emerge *during and as a result of* the clinical encounter and subsequently exacerbate the differences in care and outcomes that minorities and white patients experience.

The place to begin to unravel this curious pattern is by examining patients' communication and conduct during the clinical encounter, in the same way we have examined physicians'. Physicians report that some minority patients enter the clinical encounter with suspicion and distrust. Consider this black cardiac surgeon's description of his experience with a white patient:

> I think I've experienced that with very wealthy, white patients who have an attitude. This family had been to . . . a big name place in Minnesota. She came back and had pain in her sternum and wanted her wires removed because she had read that removing the wires might help. . . . So she came to us, even though she had had her surgery elsewhere. . . . She has just been difficult every step of the way and so my communication with her has just been minimal. Because she and her husband have been difficult every step of the way—all the way up until the last visit— everything with them is a fight.
> —African American Cardiac Surgeon, Western University Hospital

While this black physician attributes his "difficult" interaction with his white patient and her family to bias, far more often in American health care, the racial roles are reversed. White providers experience their minority patients' mistrust and "difficult" interactions as bias. However, equating white and minority patients' perceptions for similar mistrust of their physicians would foolishly ignore the centuries of racial discrimination, mistreatment, and misunderstanding at the hands of the American health care system that genuinely gives rise to minority patients' attitudes. Social scientists such as Vanessa Gamble,[17] Todd Savitt,[18] and Heather Devlin[19] have documented the historical and contemporary grounds for minority patients' medical mistrust. Nevertheless, minority patient biases cannot be overlooked by the Biased Care Model both because of the impact these attitudes have on physicians' perceptions, communication, and quality of health care and because of the effect they have on patient satisfaction. Again, a black physician's experience with white patients illustrates the impact patient bias can have on physician care:

I'll give you an example. They [white patients] were in my office, and I was running maybe fifteen minutes behind. . . . They went up to my office manager and told my staff that she didn't have time to wait for the doctor because her husband was a very busy businessman. I think that I did not give them the same level of discussion or attention as I give the farmer from Nebraska who just says to me, "Hey doc, tell me what I need to do to get better."
—African American Cardiac Surgeon, Western University Hospital

This physician's transparency and self-awareness are remarkable. He admits the involuntary nature of his patient's negative perceptions as well as his own. Note how the next doctor says that hostile patients cause him to "shut down" so that neither physician nor patient is communicating freely during the clinical encounter. In some cases, as with the physician whose narrative follows, doctors may simply refuse to treat a patient whom they perceive to be racially biased.

Even though I don't want to be that way, they just set up an offensive relationship. People do that because they regress when they get in a stressful situation. They go back to their defense mechanisms. Most of the time I can get by the defense mechanisms. . . . But for some reason when they come with a hostile attitude, then that shuts me down. I have actually given patients away when I sense that. I show them a picture of my [white] partner and tell them, "He has more experience with this," and I send them on their way!
—African American Cardiac Surgeon, Southwestern United States

More commonly however, minority physicians report that they regularly endure subtle forms of unconscious racism from patients. Some researchers describe these experiences as "racial microaggressions," a term that Dr. Chester Pierce coined to refer to the daily, subtle, and automatic insults that result from unconscious racism.[20] Again, the black surgeon's experiences illustrate minority physicians' experiences with microaggressions that grow out of implicit bias.

I have had it [implicit bias] work against me. It's interesting. There are different types. It depends on a person's level of education. I've had some people who were unsophisticated and they just seem frightened. . . . Where I think I have found more racial bias has been in some of the educated, wealthy patients. . . . And I start getting questions, "Should we get a second opinion?" "What do you think of the Mayo Clinic?" "What do you think of the Cleveland Clinic?" "How many of these have you done?" . . . I think the [most] implicit bias that I've experienced is the one where they just question you about your credentials ad nauseam. "Have you heard of so-and-so?"—some surgeon that they've known in the past. "What schools did you attend?" Fortunately I was blessed with a good academic pedigree having gone to Ivy League schools on the East Coast. And most people recognize the schools and you can see their blood pressure go down when I tell them.

This black physician concluded his narrative explaining how he responds to the implicit racial bias he encounters from patients, which admittedly is difficult to "dissect":

Well it's hard to dissect because some of it could be just their fear. Some of it could be their unfamiliarity with our hospital system as opposed to some of the more famous hospitals. I would say it's probably more body language than anything else. And some of it could be my own perception. It could be that they're just frightened and I think it's because of race. . . . So I just tend to treat everybody as if it's not a [race] issue . . . answer all their questions and treat them as if they're just a frightened patient.
—African American Cardiac Surgeon, Private Practice, Western United States

This doctor's story highlights the extent to which the physician can set the tone for the clinical encounter by either diffusing or perpetuating the effects of unconscious racism. The reciprocal feedback loop can work positively as well as it can carry a physician or patient's negative messages.

In 1988, Dr. Judith Hall theorized that providers' behavior will predict patients' behavior.[21] Basing her work on a concept of reciprocity, Hall explained that physicians' conduct, or what she called "task behaviors," such as information giving, question asking, and demonstrating technical competence, motivated patients to engage in reciprocal tasks, such as keeping follow-up visits, complying with treatment regimens, and adhering to medical advice. The empirical evidence collected over the years has borne out her theory. Thus, this fourth mechanism in the Biased Care Model describes the patient's role in a "feedback loop" between provider and patient that occurs when the patient reacts to the provider's unconsciously activated reliance on stereotypes and bias.

Implicit Bias and Verbal Reciprocity

Studies have shown that even the most egalitarian white health care providers experience emotions triggered by patients of minority racial or ethnic groups, including inadvertent feelings such as fear, anxiety, discomfort, or distrust. Researchers have observed these inadvertent reactions during clinical visits and determined that because of them, when providers interact with African American and Latino patients, they exhibit less nonverbal attention, empathy, and courtesy than with white patients.[22] These emotionally driven responses can cause providers to unconsciously communicate with a negative affect. Patients then interpret this conduct as a reason to distrust their provider and, as a result, behave in ways that confirm the provider's initial stereotype.

The feedback loop is bidirectional. Thus, just as patient responses to physician discomfort can cause the patient to return signals that confirm that initial discomfort, physician responses to patient demeanor and conduct can signal a reason for patient distrust of the physician. Especially in racially discordant physician-patient dyads, communication miscues can become cumulative, fueling the distrust between both parties. However, some research has shown that either the patient or physician is capable of breaking this feedback loop and correcting the miscommunication. For example, in a recent study mentioned earlier involving 137 lung cancer patients and their physicians, Dr. Howard Gordon found that black patients received considerably less information from their physicians, but only when the patients were less active participants in the clinical conversation. He also found a pattern of limited communication in racially discordant interactions as compared to racially concordant ones, *except* when patients took an active role in the conversations. The interaction between white doctors and black patients differed very little from conversations between white patients and white doctors when patients asked questions, raised concerns, or generally made assertions during the clinical visit; in these cases, whether the interaction was racially concordant or discordant, Gordon found little difference in the information shared by physicians.[23] Thus, physicians in this study—whether white or otherwise—engaged fully with their patients, regardless of race, when the patients were also actively engaged in the interaction. One reading of Dr. Gordon's study might be to place the onus for improving physician-patient communication on minority patients themselves. If only they were more open with their white doctors, they would receive better care. This interpretation would be a mistake.

The implications of Gordon's study must be seen in the context of other findings. Most notably, researchers in other studies have repeatedly shown that even when minority patients are forthcoming, white physicians are less likely to listen to or respect their input, perceiving these patients to be less intelligent or rational. Such a view, however unintentionally formed, is held by a majority of doctors studied. However, Gordon's evidence is promising because it suggests that changing one party's verbal patterns that are infected with implicit bias can change the verbal responses of the other party and thereby introduce positive and corrective conversational patterns. . Achieving changes in *nonverbal* communication that impacts the feedback loop, however, may prove more difficult.

Implicit Bias and Nonverbal Reciprocity

Quite possibly, the physicians most at risk for transmitting unconsciously racist nonverbal cues to minority patients are the most overtly egalitarian, liberal, and racially open-minded of all providers. These are the physicians who are most likely to expend considerable effort and attention to *avoid* falling into discriminatory patterns of behavior and communication. In some ways, their efforts to appear objective, nonpreferential, sympathetic, or sensitive may be the very means by which they communicate bias to their minority patients. Here is an example of one physician's self-correction.

I think that if I walk into a patient room and it's my patient and I see somebody who is African American my level of awareness jumps way

up. Because I recognize, this is something different than what I'm usually dealing with. I am acutely aware of race relations and issues with
disparities. And so I've become extraordinarily more introspective than
I would be with somebody who is white because I'm being very careful
about my assumptions. I don't want to make assumptions because that's
the tendency.
—Attending Physician, Internal Medicine, New England University Medical Center

In 2010, a group of social psychologists led by Dr. Louis Penner
coined the term "aversive racism" to describe a more complex and subtle communication exchange between physicians and their minority
patients.[24] An aversive racist describes the individual whose IAT tests
and survey responses show very low explicit bias scores, together with
very high implicit bias scores. This is the person who does not in any
way hold expressly racist views. In fact, this person explicitly and perhaps even emphatically rejects racial bias and preference. At the same
time, this person also holds attitudes informed by racial prejudice and
stereotypes in his or her unconscious thoughts. Racial and ethnic bias
is noxious to this person—and yet, despite this aversion, the person not
only holds subconscious, implicit biases, but also acts on them. Suggesting how aversive racism can have an especially detrimental impact on
physician-patient relationships, the Penner study may help explain the
prevalence of miscommunication between well-meaning physicians and
minority patients.

Penner's group examined the effects of implicit and explicit bias on
physician-patient relationships. His study involved fifteen primary care
physicians and 150 of their African American patients at an inner-city
clinic. The study evaluated the level of teamwork and cooperation black
patients felt with doctors who demonstrated high anti-black implicit bias
on their IATs. The physicians Penner studied were almost all non-black,
foreign-trained doctors. This is a typical demographic profile for inner
city providers who serve poor communities of color; at the same time,
it is also a limitation of the study since the physician population tested
was not representative. Moreover, because the participants were volunteers, not randomly selected, it cannot be said that this study provided a
representative sample of the health care provider or patient community.

Nevertheless, Penner's findings are informative especially in considering the potential role of aversive racism in cross-racial medical interactions.

According to the Penner study, African American patients react most negatively towards providers who exhibit the aversive racist profile, distrusting these physicians most of all. However, Penner's study did not explain why patients responded this way. Perhaps minority patients perceived physicians as disingenuous or insincere as they confidently acted from the erroneous assumption that they were free of racial bias. Perhaps physicians misread minority attempts to appear competent and formal and therefore responded by becoming distant or aloof. While further research will be needed to thoroughly understand the dynamic between patients and providers who are aversive racists, this interaction is key to unpacking health disparities, not only because it could describe the role race plays in an overwhelming majority of physician-patient dyads in the United States, but also because numerous studies have shown the connection between patient mistrust and poor health outcomes. Patients who do not trust their physicians also tend not to accept their medical advice, adhere to treatment regimes, or schedule and attend follow-up visits. Patients will not likely return to a physician who they believe discriminated against them. As a result, minority patients may disproportionately experience discontinuity in care, and therefore will generally have inferior health outcomes when compared to patients who build a trust relationship with their providers. The harm done by physicians' aversive racism offers another pathway within Mechanism #4 for implicit bias to exacerbate racial and ethnic health disparities.

Whether the emotional reciprocity between physician and patient affects verbal or nonverbal communication, the dynamic is exacerbated by the power disparity between patients and physicians. Physicians, by virtue of their knowledge, control, and authority, traditionally occupy a position of relative power over patients, who enter the health care relationship as recipients who occupy a position of vulnerability. Stereotypes are more likely to be automatically activated when situational roles place white providers in positions of relative power over minority patients holding a low situational power role.[25] Even in cases where the interaction is between actors of the same race, the relative positional status between a doctor and patient has been shown to affect implicit biases. The situational power dynamic can operate both ways. Research has also shown that those in the subordinate or "low power" position in an inter-racial interaction—such as the position occupied by a patient—generate less biased attitudes when compared to those in a powerful role—such as the role occupied by physicians, but nevertheless can display implicit bias towards their providers.[26]

The detriment that physicians' implicit bias has on patient health outcomes continues after the clinical encounter is concluded, as Drs. John Dovidio and Susan Fiske explain:

> Greater mistrust of the health care system and experiences of bias in medical encounters, whether accurate or not, can reduce use of health care services and erode confidence in the prescribed medical regimen leading to lower levels of medical adherence, less utilization of preventive services, and ultimately poorer health.[27]

Regardless of the origin, timing, or relative strength of the biases that infiltrate the patient-physician encounter, the third and fourth mechanisms have a substantial impact on the quality of care delivered to minority patients and on the disparate health outcomes that minority patients experience. The feedback loop between these two mechanisms is unlikely to be interrupted or mitigated without intervention. But the good news is that the evidence suggests that one of the parties to the reciprocal communication loop can alter the dynamic. I have shown in this chapter how unconscious racism works between physician and patient as they attempt to communicate together during the clinical encounter. The following chapter explores the evidence for Mechanisms #5 and #6—the instances when providers and patients act independently to allow unconscious racism to affect their decision-making after the clinical encounter concludes.

6

Implicit Bias beyond the Clinical Encounter

I swear by Apollo the physician, and Asclepius and Hygieia and Panacea and all the gods and goddesses as my witnesses, that, according to my ability and judgment, I will keep this Oath and this contract: . . . I will use those dietary regimens which will benefit my patients according to my greatest ability and judgment; and I will do no harm or injustice to them.
—Classical Oath of Hippocrates

I swear to fulfill, to the best of my ability and judgment, this covenant: . . . I will apply, for the benefit of the sick, all measures that are required, avoiding those twin traps of overtreatment and therapeutic nihilism. . . . I will remember that I do not treat a fever chart, a cancerous growth, but a sick human being, whose illness may affect the person's family and economic stability. My responsibility includes these related problems, if I am to care adequately for the sick. . . . I will remember that I remain a member of society, with special obligations to all my fellow human beings, those sound of mind and body as well as the infirm.
—Modern Hippocratic Oath

Despite the controversy surrounding the ancient Oath of Hippocrates,[1] some version of this declaration remains the core statement of commitment to professionalism, competence in healing, and equity that binds all American physicians to this day. Both the ancient and modern oaths eschew rigidly objective myopic patient care, in favor of compassionate concern for the whole patient, which extends to family, as well as to economic and societal concerns about injustice. Patients also must balance competing tensions as they exercise their autonomous decision-making

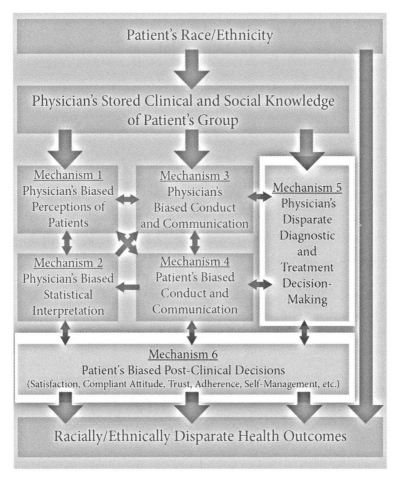

Figure 6.1. Post-clinical decision-making mechanisms.

capacity and desire to maintain control of their health and well-being, while also deferring to the professional judgment of well-trained health providers. Uncertainty and contradictions characterize physician and patient decision-making after the clinical interview concludes. Hence, both parties are susceptible to their unconsciously held biases in their medical decision-making. This chapter explores the impact implicit biases have on physicians and patients after the clinical encounter has ended. These two final mechanisms of the Biased Care Model are highlighted in figure 6.1.

Mechanism #5: Physicians' Implicit Biases Influence Their Diagnostic and Treatment Decisions

Most of the physicians I interviewed for this book would sincerely disavow any hint of implicit bias in their practices. This physician, by reputation one of the most gifted and compassionate surgeons in his region, completely rejected the notion that he held implicit biases based on gender, race, ethnicity, or wealth:

> I can truthfully answer that question and I can say "No!" to each one. And that's not true for all doctors, obviously, I am fortunate in my upbring-ing. . . . I was exposed to Asian people, to African American people. [I come from a] missionary background, but . . . I grew up with African American kids and folks and from an early age I had that interaction, and my beliefs, my parents' teaching, it wasn't a part of our thinking. And I grew up in the south, as you well know. So, no, I was blessed in my exposure to all kinds of people—all ethnicities, genders, early on, and so I didn't have that.
> —Cardiac Surgeon, University Practice, Western United States

In contrast, some physicians are familiar with the data showing the prevalence of pro-white, implicit racial and ethnic biases in America generally, and among physicians particularly; these physicians are all too rare, but they understand the frequency with which medical providers act out of unintentional, unconscious racist attitudes. Take, for instance, this pulmonologist's observations:

> As a physician and sort of talking to colleagues about what treatments they would give to some folks because they believe . . . they can afford it and they can pay for it and they have the support, and other people who they assume—because we don't know—they can't. [Some] would use other options . . . because they assume they don't have the support at home . . . based on their race and ethnicity. I mean so this is something that . . . probably it happens all the time. At the end of the day, we really are still people. We dress up in this context of the professional but when you're not aware of those biases, right, I mean you ultimately bring those

in. . . . And it goes for racial, ethnic, it goes for gender, and there are studies even to support all of these above.
—Pulmonologist, University Medical Center, Southwestern United States

To date, five published, peer-reviewed social science studies directly test the association between physicians' racial and ethnic implicit bias, and their medical decision-making. Chapter 2 contains an in-depth discussion of these five studies. I will summarize their findings here to highlight the importance of this evidence to the Biased Care Model. These studies show that implicit bias disparately affects the quality of medical care that minority patients receive; the model posits their impact on quality of care and how they can adversely affect health outcomes. First, Dr. Gordon Moskowitz demonstrated that physicians may use inaccurate stereotypes to diagnose and treat minority patients, and also may use accurate generalizations to unduly influence their medical decisions. Second, Dr. Alexander Green found that as physicians' pro-white implicit bias increased, their likelihood of treating white but not black heart disease patients with thrombolysis increased.[2] Dr. Janice Sabin reported two studies relating pediatricians' medical decision-making to their implicit race bias. The physicians tested in these studies showed generally weak, pro-white IAT levels when compared to other physicians, suggesting that pediatricians have less implicit race and ethnic bias than other specialists. Also in both studies, Dr. Sabin reported finding "no significant relationship" between implicit and explicit bias measures, thus confirming once again that physicians' intentionally held values may be entirely different from their subconsciously held biases. While Dr. Sabin found the pediatricians' recommendations for treating asthma, ADHD, and UTI's did not vary with physicians IAT levels, she found physicians' recommendations for pain medication did change with their bias levels. These results suggest that the effect of implicit biases on medical diagnostic and treatment decisions will not be uniform for all patient conditions.[3] Dr. Irene Blair confirmed that physician implicit bias may impact different diseases differently, when her studies showed that bias did not correlate with changes in physicians' provision of care or health outcomes for hypertension patients.[4]

Research beyond these five studies specifically testing the impact of implicit racial and ethnic bias confirms that physicians' decision-making can be tainted by discriminatory attitudes. A study of 495 physicians showed that providers were more likely to prescribe highly active antiretroviral therapy to HIV/AIDS patients when they perceived them as likely to adhere to a complex treatment regimen. However, the mostly white (86 percent), mostly male (76 percent) physicians studied were more likely to rate black men as not likely to adhere to such a regimen. This means these physicians made decisions to prescribe or withhold effective therapy for HIV/AIDS patients based solely on their expectations and judgments about their patients' ethnic group membership, not on any accurate data concerning adherence rates by race, nor on any information about the individual patients or their life situations.[5] To be sure, physician judgments in this study were tempered by the risk that a non-adherent patient who begins but fails to complete the treatment regimen may develop and transmit a drug resistant strain of HIV. Indeed the U.S. Department of Health and Human Services recommends that the decision to initiate antiretroviral treatment include judgments about the likelihood of adherence. At the same time, a delay in initiating antiretroviral therapy poses a significant health risk to HIV-infected patients. This study shows that given no more information than race, disease severity, and HIV-drug use history, a group of largely white, male providers made judgments about who would receive the life-saving treatments, and did so according to prior expectations that most often favored white men over black ones, rather than according to current and actual information about the patients themselves. This type of medical decision-making by physicians is as unintentional as it is damaging and even deadly. However, the empirical record explaining the extent to which physicians' biased decision-making has a negative impact on minority patient health outcomes is not well developed. Nevertheless, the circumstantial evidence for a causal connection between physicians' implicit biases and their medical decision-making is formidable.

Implicit bias must be suspected as a contributor to the fact that minorities experience more errors and avoidable complications from surgery than whites.[6] Implicit bias must be suspected as an explanation for why primary care physicians who treat predominately black patient populations more often report that they are unable to provide access to high-quality care than those who care for predominately white patient populations. Specifically, these practitioners report more difficulty making referrals to high-quality subspecialists, high-quality diagnostic imaging, non-emergency hospital admissions, and high-quality ancillary services.[7] Disparate treatment decisions involving the care mental health patients receive must be reviewed in light of the pervasive findings of implicit bias among physicians. For example, studies have shown that minorities may be more frequently exposed to treatment decisions that can cause injuries, such as the decision to use restraints. One study showed that black youths were twice as likely as white youths to be subjected to the decision to place them in restraints upon admission to a psychiatric hospital even when white patients had the same psychiatric conditions; under the same circumstances, Latino youths were 70 percent more likely to be restrained than whites.[8] At the other end of the age spectrum, studies also show that the decision to apply physical restraints on Asian or Pacific Islanders and Hispanic residents in long-term nursing homes are higher than for patients of other ethnicities.

However, accessing *direct* empirical evidence of the link between biased physician decision-making and poor health outcomes is more complicated. First, social scientists have not disentangled the respective impacts on health of providers' implicit biases regarding socioeconomic status, on the one hand, and race and ethnicity, on the other. The next physician narrative describes how this quandary plays out in hospital emergency rooms:

I had a gentleman in this past week who had a horrible catastrophic event occur. He is fifty years old and he's a business owner. . . . So, in the ER it's extremely hard to express outcomes. I more often witness the fact that there are patients who have—my expression is "have gotten jerked around by the system, or the lack of a system." For instance, the African American shop owner that I saw last week was being seen at a clinic, and my guess is not being treated that well. And I don't know what was linked to economics—you know, he's a businessman. So why was he at a sub-par doc? Why was he seeing somebody who couldn't manage his high blood pressure and then he ended up with a devastating complication of that? So I witness that. But I must say that . . . my pushback is that I witness that in poor Caucasians also. And the disparities in our health care system are so ubiquitous that it's hard for me to differentiate the racial parts of that. . . . I have to send people out who have trimalleolar fracture of the ankle which you or I would get surgery for, who are going to be mushed back together and have a somewhat dysfunctional walk for the rest of their life because they don't have insurance.

Clearly the doctor was surprised that her black patient, a financially stable businessman, was still being subjected to what she deemed to be "sub-par" medical care. Her patient's predicament would suggest that his race, more than his socioeconomic status, left him in a position to live with uncontrolled high blood pressure—a condition that certainly would diminish the quality and length of his life as it would anyone else's. At the same time, this doctor's "pushback" relates to the difficulty of ascribing the fact that this patient was relegated to inferior medical providers exclusively to his race. The doctor points to the number of poor whites who have poor health outcomes, such as the untreated ankle fracture she describes. Presumably racial biases play no part in their inferior treatment; instead, their low income is the key. At the same time, this physician's narrative points out the overrepresentation of blacks, Latinos, and other minorities among the ranks of the poor and uninsured. Thus, even to the extent that poverty, not race or ethnicity, motivates biased physician decision-making, minority patients will suffer disproportionately. The intersection of race, nationality, and poverty is a triple burden to many patients of color in the United States, as the next narrative attests:

> I had a Hispanic patient who fell off a ladder working construction in the wind two weeks ago. No insurance. We were excited when it turned out he had a . . . County address so we could send him to [County] General. And then it turned out he didn't have a social security number so he was shit out of luck with that. So all I could do was send a DVD with his x-rays and tell him, "You're on your own." And that sucks.
> —Emergency Physician, University Hospital, Western United States

Some racial effects are attenuated for some medical conditions after controlling for socioeconomic variables.[9] Yet, studies that control for patients' insurance status shed considerable light because they show the many instances when differences in treatment that minorities receive when compared to whites have nothing to do with disparities in the financial ability to *access* health care or the social determinants of good health; rather, the differences arise from differential treatment decisions that minority patients experience *qua minorities* once they have entered the physician-patient relationship. For example, this patient explains bias he perceived while being treated at a veterans' administration hospital, one of the few environments in the United States where patients are universally insured:

> I accessed care from the VA until I got care . . . at another hospital. At that time I had [HMO] insurance. . . . I always go to the doctor assuming that they have my best interest in mind but I soon found out that was not the case even at the VA hospital. The VA hospital had recommended a blood pressure medicine and I found out this was causing me to have grey spots in my vision. I tried to tell the doctor that but he really didn't make any other recommendations for another medicine. Also, at the time he didn't talk about other things like a prostate exam as I got older. I later found out that those things were common in black men and tests were readily available. I transferred to [HMO] and they immediately changed my blood pressure medication and that was a vast improvement at that particular time. But even then, my doctor who was a white female, never really asked me any questions.
> —African American Male Patient, Western United States

The African American patient in this interview is a well-educated, successful, and prominent leader in his community. His story confirms the now-familiar finding that minority patients are subjected to inferior medical treatment even when their ability to pay, income, wealth, and employment status are equal to that their white counterparts. For example, studies show that even when minority heart attack victims have access to the same insurance coverage that white patients have, they still suffer from longer wait times before doctors intervene. The "door-to-balloon" time—that is, the time between these patients' arrival at hospital to receive treatment for clogged arteries to the time they are given cardiac catheterization—is longest for black patients, and on average twenty minutes longer than for whites. This delay exists even when researchers controlled for age, sex, hospital characteristics, insurance status, and other confounding factors.[10] In discussing earlier mechanisms, we have seen that some physicians automatically perceive black and other minority patients as having fewer resources, being less intelligent, and having less ability to comply with treatment advice. Notwithstanding the difficulty of disaggregating and quantifying the effect of racial and ethnic bias on health outcomes from the impact that bias against the poor also has on health outcomes, we know that socioeconomic factors alone do not explain pervasive ethnic and racial health outcome disparities. We know that the effect of race on health outcomes grows increasingly significant as patients' socioeconomic levels improve.[11] We see further, as the African American male above who began his account describing care he received at the VA continues his story, that racial and ethnic treatment disparities persist across generations, delivery settings, and a wide variety of medical conditions.[12]

> And it wasn't until [HMO] was doing a study on black patients that she began to ask about my family history. At the same time my mother was having treatment and she got fairly good care because they . . . performed a surgery and then they had to bring her back in because there was a leak. They had to rush her back in a few hours after the surgery and at that particular time they put in a pacemaker. On my way back [home] I picked up a *Time* magazine that talked about health disparities talking about how blacks die from what should be easy to treat heart attacks. And so I thought about my mother and maybe all the questions that should have been asked but had never been asked, and I saw that not being asked about prostate exam by my new doctor at HMO was exactly the same.
> —African American Male Patient, Southwestern United States

In sum, the evidentiary record is sufficiently well developed to conclude that physicians' racially biased treatment decisions are independently associated with poor minority health outcomes, notwithstanding the confounding impact of wealth, income, education, and other measures of socioeconomic status.

Another formidable challenge to proving the causal link between physician bias and minority patients' inferior health outcomes lies with the inherent limitations of social science research. The vast majority of such research measures the strength of associations and correlations between independent variables, such as implicit bias, and dependent outcome variables, such as health disparities. Most social science methods do not generally allow any conclusion about the direct cause of a particular outcome. In principle, there is one methodological approach that could prove absolutely that physicians' unconscious racism causes inferior health outcomes. This method is called a "true experiment." A true experiment would randomly assign patients of different racial and ethnic groups to receive treatment from physicians known to be unconsciously biased, while assigning an identical control group of racially diverse patients to receive medical care from physicians who have no implicit biases—and as we have seen, no such group of physicians is likely to exist in America since we all have biases to some degree. Then experimenters would compare the health outcomes of the two patient groups over time while holding absolutely every other possible variable constant. In practice, however, the complexity and variability of possible medical treatment choices, disease patterns, patient responses, and provider practice styles, just to name a few uncontrollable variables, make such an experiment simply impossible to perform.

And yet, leading researchers such as Drs. David Williams,[13] Michelle van Ryn,[14] and John Dovidio[15] see the body of empirical evidence that physician bias and inferior minority health outcomes are associated as persuasive evidence of causation. I believe they reach this conclusion because the published findings compel them to do so. In fact, the IAT has shown variability in bias levels between groups of physicians. Also, studies show that implicit bias predicts treatment behaviors that are sufficiently correlated with adverse health outcomes to strongly infer causation. Therefore, it is more than reasonable to conclude that a preponderance of the empirical evidence shows a causal relationship between physician implicit racial and ethnic bias and health disparities. This conclusion, based on the data, fits the theoretical framework that explains the social causes of disparities.

In 1995, two social psychologists, Drs. Bruce Link and Jo Phelan, introduced the theoretical framework that asserts that some social conditions, rather than individual risk factors, may be a fundamental cause of disease.[16] They defined a "fundamental cause" as a social condition that involves and influences individuals' access to the resources that help them avoid diseases and their negative consequences through a variety of mechanisms, and they identified three essential features of fundamental social causes. First, fundamental causes involve access to resources. Second, fundamental causes influence multiple risk factors. And third, fundamental causes influence multiple disease outcomes. Importantly, Link and Phalen explained that efforts to eliminate the effects of a truly fundamental social cause of disease will be futile when focused solely on single mechanisms that link to disease, such as increased access to health care. Rather, the social conditions that involve a person's access to resources and relationships with other people must be radically disturbed to influence a multiplicity of risk factors and outcomes before the relationship between a fundamental cause and a disease outcome may be altered.

Drs. David Williams and Toni Rucker later identified racism as a fundamental cause of the disparate and inferior disease and health that minorities suffer in the United States.[17] Pointing first to the copious evidence of the impact that racial discrimination has had in producing segregated housing patterns and inferior employment opportunities for minorities in the United States, they observed that policies designed to eliminate racial discrimination in housing and employment have historically failed. Williams and Rucker then observed that despite the reluctance in the medical literature to address racial bias among providers as a causal factor, institutional as well as personal discrimination is likely a part of the complex and multidimensional explanation for health disparities as it is in the context of housing and employment. In the Biased Care Model, I extend the Williams and Rucker assertion that racism is a fundamental social cause of disease. My belief is that all racism—and specifically *unconscious* racism—is a fundamental cause of health disparities.

Unconscious racism is a fundamental social cause because it satisfies the three constituent claims important to the theory that I posit links implicit bias and poor minority health outcomes. Drs. Karen Lutfey and Jeremy Freese eloquently describe these three claims and the nature of a fundamental cause.[18] First, we know that unconscious racism is a fundamental cause of health disparities because it satisfies the "Massive Multiplicity of Connections Claim." In terms used by sociologists, we can say unconscious racism is "multiply realized and has diffuse proximate consequences" where minority health outcomes are concerned.[19] In common parlance, this means that unconscious racism operates to produce inequalities in all aspects of society that affect health, including housing segregation, education achievement gaps, employment disparities, and inequitable access to health care. More specifically, it means that unconscious racism operates throughout the relationship between minority patients and their providers. This is the message of the Biased Care Model. Second, unconscious racism satisfies what Lutfey and Freese call the "Holographic Claim" of fundamental cause theory. The disparate health outcomes that unconscious racism causes are realized over many different diseases, providers, patient populations, and practice settings. That is to say, the effects of unconscious racial discrimination can be observed even after breaking down health disparities into a myriad of subclasses throughout the health care system.

Finally, the fundamental relationship between unconscious racial discrimination and health disparities meets the critical "Predictive Claim" that Lutfey and Freese have identified. In other words, simply varying the way disparate disease outcomes occur or are treated cannot eliminate the fundamental relationship between unconscious racism and health inequality or the way in which disparate health outcomes are realized. Examples of this predictive relationship abound. Improving access to health care reduces the overall incidence of cancer and coronary heart disease but does not change the disparities due to death from these diseases experienced by whites and non-whites. Well-funded national and state-level efforts to improve access to health care, diversify the health care workforce, finance research, and make health care delivery culturally competent have only marginally succeeded in disrupting the persistent relationship between race and poor health outcomes.

A plausible explanation for the limited impact these interventions have is that they modify only intervening mechanisms rather than a fundamental cause of disparities. Increasing access to health care, for example, does not eliminate disparities because the health care itself is infected with unconscious racism. This is what it means to identify unconscious racism as a fundamental cause. Again, returning to the language of sociologists, disruption of the fundamental association between unconscious racism and inferior health outcomes requires a radical transformation, not merely changes in the resources, knowledge, or access to care that has been the focus of American health policy during the past two decades. The Biased Care Model is designed to contribute to such a radical transformation by explaining the process by which implicit racial bias works to drive the causal relationship between unconscious race discrimination and disparate health outcomes. And while there remains a need for future research to understand exactly how each mechanism contributes to disparities, the currently available evidence is enough to compel life-saving reforms.

The fifth mechanism of the Biased Care Model approaches what statisticians have called the "assumption of finite causation."[20] That is to say, the number of plausible rival hypotheses to explain disparate diagnostic and treatment decisions in the presence of physician bias is dwindling despite the growing number of independent experiments that do not disconfirm biased provider decision-making as a plausible explanation for disparities, while the variety of separate, alternative hypotheses needed to explain the persistent racial and ethnic disparities in clinical health outcomes in the absence of provider implicit bias is increasing.[21] In short, a preponderance of the scientific evidence confirms not only that Mechanism #5—biased physician diagnosis and treatment decisions— cause harm to health outcomes, but also that the Biased Care Model accurately describes the pathways that connect providers' implicit biases with racial and ethnic health disparities. Turning now to the sixth and final mechanism of the model, this chapter concludes with a discussion of why minority patients might not return to a physician whom they regard as unconsciously racist.

Mechanism #6: Implicit Biases Influence Patients' Satisfaction, Adherence, Compliance, and Follow-Up

The final mechanism linking implicit bias to disparate health outcomes focuses on patients' health care decisions *after* the clinical encounter. A patient's post-clinical decisions are related to the bias he or she perceived in their providers. The evidence shows that minority patients reduce their adherence, compliance, and future care-seeking after experiencing racial or ethnic bias. Racial and ethnic minority patients report that they have well-developed methods of coping with the stress of health care discrimination. Unfortunately, all too often these coping methods have a deleterious effect on their health.[22] For example, patients with limited English proficiency may choose to delay or avoid seeking health care altogether in order to avoid the hassle or humiliation of finding translators or being misunderstood. Patients who anticipate their medical interactions may expose them to prejudicial attitudes from their physicians or health care institutions are likely to avoid these encounters. For example, some patients suffer from measureable psychological and physiological stress responses even before they reach their doctor's office[23] just because of what they anticipate from a clinical encounter. These are the types of patients who may avoid the clinical encounter altogether.

Patient Trust and Satisfaction

The *Journal of the American Medical Association* reported a telephone survey of over 1,800 managed care enrollees who were adult patients of primary care practitioners.[24] Dr. Cooper-Patrick found that patients in race-concordant relationships with their physicians rated their physicians as significantly more participatory, respectful, and trustworthy. These variables turn out to have a great deal of influence on how a patient will respond to a physician. Studies involving African American patients have shown that these patients respond to their white providers by asking fewer questions, providing less information when asked questions, seeking less clarification of information provided by physicians, and exhibiting a less positive emotional tone in their visits with physicians.[25] Hispanic and Asian Americans, however, more often report that language barriers are the source of their communication problems with health care providers, who they report become inattentive during clinical encounters. These findings are consistent with studies showing that when patients perceive their physicians like, care about, and are interested in them, they are more likely to volunteer information and actively participate in the clinical encounter. Further, numerous studies show that these same patients leave the encounter more satisfied and therefore more compliant with provider recommendations.[26] Conversely, dissatisfied patients are more likely to change health care systems or physicians; some studies have even demonstrated that their symptoms are less likely to improve than those of satisfied patients.[27]

In interviews with young adult patients from racial and ethnic minority groups, I noted a pattern that sheds light on the differences in the way minority patients respond to physicians. Often, young adult patients explain that they accompany their parents to doctor visits, not only as language translators, but also as cultural translators even where language is not a barrier. Older minority patients may have different perceptions of authority and therefore defer to physicians without asking questions or requesting information that would help them to better manage their health. Moreover, ethnic traditions that require deference may limit a minority patient's willingness to share information that could help physicians better understand the objective medical data they receive from patient examinations. All too often, without a cultural interpreter, minority patients, especially those who are older or from socially conservative backgrounds, simply remain silent in their physicians' office, but later leave without the satisfaction of a connection with their provider that results in a shared involvement in their health management. The first-generation Indian woman whose narrative follows provides a cultural bridge for her parents, even when they visited a physician who shared her family's ethnic background. First, she explains the impact that a cultural divide between patient and physician can have on the patient's health behaviors after the clinical encounter concludes.

> I definitely have found in situations when my [Indian] doctor was not available and I was working with someone who had a different background that it was harder for them to understand our situation. They would try to get us on a diet that met the requirements of what they're supposed to tell you like x number of calories or weight level or try to get more grains in or whatever. And I knew that we weren't going to be able to follow that because it just isn't the way that our diet works. It's easier for my husband and I [sic] to follow because we grew up here, but I was also asking questions for my parents and they definitely eat Indian food all the time. And so they just can't follow the American diets.
> —Indian Female, Western United States

This woman has no difficulty concluding that her parents would not comply with a physician's dietary recommendations that did not take their culture into account. In contrast, she explains, when a physician respects the complexity and importance of her parents' cultural context, then their compliance with the doctor's recommendations increases.

> So asking doctors that had that kind of a background was extremely help-ful. . . . They were able to delve in pretty deeply in the sense that in India there are so many cultures within one country, so he was able follow up and ask questions like, "Is it a South Indian diet? Is it a North Indian diet? Do you eat more roti, which is the bread versus the rice?" So they were able to ask questions that I would have not thought about. Or the other thing is he knew things like Indians tend to reuse oil. And it cools down and then they reuse it again. And that heating and cooling process is extremely bad for you. . . . So there's no way—or it's less likely that some-one without that background would know something like that. The other thing is heating milk, to make certain kinds of food, it turns out that even if you're using skim milk or 1percent milk, when you're heating it and distilling it, it becomes thicker and the fat content becomes greater. So again, someone who didn't have that background wouldn't know that this is how we make yoghurt and this is how we make paneer. . . . So I think it's been extremely helpful.

However, the significant downside to this family's story is the fact that the vast majority of physicians in America are *not* Indian. This patient family cannot count on meeting with physicians only from their ethnic background in order to receive high quality health care. If patients from this and other minority ethnic groups are to be able to manage their health after they have concluded a clinical encounter, all physicians must be mindful of their impact on patients even after they leave the doctor's office and therefore must strive to practice unbiased medicine.

Minority patients consistently perceive they have received a lower quality of care than they would have were they white, and they often report that they have felt discrimination based on their race or ethnic-ity in health care settings.[28] However, these findings are nuanced in in-teresting ways. First, African Americans and Asians are generally less likely than other racial and ethnic groups to rate the quality of their health care favorably. Hispanics generally report the highest quality of care, despite the high numbers who report perceived discrimination. In contrast, African Americans' view of care quality is directly related to whether they perceive discrimination. For example, another study of over 36,000 California patients[29] also found that negative quality of care perceptions were "fully" explained by perceptions of discrimination among African Americans.[30] Certainly, self-reported perceptions of discrimination and quality of care are subject to widely varying definitions, standards, levels of sensitivity, and expectations. Nevertheless, patients' perceived discrimination has been linked directly and indirectly to health outcomes. The data that perceptions of health care quality profoundly influence minority patients' mental and physical health is particularly instructive.[31]

Dr. Louis Penner conducted a longitudinal study of 156 African American patient volunteers to determine how their perceptions of racial discrimination contributed to health disparities. The study tested whether discrimination leads to a sense of wariness and mistrust among black patients, which, in turn, negatively affects their responses to medical interactions, their health behaviors, or their health. Patients were surveyed prior to their interactions with physicians to determine their health status, experience with discrimination, and past adherence or willingness to follow physician recommendations. Penner's researchers next surveyed these patients immediately after their interactions with the nineteen family medicine physicians in the study. They asked for information about their satisfaction and feelings of camaraderie, or "being on the same team." The researchers then conducted two follow-up surveys to consider the patients' adherence and health status, four and sixteen weeks after the clinical visit.

Penner's first finding was revealing. The black patients' perceived levels of discrimination were significantly and negatively correlated with their general health status; as the level of patients' perceived discrimination increased, their self- reported health measures declined. Moreover, perceived racial discrimination was significantly and *positively* associated with the number of chronic illnesses, most notably diabetes, identified in patient medical records. Penner found similar correlations with patients' reported mental health as measured on Medical Outcomes Study 20-Item Short Form Health Survey (SF-20), a widely accepted self-report adherence and health measure developed for RAND Health, one of the world's largest health research groups. As predicted, based on numerous other studies, patients' satisfaction and sense of camaraderie were inversely related to their perceptions of past discrimination. Also unsurprisingly, patients with greater levels of perceived discrimination showed poorer adherence to physician recommendations at the four-week and sixteen-week follow-ups, while a significant positive association was found between patient satisfaction and adherence at follow-up. The study confirmed that perceived discrimination has a direct and indirect effect on patient adherence, which in turn influences patient health status. Four weeks after their clinic visits, poor health outcomes were associated with higher levels of perceived discrimination. These findings were replicated at the sixteen-week follow-up, but because of patient attrition, they were not statistically significant.

Certainly, other researchers have found that mistrust and the expectation of stigmatization can have a significant impact on black patients' use of medical services. For example, existing studies have shown that blacks who perceive higher levels of medical discrimination are less likely to make the decision to get cancer screenings and cholesterol and diabetic testing, as well as to receive flu shots. The Penner study, however, uniquely connects patients' perceptions of racial discrimination with their satisfaction with the quality of care they receive, their subsequent adherence to treatment regimens, and ultimately, their health outcomes longitudinally. Therefore, this study powerfully connects the disproportionately poor health outcomes that minority patients experience to their perceptions of discrimination and distrust in their providers. Said another way, minority patients' responses to providers' implicit biases will ultimately have a deleterious and disparate effect on their health outcomes.

Patients Who "Vote with Their Feet"

My interviews revealed that several minority patients simply gave up seeking medical treatment from providers whom they perceived to be biased. In some cases, these disaffected patients sought medical care from others in the American health system. In another case, the patient finally resorted to alternative cures. These stories are important for the obvious health impact that each patient's decision to leave a provider's care represents. Moreover, these decisions should also inform the study design that social science researchers choose to investigate the causal link between minority patient health outcomes and providers' implicit biases. Minority patients appear very willing to stop seeking care from a physician who they believe to be biased, and therefore may not be present in studies examining the impact a biased physician may have had on their health.

The first example of just such a patient begins in China.

> One night I just found I got some clinical disease like recurring to me, which is caused from the countryside back in China. The mosquito— very tiny thing—I don't know the term for that illness. Basically it's hidden in the liver. It can be periodically, one day you have very high fever, suddenly you feel very cold, and after a while you feel so hot. And then you're exhausted and you get to sleep and the next day it seems everything is fine but it may occur the same thing the next evening. I got this thing from the countryside. I was from Shanghai but during the Cultural Revolution I was sent to the countryside. And then I got that thing. And it seems sometimes this disease can be hidden for fifteen years and then it comes back. . . . It's like an Asian disease, or something like that. But when I came here, I got this thing back. I knew what it was. I knew everything for sure. But when I got to the hospital, nobody believed me! And then they take my blood and they say, "You know I can find nothing."

The patient in this interview holds a Ph.D. in material engineering earned from a prominent United States university. Yet, the first part of his narrative implicates the first and third mechanisms of the Biased Care Model. His intermittent symptoms, unfamiliar to Western care providers, were simply disbelieved when the blood tests used by American physicians could not identify the source of the problem this patient described.

> But this thing, it's true; . . . you cannot find anything from the blood but if you look very carefully at the liver you can see. But I don't think that they bother to do that. And of course, just like right now I cannot really remember the name or the academic terminology. So I think I took the dictionary and found the word to tell the doctor. But they just say, "No way, I cannot give you any kind of treatment. When you get this thing again, come back." But on the other hand, in this system, if you have something

very urgent in symptoms, typically they just kill the symptoms, not that they just find out something. And also, if you don't speak English very well, you have less chance of making them understand.

This patient's comments recall the communication biases from Mechanisms #3 and #4. Nevertheless, like most minority patients studied, this interviewee was eager to discount the possibility that his providers were overtly or deliberately discriminating against him based on his ethnicity.

> This is not saying that they really hate Chinese. But they have got some kind of prejudgment. They say you are wrong because you're not a professional. . . . Plus maybe your whole life in the United States you never meet anyone like this. So I just go back without any kind of treatment. It really can make you so weak. You really cannot walk. You don't have the strength. . . . If you are so weak originally it can kill you but if you are strong the thing can go.

It is difficult to determine whether the patient is describing being weak as a symptom of his illness or as a result of repeated efforts to obtain treatment from his providers who were not forthcoming. Both explanations are plausible. In either case, the patient relates the deleterious impact of his physician's perceptions of ethnic minorities as described by Mechanism #1.

> So after fifteen years I came here and I got this thing again. . . . But I decide I'm not going to the hospital because this really makes things worse because I have to make effort to go there and I know the result. So I just call a friend in Shanghai and tell him I need this medicine. . . . After like half a month somebody brought the thing to me. . . . I think quite a few doctors don't really feel like dealing with someone who cannot communicate well, is a waste of effort. . . . I'm a professional in my area at least I can say I'm well educated.
> —Chinese American Male Patient, Northwestern United States

The frustration with providers that this patient felt prompted him to opt out of the American medical system entirely, at least with respect to the ailment he described in this interview. Other patients interviewed confirmed that minority patients may simply refuse to return to providers they perceive as biased.

In one interview with the next patient, he related the stories of three black patients who terminated their relationships with physicians based on their views that these doctors were implicitly biased. The first patient was the interviewee himself. After explaining that he thought doctors at a particular clinic exhibited implicit bias by not seeking alternatives that he described as "more progressive" treatments before resorting to surgery, he decided not to return for the recommended surgery.

> Yeah I did [decide not to go back]. I basically did. I basically did withhold going back there. With my understanding from the experience while these people are very good at finding out what's going on, I did not think that they were balanced in their approach about the treatment because they could have, in my opinion, taken this a more progressive way and got more data before they decided to do this kind of removal.

The second patient in his account was this man's daughter, who also declined to remain with doctors when she felt they disrespected her treatment preferences. Finally, when this patient shared his experience with an African American colleague who was being treated by the same internist who held implicit biases in the patient's view, that colleague—the third patient—similarly decided to terminate physician-patient relationship.

> The funny thing about it was that the president of the university at that time . . . was also seeing the same doctor. And when I told him finally about what had happened, he started asking questions and I think also switched to the doctor that I was seeing of Nigerian background . . . because he was really concerned.
> —African American Male Patient, Midwestern United States

The findings from the two patient interviews cited above point out the important impact that unconscious racism operating through Mechanism #6 may have on patient health outcomes. The sixth mechanism of the Biased Care Model is an important vector connecting physician bias to poor minority health outcomes. If minority patients frequently change physicians to avoid implicit bias, they are also likely to suffer discontinuities in their care. Minority health outcomes may also be affected by this mechanism as they delay care in order to seek out minority providers whom they perceive as nonracist. Finally, if this finding turns out to be generalizable, the sixth mechanism will provide a powerful explanation for the limited association some researchers have noted between physician implicit bias and quantifiably poor minority health outcomes. It may simply be the case that minority patients do not remain in clinical relationships with biased physicians, thereby precluding any finding of the association between implicit bias and poor biomedical health outcomes. Taken together, the Biased Care Model's six mechanisms operate to reduce the quality of minority patient health and health care. The final section of this chapter ties all six mechanisms of the Biased Care Model together, to show how they interact to affect health disparities.

Applying the Biased Care Model to Pain Management

Pain treatment provides an excellent case for seeing how the Biased Care Model's six mechanisms work together to produce disparate health outcomes. Numerous studies show significant racial and ethnic disparities in physicians' evaluation and treatment of pain, even after controlling for socioeconomic status, medical comorbidities, insurance status, and patient preferences. These studies show that racial and ethnic minority patients of all ages are significantly more likely to be undertreated for all kinds of pain—whether postoperative, chronic, acute, or end-of-life pain—in a wide variety of settings.[32] Therefore, pain treatment provides a platform to see how implicit bias infiltrates each of the six mechanisms to produce disparate health outcomes.

The first mechanism—physicians' perceptions—operate as a strong factor in transmitting implicit biases into unequal pain management outcomes because physicians who treat pain work in settings that are particularly amenable to the use of stereotypes in making clinical decisions. Treating pain involves gathering ambiguous evidence, largely from patients' subjective reports, to make complex medical judgments. The clinical uncertainty of this endeavor is compounded by the risks associated with mistakes. Morphine, heroin, Percocet, Valium, and other controlled substances are the drugs that pain doctors regularly prescribe. These medications are addictive, as well as being attractive to people who misappropriate medication for illicit uses. In addition, pain is difficult to quantify. Physicians rely upon imprecise questions such as "Can you rate your pain on a scale from one to ten?" while knowing that no two individuals have identical scales. At the same time, the danger associated with potential drug abuse and addiction raises the stakes for physicians who seek to prescribe narcotic pain medicine only when necessary, justifiable, or appropriate. Thus, the combination of clinical uncertainty and perceived risk places great weight on the physicians' ability to make judgments about the patients' honesty and likelihood of compliance, and increases the probability that physicians will use racial, ethnic, and other stereotypes to make difficult judgments and predictions about patients' behavior.[33] When providers must make high-risk judgments in the face of uncertainty, they are more likely to access stereotypes and stored social knowledge to fill in the information gaps. When these judgments and predictions are informed by implicit biases, minority patient health outcomes may suffer.

The third and fourth mechanisms that operate during the clinical encounter are exaggerated in the pain management context because of the extent to which providers must rely upon patients' communication tone and affect in order to judge their future health behavior and amenability to treatment. One pain treatment study powerfully confirms the emotional reciprocity that the Biased Care Model predicts is present when patients seek help managing their pain from physicians. Dr. Diana Burgess tested the interaction between patient behavior and physician decision-making when prescribing opioids to treat low back pain. The 382 primary care physicians were presented with vignettes about cooperative and uncooperative patients and randomly assigned black or white subjects. Some were assigned patient hypotheticals in which the subject acted in a challenging manner—demanding Percocet by name, evincing use of a relative's prescription, and appearing angry during the interview. Others were assigned patients who acted in a non-challenging manner—showing calm confidence. The treatment decision tested was whether physicians would change patients to a higher dosage or different type of opioid medication. The outcome was surprising.

For black patients, physicians were more likely to switch challenging patients to a stronger opioid than they were to switch cooperative patients. For white patients, the opposite was true—higher doses were given to cooperative rather than to challenging patients. What explains this disparity? Perhaps black patients who communicate direct demands may reduce clinical uncertainty during treatment. Alternatively, assertiveness by black patients may get physicians' attention or help physicians become aware of their own racial stereotypes and avoid them. A third explanation suggests that physicians do not lend credence to pain complaints from black patients until they aggressively impress their need for treatment on their physicians. The importance of Mechanisms #3 and #4 is demonstrated by this research. All of these three explanations confirm that the Burgess study shows the physician and patient relationship in pain management offers two avenues for implicit bias on both sides of the physician-patient dyad to affect health outcomes.

The second mechanism—biased statistical interpretation—has been demonstrated by Dr. David Moskowitz's study of pain treatment provided for 169 HIV-infected indigent patients. Dr. Moskowitz used the Physician Trust in Patients Scale, a validated scale that measures providers' trust in patients, to show that primary care providers trust non-white patients less than they trust their white patients, despite similar rates of reported illicit drug use and opioid analgesic misuse.[34] Moskowitz observed that "in this study of socially marginalized patients, PCPs' trust in patients appears to be guided in part by perceptions of racial/ethnic groups, and not solely by individual patients' illicit drug use or opioid analgesic misuse."[35] Other evidence suggests that pain management often involves stereotype bias that is more difficult to combat because it arises from what psychologists call "rule-based inferences." These stereotypes are the result of cognitive reflection and are influenced by the physician's goals for patient interaction. In the pain management case, providers are likely to apply racial and ethnic stereotypes to help comprehend uncertain or subjective information from patients or to process complex decisions where knowledge or consensus is lacking. If a provider must determine whether a patient is under-reporting or exaggerating pain, has a history of past substance abuse, or possesses a strong (or lazy) work ethic, stereotypes may be useful. Thus, in some studies, evidence strongly suggests that automatic stereotyping results in inadequate pain treatment in clinical settings where negative aspects of racial biases are reinforced. For example, inner-city emergency rooms with large indigent populations generate higher levels of unconscious bias among physicians than settings where the case mix is more diverse. In any settings, however, stereotypes can falsely appear to provide clinically relevant information to the decisions doctors make to treat pain. The physician may call upon stereotypes about low-income patients' access to pharmacies or about the incidence of drug abuse by African Americans when making decisions about pain treatment. Thus, the physician might even decline to conform treatment decisions to the well-described clinical risk factors associated with increased opioid analgesic misuse, and instead trust "gut feelings" to drive clinical judgments.[36] In truth, any stereotypes overlap imperfectly with the information doctors need to treat pain; they also introduce dangerous implicit biases into medical decision-making.

The sixth mechanism—patients' cognitive and behavioral responses to physician implicit bias—has not been extensively studied. Nevertheless, there is some evidence that when minority patients perceive provider discomfort and uncertainty, they may choose to avoid follow-up care, and return instead to providers for pain treatment when they are in extremis, rather than when preventative care could have forestalled acute episodes. Recall Penner's study linking physician's implicit racial bias to patient's reactions following clinical interactions discussed earlier.[37] Low patient satisfaction is, of course, associated with inefficient use of health services and poor health outcomes.[38]

Scores of pain management studies have found evidence that the fifth mechanism of the Biased Care Model may introduce implicit bias into doctors' treatment decisions, and those studies furnish support that this mechanism is linked to disparate health outcomes.[39] Diagnostic and treatment decision-making in the pain treatment setting is further complicated by differences in physician perceptions of pain based on its origin and verifiability. For example, Burgess reported a study that involved hypothetical patients with pain from kidney stones, nontraumatic back pain, ankle fractures, and migraine headaches and found that male physicians provided pain relief to white patients more readily than to blacks, while female physicians provided more pain relief to black patients with kidney stones and back pain. However, differences were less pronounced when complaints were linked to objectively verifiable injuries such as an ankle fracture. In a second study, patients' race was unrelated to the physicians' decisions to provide non-opioid based pain medicine, but disparities appeared when physicians prescribed opioids, especially in cases where there were fewer objective findings available.[40] The majority of pain studies have found disparate treatment for blacks and Latinos when compared to white Americans, and most have found that minority patients are more likely to be undertreated for pain than whites. Now that the Biased Care Model has been useful in understanding these data, the next chapter turns to building the case that the Biased Care Model is also useful as a guide in constructing practical solutions to reduce and even eradicate health disparities.

7

From Inequity to Intervention

What Can Be Done about Implicit Bias

Mr. Thompson is a 50-year-old man with a history of well-controlled hypertension and smoking, but no other risk factors for coronary artery disease (CAD). He presents himself to the emergency department, complaining of chest pain. He appears to be in a lot of pain, describing it as "sharp, like being stabbed with a knife" and pointing to the mid-sternum. He has had it about 3 hours and it has waxed and waned but now is an 8 out of 10 in intensity. The pain doesn't change with movement or deep breathing. It does not radiate and is not accompanied by shortness of breath. His vital signs, oxygen saturation and physical exam are normal except for mild sternal tenderness to palpation. His ERG shows 2 mm horizontal ST elevations in the anterior leads, but there is no prior EKG for comparison and there is no time for cardiac enzymes. He did not have access to a cardiac catheterization lab. He has no absolute contraindications to thrombolysis, the treatment of choice that breaks up clots of blood that can cause stroke or heart attack.
—Alexander R. Green et al., "Implicit Bias among Physicians"

We know from the evidence explored thus far that if the patient, Mr. Thompson, described in this vignette is an African, Hispanic, Asian, or Native American, he is much less likely to receive thrombolysis than if he were white.[1] We know that this is due in no small part to the unconscious biases Mr. Thompson's doctor holds. However to this point, we have focused on the automatic and ubiquitous aspects of unconscious racism, ignoring the question of whether Mr. Thompson's physician might be able to control his biases. This chapter shows that he can. This chapter challenges the prevailing narrative that has left the American health care system generally tolerant of, if not complacent about, this form of race bias. The assumption that discrimination due to implicit biases operates without intention or conscious awareness has lulled us to conclude that unconscious racism is also unavoidable, intractable, and beyond conscious control. It is not. The prevailing narrative about unconscious racism wrongly assumes its inevitability and thus leaves Mr. Thompson, if he is not white, to suffer the most harmful and insidious forms of discrimination.

After Mr. Thompson is turned down for thrombolysis treatment, he is unlikely to receive adequate medication for his chest pain as he departs the cardiologist's office. If he returns to his primary care provider, he is less likely than a white patient to receive educational counseling about smoking cessation, moderating his diet, and increasing exercise, because his providers are likely to assume that Mr. Thompson is not well-educated enough, wealthy enough, or motivated enough to benefit from this type of life-prolonging counsel. The evidence shows that Mr. Thompson is more likely to be dissatisfied with his provider interactions and that he is also likely to feel he has experienced racial discrimination. Thus, Mr. Thompson most likely will not place his trust in his physician, may not adhere to the doctor's recommendations, may not attend scheduled follow-up visits, or may even decide to stop seeking medical care for his condition altogether. Should Mr. Thompson's condition deteriorate significantly, he is less likely to receive a heart transplant because as a black American, he is statistically less likely to be evaluated for, counseled for, or put on a waiting list to receive a solid organ transplant than his white counterparts. Ultimately, Mr. Thompson is likely to die several years before a white patient with the same initial medical condition. In short, because we assume that nothing can be done to mitigate unconscious racism in health care, the length and quality of Mr. Thompson's life still depends on whether his skin is black, brown, or white. This chapter explains why this injustice is avoidable.

Evidence that Implicit Biases Are Malleable

Social scientists have developed a body of empirical evidence that shows implicit biases are malleable over the past quarter century.[2] The empirical record is now well established and offers strong evidence that implicit attitudes are neither inaccessible nor inescapable; they are not impossible to control; they are not out of reach. In fact, implicit associations can be influenced both by the individual who unconsciously holds these stereotypes and prejudices and by external factors. Researchers have reported and reviewed numerous studies[3] that put two important misconceptions about implicit biases to rest. First, the evidence demonstrates that unconscious implicit attitudes are responsive to the deliberate choices and influences of an individual even though that person is not consciously experiencing the bias. Second, implicit biases are not impervious to relatively short-term change even though they arise from social knowledge that was acquired slowly, and over a lifetime. In fact, the evidence reveals that learning can continue to take place and alter social group knowledge, after initial attitudes and associations are formed. Take, for example, a person who developed bad driving habits over time and subconsciously incorporated those habits into driving behavior for many years. If this person chooses to be mindful of improving his or her driving, either out of a conscious decision to do so or in response to external influences, those bad habits can be altered. External authorities may incentivize improvement through a media campaign, new rules of the road, prosecution for reckless driving, or a driver's education class. Thus, malleability describes an ongoing learning process in which people with old, objectionable implicit biases learn to respond to newer, more appropriate attitudes and beliefs. Put another way, long-standing and unconscious thinking can change.

This understanding of malleability is called the "connectionist" model of implicit bias. Unlike the prior notion that implicit associations are static and inaccessibly fixed, the empirical record reveals that stereotypes and prejudicial beliefs to which we may adhere at any given time are "states" of thinking that form based on past experiences and current inputs. Biases can be revised depending upon current informational inputs gathered and weighed with each new encounter. This flexible view of stereotyping replaces an outdated rigid one and allows for the evidence that individuals can constantly update the stored group knowledge that produces implicit biases. The connectionist model explains that a stereotype is merely a pattern of activation that, at a given point in time, is jointly determined by *current input* (i.e., the context) and the *weight* of the new information's connection to existing and underlying beliefs.[4] Psychologists now conclude that "stereotypes are quite elastic and thus any individual could hold and even change an infinite number of representations of social category's members, when viewed across time and place."[5]

The connectionist model contrasts with early theories of implicit bias, which focused on their automaticity. "Automaticity" refers generally to the way that individuals make associations without any awareness, without intentionality, and without responsibility for the influence the associations have in directing their conduct and choices.[6] Early researchers concluded that automaticity meant inevitability. For example, one researcher said, "a crucial component of automatic processes is their inescapability; they occur despite deliberate attempts to bypass or ignore them."[7] This view is no longer correct. Over the past twenty years, researchers have collected a strong record to contradict this notion that implicit attitudes change slowly, if at all, simply because they develop slowly over time. This idea has been replaced by what Dr. Irene Blair has called "the now-bountiful evidence that automatic attitudes—like self-reported attitudes—are sensitive to personal, social, and situational pressures."[8] Blair points out that "the conclusion that automatic stereotypes and prejudice are not as inflexible as previously assumed is strengthened by the number and variety of demonstrations. . . . The fact that the tests were conducted in the service of many different goals, and by the similarity of findings across different measures."[9]

The importance of understanding that implicit biases are malleable cannot be overstated. First, malleability means that interventions may be strategically introduced to provide current inputs that alter implicit biases. Thus, we can expect that implicit biases can be reduced. To say that biased attitudes may be "reduced" is to say that current informational inputs can be adjusted so that the resulting stereotype patterns no longer conform to traditional, discriminatory, or inequitable stereotypes, but instead lead individuals and institutions to more equitable judgments and more equitable conduct. Furthermore, malleability also means that the discriminatory impacts that result from implicit biases also may be reduced. The research that gave rise to the connectionist model has provided important insights concerning the several methods available to individuals and institutions wishing to ameliorate the discriminatory impact of decisions and conduct informed by implicit biases, stereotyping, and prejudice. Finally, by demonstrating that even subconscious racial biases are within reach and control, researchers have provided a sound basis for holding individuals and institutions responsible for reducing implicit racial and ethnic biases and for reducing the discriminatory harms caused by unconscious racism.

Interventions to Transform Biased Care

The social science literature includes several studies of a wide variety of intervention strategies that have been tested for their efficacy in reducing implicit biases. Borrowing from the work of Dr. Allison Lenton, I propose a model here that organizes the interventions shown to be most effective and that have the clearest practical application. I use three categories that I call Type A, Type B, and Type C interventions based on the timing of the intervention. Figure 7.1 shows when the intervention occurs during the cognitive process. This model provides a way for health care providers to bring their treatment decisions, communication, and statistical interpretations, which had been tainted by subconscious bias, into alignment with their explicit preferences for providing the best medical treatment available to all patients, regardless of race or ethnicity. Remarkably, the interventions that can alter implicit biases have not ever before been brought to bear on the discrimination that has caused racial and ethnic health disparities. Scholars and clinicians have missed this important key to reducing discriminatory harms caused by implicit bias. The model in figure 7.1 repairs this unfortunate oversight, combining the knowledge of how implicit bias works with the understanding of how implicit biases can be interrupted before they produce health disparities. As researchers Ana Balsa and Thomas McGuire have explained, "Policies to address disparities will work differently depending on which mechanism is responsible."[10] In fact, each of the three types of malleability interventions described here maps onto the mechanisms described in the Biased Care Model presented in chapters 4, 5 and 6. Figure 7.1 illustrates how intervention policies can be used to address each of the mechanisms responsible for transmitting the implicit biases that cause discrimination and inequity in American health care.

TYPE A   TYPE B   TYPE C

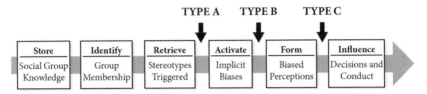

Figure 7.1. Three types of interventions that reduce the impact of implicit bias.

Type A methods reduce implicit biases by intervening before stereotypes are subconsciously activated. This category includes distraction methods, aimed at increasing the cognitive busyness a person experiences so that the encounter with stimuli that invokes automatic negative stereotypes is less direct and prolonged. Type A also includes a priori training that seeks to negate stereotype activation; such training is the most effective of this category of interventions. The strategies that are introduced after stereotypes are activated, but before implicit biases are formed, are Type B interventions. This second type depends on heterogeneity within the activated automatic stereotypes in order to bring opposing examples to bear on older learned patterns of categorization. Type C interventions describe those methods introduced after implicit biases are formed but before the biases influence judgments and behavior. Psychologists explain that the goal of these interventions is to inhibit expression of implicit biases and prejudices after they have been formed. Rejection campaigns, such as a "Just Say No," approach fall into this category and are notoriously ineffective. However, other Type C methods that alter individual and social motivations do work to reduce the discriminatory impact of implicit biases. Interventions of all three types can be useful to reduce implicit racial, ethnic, and other biases.

Type A Intervention: Stereotype Negation Training

Researchers have demonstrated that stereotype negation training can significantly reduce the automatic activation of stereotypes. As early as 1989, psychologist Patricia Devine directed a series of three studies that demonstrated how automatic racial stereotypes and prejudices against blacks could be controlled and ultimately changed by an individual's willingness to invest "intention, attention, and time."[11] Devine demonstrated that a process called stereotype negation training could effectively inhibit automatically activated attitudes and beliefs and replace them with nonprejudiced ideas and responses. Her explanation of the change process succinctly describes the premise underlying stereotype negation training:

> Inhibiting stereotype-congruent or prejudice-like responses and intentionally replacing them with non-prejudiced responses can be likened to the breaking of a bad habit. That is, automatic stereotype activation functions in much the same way as a bad habit. Its consequences are spontaneous and undesirable, at least for the low-prejudice person. . . . Elimination of a bad habit requires essentially the same steps as the formation of a habit. The individual must (a) initially decide to stop the old behavior, (b) remember the resolution, and (c) try repeatedly and decide repeatedly to eliminate the habit before the habit can be eliminated. In addition, the individual must develop a new cognitive (attitudinal and belief) structure that is consistent with the newly determined pattern of responses.[12]

Devine's description of the methodological principles that make stereotype negation training effective distinguishes this training from cultural competency programs currently in use throughout the American health care system.[13] Such programs typically provide brief episodes of exposure to factual information about health disparities and minority communities. Their curricula encourage "color blindness" or suppression of anti-group attitudes in order to achieve equality of care. These methods are aimed primarily at affecting explicit rather than implicit biases and prejudices.[14] As a result, the effectiveness of cultural competency programs has been mixed at best.[15] In contrast, stereotype negation aims to remove and replace automatic, implicit, subconscious attitudes and beliefs through repeated and prolonged exposure to new structural models of association. Studies show this latter method works to reduce and replace implicit biases.

A research team led by Dr. Kerry Kawakami, for example, conducted a series of experiments in which participants were asked to associate stereotype words with images of skinheads and African Americans before and after negation training.[16] These researchers theorized that just as negative stereotypes are learned through repeated exposure, introducing repeated training to denounce stereotypes and replace old automatic attitudes with newly learned ones could reduce automatic activation of negative stereotype traits. It worked. Participants in the studies who received extensive training in negating stereotypes were able to reduce stereotype activation, and furthermore the effect lasted and was still clearly visible twenty-four hours following the training session.[17] The researchers concluded optimistically, saying, "These findings provide support for the assumption that with instruction and repetition individuals can become adept at responding negatively to stereotypes. In short, practice does make perfect—or at least very good—stereotype negators."[18]

A later study demonstrated similarly effective outcomes using live student participants. This study involved two quasi-experiments that followed college students enrolled in a prejudice and conflict seminar. Control group students were enrolled in a research methods class. Drs. Laurie Rudman, Richard Ashmore, and Melvin Gary found that training significantly reduced both implicit and explicit anti-black biases.[19] These researchers measured students' implicit biases twice. Students in both classes were tested at the beginning of the semester to confirm that neither group was less affected initially by implicit bias than the other, and then they were retested at the end of the fourteen-week course. This study measured implicit preferences using the Implicit Association Test, as well as the Lexical Decision Task (LDT), which is used by psychologists to observe how quickly people classify words and thereby to measure automatic stereotyping.[20] The stereotype negation training in this study included journaling exercises that required students to document and discuss their own biases, motivations for bias, and ways to counteract their biases. Social contact with members of other racial and ethnic groups, including an African American male professor, played an important role in the training. Discussion that focused on personal views and experiences sometimes resulted in heated exchanges among students but allowed them to encounter, share, and process personalized experiences as well as information about prejudice. Importantly, the stereotype negation training class met regularly over the course of a full academic semester. This quasi-experiment featured the components of a negation program that works to reduce implicit bias.

Researchers seeking to refine the understanding of how negation training works have looked more closely at the types of training that are most effective,[21] the precise memory functions affected by negation training,[22] and the types of people most likely to succeed in reducing their implicit biases.[23] The sample of the leading studies on stereotype negation training presented here is not intended to treat the subject exhaustively. The point is to demonstrate the strength of the social science record that supports the conclusion that individuals who exhibit automatic, implicit racial and ethnic biases can be trained to think and behave differently.

Type B Intervention: Promoting Counter-Stereotypes

Increasing the accessibility of counter-stereotypes decreases automatic negative stereotype associations. This has been confirmed in numerous laboratory studies, including one conducted by Drs. Nilanjana Dasgupta and Anthony Greenwald.[24] Their study demonstrated that automatic negative attitudes could be reduced by more than 50 percent by repeatedly showing study participants photographic images of famous and admired blacks, such as Martin Luther King or Denzel Washington, and photographs of infamous and disliked whites, such as Charles Manson. Moreover, in a follow-up experiment, Dasgupta and Greenwald showed these findings were not limited to racial attitudes, but were applicable to subconscious age-related attitudes. In both instances, significant reductions in automatic preferences were modified for at least twenty-four hours. These are useful findings that have been replicated by other scientists studying race,[25] gender,[26] and age[27] implicit biases. However the practical importance of counter-stereotype research becomes most plainly apparent when the experiments move from controlled laboratory settings into actual "real-life" field settings.

In a study of the impact that counter-stereotypes have on gender biases, Dasgupta and colleagues tested the extent to which exposure to women in positions of leadership on a college campus changed female students' implicit gender biases.[28] One of the two studies in this series was conducted in a laboratory, while the other took place on the campuses of coeducational and women's colleges. In the first study, women participants were exposed to biographies and photographs of high profile women in leadership positions. Women in a control group were shown descriptions and pictures of a variety of flowers. The participants then completed gender-IATs to measure their implicit biases. The study was designed to determine whether exposure to admired members of a disadvantaged group—women—would affect automatic attitudes and beliefs about members of that social group. In the second study, fifty-two college students were asked to complete gender-IAT studies, identical to the test used on the first group of participants. The students were then asked to describe their course load, extracurricular activities, and role models on campus. In contrast to the group in the first study, these college students were exposed to counter-stereotypes of women in leadership roles in their everyday lives. On both campuses studied, women occupied leadership positions as deans, math and science professors, college presidents, and other counter-stereotypical roles. However, women more frequently occupied these leadership positions at the all-women's college. The students were followed a year after their initial study to see how their stereotypes and prejudices had changed. At the end of both studies, Dasgupta related that "both the laboratory study and the field study reported in this paper converge on the same message—women's automatic stereotypic beliefs about their in-group can be undermined if they inhabit local environments in which women frequently occupy counter-stereotypic leadership roles."[29] This gender-bias study importantly replicates results that test the malleability of implicit race bias in controlled laboratory settings.

For example, Dasgupta and Greenwald showed that not only images of counter-stereotypical individuals (such as a photograph of an admired black, elderly, or female subject), but also videos showing counter-stereotype *conditions* can effectively reduce automatic stereotyping. Their finding replicated a study conducted in 2001 by Bernd Wittenbrink, Charles Judd, and Bernadette Park. In that earlier study, some participants watched a short video that showed African American families enjoying a family barbecue or attending church before their implicit associations were tested. Other participants saw videos of blacks in gang-violence scenes. Those who had watched the first videos demonstrated significantly lower implicit preferences for whites when compared to participants who had watched a video of blacks engaged in stereotypical activities.[30] These studies provide important information for antidiscrimination efforts: Counter-stereotypes can reduce implicit biases whether they are externally introduced or internally generated.

A variant of counter-gender stereotype training called "imagining" allows individuals to think up their own counter-stereotype images. Drs. Irene Blair and her colleagues performed five experiments to show that an individual who focuses attention on creating a counter-stereotypical mental image of a strong and capable woman can effectively reduce his or her own access to automatic stereotypes and alter the implicit associations that direct judgment and behavior toward women.[31] Put another way, this series of experiments shows that individuals can reduce their implicit biases by what they choose to think. In three of the five experiments, these researchers asked undergraduate students to spend several minutes imagining what a strong woman is like, including her hobbies, what she is competent at doing, and other characteristics that came to mind. A control group of student participants was asked to spend the time thinking about neutral images such as a Caribbean vacation. In all cases, the students reported that they had no difficulty developing mental images of counter-stereotypes, which included businesswoman, athletes, warriors, or simply women who balanced family, career, and friends well. Participants then took gender-IATs to measure the speed of their associations with words and pictures that contradicted stereotypes about women (e.g. "strong," "leader," "muscular," "in charge") and the speed of their associations to terms and images that were consistent with gender stereotypes (e.g. "feminine," "weak," "dainty," "quiet").

The results of the first three experiments demonstrated that mental imagery moderates implicit stereotypes, reducing their impact on judgment and behavior. In their remaining two experiments, Blair's research group tested the strength of their results using measures of implicit bias other than the IAT.[32] Overall, they concluded that implicit stereotyping was "substantially diminished by counter-stereotype imagery." The implications for this research are profound because they demonstrate that whether the counter-stereotypes are provided externally or are self-generated by one's own deliberate imagining, it is possible to intervene, interrupt, and reverse the impact that unconscious biases have on one's judgments and conduct. Thus, as a policy matter, both individuals and institutions could use counter-stereotypes to reverse the impact that implicit biases have on unintentionally discriminatory decision-making and behavior.

Type C Intervention: Social and Self-Motivation

Researchers have repeatedly confirmed that individuals who are highly motivated can modify their automatic responses to implicit stereotypes and prejudices. Type C interventions are particularly interesting from a scientific point of view because they operate despite automatic reactions—even after individuals have unconsciously activated long-standing biased attitudes and beliefs. From a law and policy perspective, these interventions are intriguing because they do not require any change in a person's stored group knowledge or memory in order to be effective; thus, they avoid what implicit bias critics have called "the perils of mind reading."[33] Studies of various Type C interventions offer three important insights. First, individuals can inhibit negative stereotypes and activate positive ones when doing so is beneficial to their self-image and responsive to social demands or relationships. Second, social context can produce the requisite motivation to achieve these modifications. And third, merely suppressing negative race biases by ignoring or forgetting about racial and ethnic differences does not work.

The classic example of interventions that change self-motivation involves research that demonstrates that people show less automatic negativity and give more favorable racial responses about blacks in the presence of black experimenters.[34] However, even beyond this one-on-one example, other researchers have shown that individuals who deliberately work to internalize egalitarian norms communicated from the environment around them can show lower levels of implicit prejudice.[35]

In a series of studies performed by Drs. Gretchen Sechrist and Charles Stangor, when participants learned that their unconscious use of automatic stereotypes served to discredit them, their interest in a positive self-image motivated them to inhibit these stereotypes. These experiments demonstrated the extraordinary influence that perceived social consensus can have on reinforcing or dismantling implicitly held race stereotypes and, further, how consensus can reinforce or diminish participants' resulting negative racial behavior. The study tested white students enrolled in a university's introductory psychology class at the beginning of a semester for their high or low explicit anti-black preferences as demonstrated on a mass-administration of a computerized questionnaire. After the participants completed the online questions,

Sechrist and Stangor selected students to participate and divided them into low-prejudice and high-prejudice groups according to their levels of explicit prejudice. The selected students were then randomly assigned to receive feedback to indicate either that 81 percent of university students agreed with their assessments or that only 19 percent of students agreed with their judgments. This feedback signaled the level of social consensus around the subjects' explicit views on race. Experimenters then asked each student individually to follow an African American student who entered the study room, ostensibly to usher the subject to the next phase of the test. However, the interaction between the escort and the student subject was actually a part of the experiment. This phase tested the effect consensus had on the stereotypes about blacks that students held and the way those stereotypes informed students' behavior.

Researchers reviewed the interaction of low-prejudice and high-prejudice subjects, who had received either low-consensus or high-consensus feedback. The researchers watched, for example, how close each subject chose to sit next to the African American escort when given a line of seven available chairs during the waiting period. Later, the student subjects were asked to predict the percentage of African Americans who possessed favorable stereotypical traits such as "fun-loving" or "hard-working," and what percentage of blacks were described by negative stereotypes such as "irresponsible" or "violent" or "hostile." The results of Sechrist and Stangor's first experiment demonstrated that the white students' negative race prejudices were weakest when participants perceived low social consensus on such negative views; conversely, students' prejudices were strengthened by perceived high consensus.[36] Importantly, Sechrist and Stangor's results also reflected the impact that stereotypes have on conduct. In their first experiment, low-prejudice participants who received high-consensus feedback sat in chairs closer to the African American target, as compared with individuals who did not have their beliefs confirmed. In contrast, high-prejudice individuals in the high-consensus group sat farthest away from the African American target when compared with individuals who did not have their beliefs validated. The analysis these researchers performed showed that negative implicit attitudes and behavior were greatest for students who believed their views were widely shared. In the second phase of this first experiment, the group of students who believed their high-prejudiced views were widely shared also more readily held unfavorable stereotypes about blacks' traits when compared to the students whose negative race views were not validated by consensus.

Sechrist and Stangor's second experiment tested the accessibility or ease with which the automatic stereotypes could be recalled consciously when triggered by priming. As in the first experiment, white students were asked to indicate the percentage of African Americans who possessed stereotypical traits, and then were provided feedback that randomly showed their views were broadly shared or contradicted by their peers. In the next phase of this experiment, using the Lexical Decision Task test to measure these students' implicit biases, researchers assessed their reaction times to other stereotypes that had not been expressly identified previously. The researchers found that automatic stereotype associations with negative traits came more quickly to students who perceived their individual prejudices were validated by consensus. Thus, the researchers concluded that their two experiments demonstrated that "intergroup beliefs and behaviors are determined by the perception that those individual beliefs are or are not shared with others."[37] Moreover, both experiments show that perceived consensus not only influences accessibility of implicit attitudes and cognitions, but also changes the expression of explicitly held stereotypes and beliefs.

Ironically, researchers have observed that interventions based upon strategies that stress appreciating or ignoring group differences, rather than eliminating and replacing implicit stereotypes, have a rebound effect. Merely instructing subjects not to think about stereotypes backfires, showing an increase rather than decrease in implicit bias measures.[38] The fact that studies show this Type C intervention is likely to fail should caution against the very approach that many cultural competency curricula health providers now rely upon.

The research reviewed here has far-reaching implications for informing new methods of reducing racial bias due to implicit and unconsciously held prejudices. Social scientists have dedicated considerable attention not only to testing the efficacy and operation of various interventions, but also to drawing practical lessons from the scientific literature to inform changes in policy and practice. In particular, Diane Burgess, Michelle van Ryn, John Dovidio, and Somnath Saha suggest a catalog of strategies that empirical evidence confirms can reduce implicit racial biases among physicians.[39] They caution that current programs, which focus on crosscultural communication skills, will have limited effect on cognitive bias. They also advise that accusatory or "politically correct" messages are likely to backfire, while enhancing providers' understanding of the psychology of implicit bias will not. Their work includes a number of strategies that might be integrated into a strategy that incorporates Type A training interventions with Type B and Type C contextualizing strategies.

The salient question raised by this body of malleability literature concerns accountability. Arguments that unconsciously driven discrimination is involuntary do not hold up in the face of the evidence that implicit biases can be internally and externally influenced. Also, evidence showing that individuals can choose to alter their responses to bias, lays open the question of whether the institutions that employ or contract with implicitly biased physicians should be held accountable for externally incentivizing physicians and other health workers to take advantage of the interventions that reduce implicit bias. Since the discrimination that results from implicit biases is at least as damaging to minorities as blatant prejudice, the question becomes whether the scientific evidence of malleability should go so far as to inform the law pertaining to racial and ethnic discrimination. There are compelling reasons to conclude the law should account for unconscious racial and ethnic discrimination. First, remedying racial discrimination in health care has been the purview and central objective of American civil rights law since 1964, as noted in this book's opening chapter. Second, malleability evidence provides a rational basis for imposing legal liability for discrimination based on implicit bias. Borrowing from the widely accepted method of improved medical decision-making that physicians call "evidence-based medicine," legal scholars have begun to recommend that evidence-based conclusions should also inform legal disputes and decision-making.[40] Third, the malleability literature provides policy-makers with a systematic body of scientific research that will enable them to align the remedial interventions that can effectively disrupt the discriminatory impact from implicit biases with the mechanisms that cause discriminatory harm. Thus, it is possible to determine how complex empirical evidence can be realistically translated into social interventions.[41] However, before considering the exact impact malleability evidence has on the implicit biases that produce health and health care disparities, we must consider the limitations of the malleability evidence, and then turn to understanding the health care landscape from a phenomenological perspective in order to evaluate whether the interventional strategies discussed here could mediate implicit bias in that setting.

Limitations

While the evidence that implicit biases can be affected and even reduced by interventional strategies is promising, some important qualifications should be noted. First, no studies suggest that implicit biases can be reduced to zero. Thus, we cannot speak in terms of eliminating implicit biases entirely, nor can we precisely quantify the disparities that flow from the discrimination they cause. Nevertheless, the malleability literature speaks collectively of significant reductions in implicit bias and in race-conscious behavior. Second, not all the methods researchers have used to demonstrate the malleability of implicit bias are created equal. Some have no immediately obvious practical applications; others are not sufficiently understood to warrant their inclusion in policy or law. For example, evidence that automatic prejudices decline when the features of a black person's face change from "Negroid" (darker skin, wider nose) to European (lighter skin, pointier nose) are practically useless or would produce ridiculous, morally unsound and objectionable solutions to the implicit bias problem if applied. Still other interventions may prove efficacious to reduce some types of implicit bias within or toward some populations, but not all. For example, researchers do not yet understand the reasons that some interventions, which operate to reduce unconscious stereotypes towards blacks, do not vary implicit prejudices towards Asians.[42] Other research may be theoretically important, though limited in its practical usefulness. For example, several studies have shown that when a person's focus of attention is manipulated by distractions in laboratory experiments, that person will become "cognitively busy" and produce fewer stereotypical associations during the experiments. At the same time, however, the variety of distractions that could produce busyness, the variety of implicit biases that might be responsive to distractions, and the lack of field applications limit this method's applicability to policy interventions. Nevertheless, the fact that little doubt remains concerning the power of a person to focus to reduce automatic stereotypes empirically confirms the validity of viewing unconscious biases and prejudices as flexible and subject to external influence.

The malleability literature has its detractors within the social science community. In a recent article, researchers from the University of Virginia appeared to attack the scientific record reviewed here to assert that the malleability of implicit racial bias is overestimated.[43] In fact, the three experiments these scholars reported were limited to, and sought to raise questions only about, the counter-stereotype method studied by Dasgupta and Greenwald, and their results were not nearly as robust as the title of their paper suggests.[44] Other researchers have suggested that malleability is unidirectional; they observe that automatic preferences are easily formed but less readily reversed.[45] However, their conclusion is contrary to the weight of the empirical record. Another group has asserted that declining IAT measures after interventions are evidence of neither a changed mindset nor a guarantee that a decrease in discriminatory behavior will follow.[46] They argue that the nonindividualized labels assigned to test photographs (such as "good" or "bad") are ambiguous and that therefore the IAT results most likely reflect "extra-personal associations" that precede the test and have nothing to do with implicit attitudes. However, even these critics admit that their objections, as far as they go, may recommend changes in the IAT methodology or algorithm; they do not counsel discarding the use of the IAT or its results entirely. Moreover, these objections go to the validity of the IAT, which has been debated so extensively in the literature that one well-known and respected researcher has described the test's validity as a "scientific certainty."[47]

The study of implicit bias presented here contradicts the perception that racial bias is a thing of the past. Nevertheless, evidence of malleability directly challenges the firmly entrenched notion that prejudice due to implicit bias is beyond the reach of intentionality. Moreover, taken as a whole, the malleability literature significantly adds to the current understanding of the extent to which individual and institutional influences can change the discriminatory conduct that flows from implicit biases. Simply put, implicit biases can be *intentionally* reversed. Therefore, the preponderance of malleability evidence warrants a complete

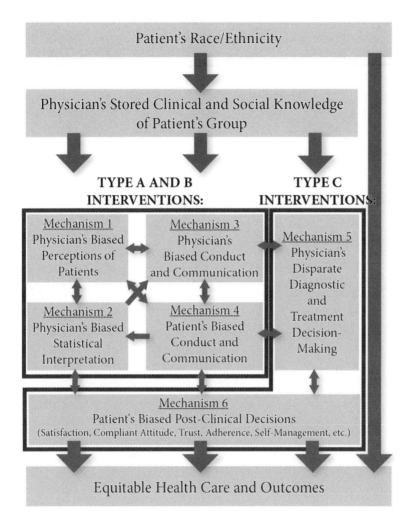

Figure 7.2. Malleability interventions that transform biased care into equitable care.

reconceptualization of when and how providers could and should be held accountable to intervene and thwart the discriminatory impact of unintentional racial and ethnic discrimination. Figure 7.2 graphically depicts the types of interventions that match the Biased Care Model's six implicit bias mechanisms that produce disparate health outcomes.

The solution described here seems simple: Impose the interventions that reduce implicit bias on the mechanisms in which they cause disparities. Yet, the theoretical simplicity of this solution is belied by the political, administrative, and practical challenges of implementing it. Although these challenges are formidable, they are now compelled by the urgency and severity of the persistent and pervasive problem of ethnic and racial health and health care disparities that plagues this nation. Implementing the transformation to an equitable health care model must be borne of the conviction that continued avoidance of the evidence that implicit bias causes disparities, and that disparities ruin lives, will be unethical at best, unjust in deed, and patently unforgivable.

8

A Structural Solution

I wish I could say that racism and prejudice were only distant memories. I wish I could say that this Nation had trav-
eled far along the road to social justice and that liberty and
equality were just around the bend. . . . America must get
to work. In the chill climate in which we live, we must go
against the prevailing wind. We must dissent from the indifference. We must dissent from the apathy. We must dissent
from the fear, the hatred and the mistrust. . . . We must dissent because America can do better, because America has no
choice but to do better.
—Justice Thurgood Marshall

God, give us grace to accept with serenity the things that
cannot be changed, courage to change the things which
should be changed, and the wisdom to distinguish the one
from the other.
—Reinhold Niebuhr

The task of defeating discrimination due to unconscious racism in
American health care will not be an easy one. And yet, the message of
this chapter is that America is morally compelled to confront unconscious racism in health care, and nothing short of a radical paradigm
shift, in healthcare and beyond, will succeed. Therefore, I open this
chapter by quoting Associate Justice Thurgood Marshall's call to action
against racism[1] to underscore the gravity of the societal disease that
unjust medicine represents, and with the familiar words composed by
the American theologian Reinhold Niebuhr[2] to acknowledge the mag-
nitude of the challenge that curing inequality in health care represents.
While we may not, on the one hand, change the seemingly infinite
number of incessant and pervasive messages that result in our involun-

tary acquisition of implicit biases, we must, on the other hand, have the courage to change the medical, social, and political environments that now tolerate the invidious racial discrimination those biases cause.

Niebuhr's petition, first formally published in 1951, but written and apparently circulated before the Second World War, has been the stalwart inspiration for many facing impossible odds. For example, the invocation was officially adopted as a prayer by the United Service Organizations (USO) to distribute to soldiers during World War II, and later by Alcoholics Anonymous to motivate people fighting addiction. Niebuhr's words are an apt inspiration for the fight against racial and ethnic health disparities. They are a fitting encouragement for those working to end discrimination due to implicit racial and ethnic biases because this may at times seem to be an impossible cause. But equality is not impossible. Niebuhr admonishes that a workable solution to unconscious racism must accept and acknowledge there are things that cannot be changed. The omnipresent climate of racial and ethnic division that feeds unconscious racism in America cannot be completely changed. Nevertheless, Niebuhr's words also counsel courage; the implicit bias and discrimination that arise from this climate should and can be changed. First, we can change our defensive resistance to admitting that racial discrimination persists. We can also change our insipid urge to absolve all but the frank bigot from the responsibility to avoid deeply wounding racial injustice. To accomplish these changes, we must recognize that while the environment that produces implicit bias may remain entrenched, the social norms that tolerate the resulting discrimination need not.

Eliminating health care discrimination should theoretically be a "winnable war" since the overwhelming majority of participants in the health care system share and espouse a commitment to deliver high quality medicine fairly. Indeed, many have advocated and implemented costly programs and policies aimed at reforming health inequity. Yet, these attempts have all fallen far short. This chapter will present a framework for public health action that explains the shortcomings of past attempts to address health care disparities. However, I do not believe these efforts were futile, nor should they be abandoned. Rather, I assert that existing antidiscrimination policies will succeed in producing health equality only when accompanied by a new structural approach that can change

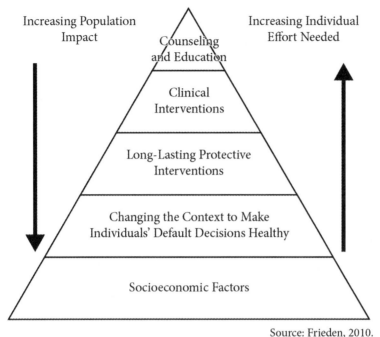

Increasing Population Impact

Increasing Individual Effort Needed

Counseling and Education

Clinical Interventions

Long-Lasting Protective Interventions

Changing the Context to Make Individuals' Default Decisions Healthy

Socioeconomic Factors

Source: Frieden, 2010.

Figure 8.1. Frieden's Health Impact Pyramid. Source: Thomas R. Frieden, "A Framework for Public Health Action: The Health Impact Pyramid," *American Journal of Public Health* 100, no. 4 (April 2010).

the context in which unconscious racism occurs. The structural solution I advance is derived from a public health framework introduced by Dr. Thomas Frieden's seminal work describing varying levels of impact that public health interventions can have on health outcomes.

In 2010, Frieden published "A Framework for Public Health Action,"[3] which introduced a pyramid to illustrate five possible tiers or levels of public health interventions and the corresponding impact each might have to improve health. The Health Impact Pyramid is pictured in figure 8.1.

Generally, Frieden's framework posits that the effectiveness of public health interventions decreases at the higher levels of the pyramid, while interventions aimed at the broad, lower levels of the pyramid have the greatest potential to improve population health outcomes. Applied to the interventions that address health care disparities, the pyramid illustrates the principle that structural interventions to change the socioeconomic disparities in housing, education, employment, food security, and other social determinants of health will have the greatest impact on eliminating health disparities, while clinical and individualized educational interventions shown at the top of the pyramid have limited potential for affecting lasting improvement. Frieden's Health Impact Pyramid is useful for understanding the limited impact of current approaches to health disparities.

Counseling and Education Interventions

According to Frieden, "Interventions at the top tiers are designed to help individuals rather than entire populations, but they could theoretically have a large population impact if universally and effectively applied." A recent *New York Times* story reported one such intervention. All aspiring physicians in the United States must take the Medical College Admission Test (MCAT). MCAT administrators have announced the test will soon incorporate a series of questions concerning implicit bias into the newly revised examination. The IAT questions are planned to be part of the "social thinking" section of the new test.[4] Described as "a better test for tomorrow's doctors," the new MCAT content will introduce the science of implicit bias and communicate the important message that physicians should beware of personal barriers to delivering equitable health care to all patients. Certainly, adding an IAT question to the MCAT will exponentially increase the number of new physicians who are aware of implicit bias. But this test change will not necessarily make those preprofessionals aware of their personal susceptibility to implicit bias. Nor will increasing physician awareness to the general threat posed by implicit bias establish accountability for minimizing the resulting discrimination. Therefore, the MCAT changes, though important and positive, fit within the top tier of individualized education reforms and are not enough to yield broad changes in health disparities.

Similarly, the proposals that social and clinical scientists offer as a result of their research belong in the top tier of Frieden's health impact pyramid. Most sociologists, physicians, and social psychologists whose studies reveal the influence that implicit bias has in health care conclude their discussions by encouraging others to learn more about attitudinal processes[5] or by making incrementalist recommendations that counsel cognitive changes on an individual level.[6] Their pragmatic remedies typically involve admonishments to educate physicians, "raise awareness," improve data collection, or encourage further research. Some may advise implementing workforce diversification to increase the likelihood of race-concordant clinical encounters. Recommendations that go beyond individualized cognitive proposals are rare.[7] While nothing is wrong with these suggestions as far as they go, the point is that they do not go very far at all.

Social psychologists, for example, describe experiments that show that race and gender determine who gets to live and who gets to die and then end their studies with stunningly tepid conclusions such as "Our data indicate that participants do differ in the strength of negative versus positive associations with African Americans relative to White Americans,"[8] or "More work bridging the psychological literature and medical practice may offer new theoretical insights and practical ways to combat bias in health care."[9] Some social scientists may acknowledge that their data will have some limited, immediate usefulness, such as the researchers who said, "Their findings have implications for cultural competency training programs. . . . This has been a concern of the legal community, police academies, and medical and nursing schools."[10] However, for the most part, fashioning concrete solutions to the destructive impact of unconscious bias on the real lives and real deaths of minorities in America seems to be a task beyond the social science gaze.

Researchers' recommendations dramatically underestimate the structural constraints on individual change and the concomitant need for macrolevel interventions to address health disparities. Because the dominant social cognitive theory explains these individual attitudes as inadvertent, inevitable, and ubiquitous, the literature makes unconscious racism seem irrational and exceptional. In truth, researchers have missed the very rational, functional, and structural bases for racism in America and in American health care. The systemic divisions by race and ethnicity in health care preserve power and protect the institutional health care delivery system from economic and social destabilization.

I do not believe that the reason for researchers' shortsightedness is malevolence. On the contrary, this research, which is necessary to support truly effective social change, is motivated by a desire to elucidate the dynamics that underlie human interactions. Yet, the level of structural change needed to accomplish reform in health care is not susceptible to scientific proof or testing. The social scientist's tools are sufficient to show associations, quantify probabilities, and tease out patterns in data. However, the methodologies social scientists employ, and even the questions they pose in the form of hypotheticals, are designed to illuminate a problem, not necessarily to correct it. For these reasons, I believe the copious social science record addressing health disparities and implicit bias rests in the top tier of Frieden's health impact pyramid. Social scientists' evidence can support changes that require individual effort such as counseling, education, and clinical interventions. Over time, social scientists are able to amass evidence to inspire long-lasting, protective interventions. But without more, even the weight of the social science record that has revealed the impact of implicit bias on our American health care system cannot, alone, drive the contextual changes or alter the most fundamental factors needed to address unconscious discrimination in health care. Social science research is a necessary but insufficient component of the social changes needed to eradicate unconscious racism; the knowledge researchers provide is invaluable and essential to understanding disparities, but the proposals and recommendations that researchers advance have aimed only at the proverbial tip of the iceberg—literally.

Clinical Interventions: CLAS and Professional Ethics Standards

When I decided to write a book about implicit bias and health disparities, I met with a physician who I know to be a brilliant, passionate, and conscientious advocate for justice in health care. However, her prognostication was dismal. I told her I wanted to describe a way to repair the impact of implicit bias on health disparities, and she enthusiastically expressed interest in hearing more. But when I told her my purpose was to design systemic interventions to require health providers to address health disparities, she was appalled. She virtually told me to forget it. Knowing I am trained as a lawyer, she eyed me with suspicion and demanded, "What more can law do? We already have all the laws we need and nobody follows them—they don't make one bit of difference!" And that's when it hit me: Absolutely every physician I interviewed during this project—every single one—expressed some version of exactly the same sentiment. They all said the solution, if there is one, lies with health care self-regulating, not with more laws to regulate "us." They asserted that doctors know best how to fix whatever is wrong with health care. Certainly, absolutely, and unequivocally they spoke in unison on this one point: "We don't need any more laws controlling health care disparities—we can solve this ourselves!" It turns out that the health disparity "laws" these practitioners were talking about are actually administrative regulations promulgated by the Department of Health and Human Services (DHHS) to influence the clinical care in publicly funded hospitals.

In 2001, the DHHS Office of Minority Health published the National Standards for Culturally and Linguistically Appropriate Services in Health Care, commonly called the "CLAS standards."[11] These standards include a preamble and fourteen mandates, recommendations, and guidelines that health organizations and individual providers are encouraged to adopt.[12] The operative word, however, is "encouraged." The CLAS standards are aspirational. In the preamble accompanying the first edition of the CLAS standards, the DHHS Office of Minority Health explained that its purpose was to "respond to the need to ensure that all people entering the health care system receive equitable and effective treatment in a culturally and linguistically appropriate manner."[13] The preamble continued to say that the standards are primarily directed at health care organizations; however, individual providers are also *encouraged* to use the standards to make their practices more culturally and linguistically accessible."[14]

The CLAS preamble clearly signaled that the standards added no new legal requirements, but merely restated existing ones accompanied by aspirational recommendations. The DHHS described the CLAS standards "as *one* means to correct inequities that currently exist in the provision of health services,"[15] leaving open the possibility for federally funded health care organizations to adopt other approaches. Therefore, of the three types of standards CLAS includes—mandates, guidelines, and recommendations—only the four mandates carry the force of law and even these merely restate current federal requirements pertaining to Limited English Proficiency (LEP) patients. The remaining ten CLAS standards are suggestions. That means even though language in the CLAS guidelines refers to patients' "rights" or health care organizations' "requirements," in truth, hospitals, health centers, and all providers' compliance with at least ten CLAS standards is completely voluntary. Moreover, compliance with the remaining four mandates is no more enforceable than they were before the DHHS repeated their terms in the CLAS standards. From the outset, the DHHS Office of Minority Health (OMH) acknowledged that the CLAS standards are intended only to guide federally funded organizations as they each chart their own chosen paths toward health equity. Thus, the approach the federal government has taken to addressing disparities through CLAS is a weak, "hands-off" form of regulatory oversight.

In 2004, the OMH and the Agency for Healthcare Research and Quality (AHRQ) commissioned a study to measure how the CLAS standards were affecting health outcomes.[16] The results were disappointing. The AHRQ researchers asked all the right questions: Did the CLAS interventions affect care? Did they improve access? Did they affect patient health outcomes? However, at the end of the day, the AHRQ study summed up the research record evaluating the effectiveness of the CLAS program by saying, "certain cultural competence interventions appear to affect health services utilization, satisfaction, and increases in knowledge, although subsequent impacts on provider or patient behavior and/or health outcomes were not explored."[17] Said another way, the record shows little evidence that the CLAS standards have any impact whatsoever on discriminatory health behaviors or inequitable patient health outcomes. One reason CLAS standards have had such limited impact is because their implementation has been spotty. On the one hand, hospitals, managed care organizations, and medical schools across the country have worked to adopt expensive and broadly touted cultural competence training initiatives. In this way, the CLAS standards have made "cultural competence" a part of the national discourse and an essential element of health programs across the country. On the other hand, the flexibility incorporated in the standards has resulted in widely variable approaches to cultural competency programs. Also, we have seen earlier that cultural competence programs have limited impact. Though they may reduce explicit prejudices, they are not the kind of sustained interventions that work to address implicit racial and ethnic biases.

When independent researchers looked at the effectiveness of CLAS standards, they found the same lackluster results that federal researchers had reported. One group asked, "Do Hospitals Measure Up to the National Culturally and Linguistically Appropriate Services Standards?" in a study that surveyed 239, primarily large, nonprofit hospitals in the southern and western United States. The study concluded,

> Our findings indicate that hospitals are not fully meeting the expectations for language service provision as set forth by Title VI[of the Civil Rights Act of 1964], even hospitals that were identified by an expert panel as 'gold standard' hospitals. . . . The ability to provide language access services in a timely manner varied considerably [CLAS Standard 4] . . . [and f]ew hospitals in our study informed patients of their right to language services in the patients' preferred language. [CLAS Standard 5]. . . . Hospitals in the stratified national sample rarely assessed or assured the adequacy of the skills of the interpreters they employed. . . . In addition, policies against use of family members especially children need to be enforced. In many cases family members were used as interpreters despite the fact that most policies explicitly prohibiting their use [CLAS Standard 6].[18]

Another study that looked at the effectiveness of CLAS standards in family medicine practices in two urban centers concluded, "family medicine practices studied are frustrated and challenged to integrate cultural and linguistic competence into patient care. Organizational pressures, multiple competing demands and resource constraints inhibit preparedness to address the CLAS standards and important new national requirements and guidelines."[19]

Some professional associations have weighed in to voluntarily support CLAS standards, while others have debated their need to do so. In 2009, for example, the American Medical Association (AMA)—the professional association that represents physicians—collaborated to form a "Commission to End Health Care Disparities," which generated another set of recommendations based on the CLAS standards. In contrast, the American Hospital Association disputed CLAS's applicability to its five thousand member hospitals, health systems, and health care organizations while testifying before Congress in support of the Affordable Care Act.[20]

National accrediting organizations adopted only some of the CLAS standards and were quite slow in doing so. For example, the Joint Commission (formerly, the Joint Commission for the Accreditation of Health Care Organizations, or JCAHCO) initially adopted the language and communication standards, but not those that covered race or ethnicity until 2010. Because the Joint Commission has the authority to withdraw accreditation from over 20,500 health care providers and make them ineligible to receive public and private insurance reimbursements, this organization's voluntary adoption of the CLAS standards seemed promising. Similarly, the National Committee for Quality Assurance included CLAS in a voluntary accreditation module that became available in 2010. However the promise of CLAS enforcement by accreditation organizations has proved illusory. In fact, when the Joint Commission "adopted" the CLAS standards, they first appeared in draft form, [21] and then the accrediting organization *finalized* its own set of standards advancing effective communication and cultural competence. The final document, titled "A Roadmap for Hospitals," did not ignore the CLAS standards completely, but studied them beginning in 2003 with a "gap analysis" that concluded that not enough was known about whether health care organizations had the capacity to adopt CLAS. In the end, the Joint Commission's "Roadmap" added CLAS standards for *voluntary* implementation in 2011, to replace the previous draft standards.[22] These new standards include a few vague references to efforts to reduce disparities, such as the requirement that hospitals train staff members on "sensitivity to cultural diversity"[23] and focus primarily on effective communication for patients with limited English proficiency.[24] The Joint Commission does not ignore other disparity-related goals entirely, adding a new "requirement" that hospitals prohibit discrimination based on age, race, ethnicity, religion, culture, language, physical or mental disability, socioeconomic status, sex, sexual orientation, and gender identity or expression.[25] However, in addition to this new requirement, the Joint Commission notes that the 2003 study that led to these new requirements "did not affect the accreditation decision" for any hospital. Therefore, failure to prohibit discrimination also "will not affect the accreditation decision," [26] and compliance with these new standards continues to be voluntary and unenforceable. In the final analysis, although the DHHS's implementation of the CLAS standards has inspired a swirl of activity dedicated to cultural competency and linguistically appropriate services, most providers and institutions only selectively follow through. The public and private regulatory systems have essentially relegated their enforcement authority to the health care institutions themselves.

Other efforts at clinical self-regulation have similarly resulted in more form than substance. The American Medical Association first issued a report on race disparities in health care in 1995[27] and adopted an opinion calling on physicians to act to eliminate disparities in 1994. Most recently, the AMA's Council on Ethical and Judicial Affairs published an opinion in June 2005 that included laudable recommendations such as "physicians should not rely upon stereotypes; they should customize care to meet the needs and preferences of individual patients"; "physicians must strive to offer the same quality of care to all their patients irrespective of personal characteristics such as race or ethnicity"; and "physicians should work to eliminate biased behavior toward patients by other health care professionals and staff."[28] Despite the AMA's recognition that doctors' ethical obligations "typically exceed legal duties," and the clear statement that "when physicians believe a law is unjust, they should work to change the law,"[29] the strength of the aspirational statements contained in this opinion have not translated into changes in disparate health care or outcomes. The AMA statements as well as CLAS regulations represent clinical interventions designed to encourage providers to practice nondiscriminatory medicine. Frieden's health impact pyramid correctly predicts these approaches' limited impact: "Although evidence-based clinical care can reduce disability and prolong life the aggregate impact of these interventions is limited by lack of access, erratic and unpredictable adherence, and imperfect effectiveness."[30]

Long-Lasting Protective Interventions: Universal Coverage

Reforms at the third tier of the health impact pyramid represent long-lasting protective interventions. These are large-scale, often one-time changes that may address some structural issues, but do so by reaching people as individuals rather than changing their collective economic or medical contexts. The third tier interventions are the societal changes that are likely to have some impact on improving health disparities; however, these reforms are also unlikely to fundamentally transform the history and culture of racial and ethnic discrimination in health care.

184 | A STRUCTURAL SOLUTION

The American effort to achieve universal health insurance coverage is one such example.

U.S. presidents throughout America's political history have futilely engaged in the rhetoric of health equality and justice for over a century. In 1912—ironically, the year the British Parliament passed that country's National Insurance Act—President Teddy Roosevelt introduced "social insurance" in an effort to provide universal medical coverage "against the hazards of sickness" as part of the Progressive Bull Moose platform, which declared, "The supreme duty of the Nation is the conservation of human resources through an enlightened measure of social and industrial justice."[31] In 1945, President Harry Truman delivered a special message to Congress recommending a comprehensive national health program as part of an Economic Bill of Rights that ensured "the right to adequate medical care . . . the opportunity to achieve and enjoy good health . . . [and] the right to adequate protection from the economic fears of sickness."[32] When President Lyndon Johnson signed the Social Security Act of 1965 into law, establishing the Medicare and Medicaid health insurance programs, his words described a reform aimed at eliminating "the injustice that denies the miracle of healing to the old and to the poor."[33]

President Richard Nixon, speaking to Congress in 1974 to introduce his Comprehensive Health Insurance Plan, began by declaring that "one of the most cherished goals of our democracy is to assure every American an equal opportunity to lead a full and productive life"[34] as he implored the legislature to expand Medicare, Medicaid, and mandatory employer-based insurance coverage. In 1979, President Jimmy Carter proposed a "National Health Plan," citing the challenge to "secure for all Americans access to quality health care as a matter of right."[35] A decade later, President Bill Clinton introduced the Health Security Act of 1993 in a bid to achieve universal coverage through managed competition.[36] Most recently, upon passage of the Patient Protection and Affordable Care Act which enacts insurance reforms intended to expand health coverage to 25 million previously uninsured Americans, President Barack Obama declared, "Tonight's vote is not a victory for any one party—it's a victory . . . for the American people." The president's remarks reinforced the equality objectives that underlie this act, calling the new reform a "system that works better for the American people."[37]

The American political effort to achieve health justice through universal access has spanned decades and crossed the political spectrum.

Nevertheless, our nation's focus has been on achieving equal *access* to health care, not on achieving equal health care *quality* for all Americans. The political goal has been to expand access to health insurance so that a larger number of Americans can purchase health care. While achieving equitable access to health care encounters is essential, true equality in health care demands more. Equal access to health care will not change the disparate health outcomes that minority patients suffer as long as the quality of the care to which they are afforded access remains substantively inequitable. Political leaders have given little attention to the injustices that will persist even if we succeed in universalizing access to medical insurance. These include the systemic inequities that affect minority health, such as poor housing, employment, education, and food security, as well as inferior medical treatment. Interventions to correct inequities in these social determinants of health are at the bottom-most tier of Frieden's health impact pyramid. The effort to universalize access to health insurance, in contrast, represents a protective intervention situated in the center of the health impact pyramid. Universal health insurance importantly will reach individuals needing access to health care services, but it will not change the collective attitudes that permeate the health care services they access.

In point of fact, the theory of distributive justice that motivates efforts to enact universal coverage actually supports a much broader view of the nature and the moral importance of health and health care equity than our legislative efforts have addressed. Recognizing that it is beyond the capacity of any health care system to guarantee all its citizens will get all the health care that they want, or even all that they need, ethicists have explored the principles that must guide any society's difficult decisions concerning the fair distribution of scarce yet life-saving medical resources. Health justice advocates recognize there is a difference between the obligation to guarantee just and equal access to health care and the impossible goal of guaranteeing just and equal access to health itself. Some differences in health care and health outcomes are inevitable and are neither the evidence for nor the result of injustice. Norman Daniels provides one of the most widely accepted descriptions of the nature of true health justice. He argues that just access to health and health care needs is especially important because it allows each individual member of society equal enjoyment of the normal range of all other opportunities the society has to offer. Daniels goes further to identify the level of responsibility for ensuring just health care:

> I shall urge a normative claim: we ought to subsume health care under a principle of justice guaranteeing fair equality of opportunity. . . . If an acceptable theory of justice includes a principle providing for fair equality of opportunity, then health-care institutions should be among those governed by it.[38]

Importantly, Daniels's concept of health justice does not focus or operate exclusively on the individual level, but instead also incorporates institutional accountability. Even though Daniels's is a theory of distributional justice—arguing that society must fairly allocate health care in order to equip all members of society to participate in the normal range of life's opportunities—his theory requires systemic, institutional level changes in order for justice to be achieved. Daniels admits to the need for exogenous governance to achieve health justice. In short, distributional fairness alone will not eliminate racial and ethnic health disparities. Establishing a just health care system will require rooting out implicit biases that affect patients differentially. The goal must be to achieve *substantive* as well as distributive justice in American health care.

Neither expanded MCAT testing, nor additional research, nor complex clinical regulations, nor principled professional standards, nor political efforts to expand health care access has proved effective to reduce, much less eliminate, racial and ethnic health care disparities. These reforms address disparities through interventions at the top three tiers of the health impact pyramid. Although the fundamental reforms in socioeconomic factors are beyond the scope of this book, the need to change the context in which health care is delivered—the fourth tier of the health impact pyramid—is well within reach and acutely indicated by the data and narratives collected in this book. The physician and patient narratives assembled here qualitatively describe the injustice and daily damage visited upon minority patients by health care disparities. Furthermore, the enormity of these inequities can also be quantified. One source has estimated that over 30 percent of the direct medical costs that African Americans, Hispanics, and Asian Americans incur are excess costs due to health inequities—nearly $230 billion over a three-year period between 2003 and 2006.[39] In 2005, Dr. David Satcher estimated that 83,570 deaths occur each year as a result of racial and ethnic health disparities.[40] In other words, inferior, racially biased health care kills people of color and costs them lots of money while doing so! Improvements in the overall quality of medical care in the United States have narrowed persistent gaps in some key disparities indicators.[41] Yet, our nation is making disturbingly little progress finding an effective solution to the structural nature of these injustices.

Evidence of a Structural Problem

Despite the serious responses to a serious disparities problem, in 2012, for the tenth year in a row, the United States Department of Health and Human Services' Agency for Healthcare Research and Quality (AHRQ) released evidence that the fight against health disparities is stalled. AHRQ's annual report on National Healthcare Quality and Disparities gives data that describes the progress American health care has made in reducing health care disparities. The 2012 report records changes in disparities over the period from 2002 to 2010 by racial and ethnic groups, basing these changes on measures of quality such as the number of deaths due to cancer and heart attacks and the incidence of end-stage renal disease due to diabetes. The AHRQ also reports changes in disparities in access to health care for the period from 2002 to 2009. Figure 8.2 depicts the lack of progress. The graph on the left shows the number of quality measures that represent a gap between health care delivered to minority and white Americans and how those measures are changing. The graph on the right shows the number and extent to which measures of disparaty have improved. Both graphs also show changes in the gap between high- and low-income groups for the quality and access measures. The disquieting message presented is that the overwhelming majority of disparities by race and ethnicity are static. In spite of focused attention from law- and policymakers, health care providers, and scholars, figure 8.2 paints a dispiriting picture of how far we have *not* come.

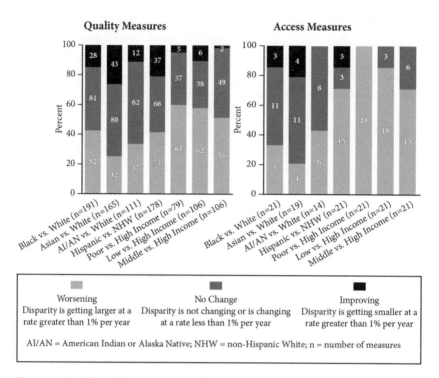

Figure 8.2. Quality and access measures by age, race, ethnicity, and income: Number and proportion for which disparities are improving, not changing, or worsening. *Source*: Agency for Healthcare Research and Quality, U.S. Department of Health and Human Services, *National Healthcare Disparities Report 2012,* May 2013, AHRQ Publication no. 13–0003. Used by permission of the AHRQ.

According to figure 8.2, well over 80 percent of the measures that describe quality and access disparities for health care have remained unchanged or have grown worse over the report period. Disparate health care quality measures have improved in absolute terms between 2002 and 2010. However, the gap between quality improvements for whites and people of color has been relatively constant. A few disparities in quality of care are getting smaller. The disparity quality measures that are improving generally have to do with acute hospital care. However, the rates at which minority and white adult surgery patients receive preventative care are not improving. Some examples of widening gaps between whites and minority patient quality outcomes include the number of maternal deaths in childbirth, the number of infants who receive vaccines, the number of diabetic adults who get their glucose levels tested annually, the incidence of breast cancer diagnosed at advanced versus early stages, the number of adults over age fifty who receive preventative care in the form of colonoscopy or other diagnostic procedures, and the number of children for whom a health provider gave advice about using car safety seats. Perhaps there is some comfort in the fact that a greater number of measured disparities are improving than are worsening. Still the short and troubling story is that most disparities in the quality of health care delivered to whites as compared to patients of minority racial and ethnic groups are not changing at all. Sadly, the data shows that even less progress is being made equalizing disparities related to access to care. The access gap between Asians and whites grew smaller for four of the nineteen categories measured, improving disparities for that group by 21 percent. But over the period between 2002 and 2009, virtually none of the disparities between other minority populations and white Americans have improved.

I submit that the only reforms that will significantly and effectively narrow the health disparities that AHRQ has reported over the last decade must fit into the bottom tiers of Frieden's health action pyramid. I propose a fourth tier intervention that will change the health delivery context to make individual physicians' default decisions healthier. My proposal aims to change the social norm surrounding unconscious racism and to affect the context in which health decisions are made, following the tradition of public health successes. For example, when a municipality fluoridates its water supply or implements clean air regulations, individuals in the community can benefit without having to exercise their individual agency to choose a health-enhancing option. I propose changing the context in which health care delivery occurs by reforming antidiscrimination law. Legal reforms will impact social norms and will incentivize long-lasting protective interventions by institutional health care providers. Institutions will create a climate for change because they will be corporately incentivized to articulate nondiscriminatory goals clearly and adopt compliance policies, procedures, and infrastructure to implement nondiscriminatory training, assessment, and enforcement. The solution I propose is designed to maximize the population-wide impact of reducing implicit biases, while also requiring individual effort to address the cognitive formation of these biases and the discriminatory conduct that they inspire.

The Courage to Make Unconscious Racism Illegal

Let us return to the theme raised in chapter 1: Bad laws allow discrimination to flourish, harming the health and shortening the lives of racial and ethnic minorities. Good laws can reduce discrimination in health care and ultimately change the social climate in the way that civil rights laws eventually made explicit prejudice intolerable. Throughout this book we have seen the tenacity of health disparities and the serious injuries they cause. The Biased Care Model identified six mechanisms through which implicit biases operate to produce health disparities. The literature on malleability defined the types of interventions that can alter the cognitive processes that form implicit biases and translate them into harmful discriminatory conduct. However, we have yet to see how these interventions can be generalized to affect broad contextual changes in the health care industry. We have yet to see how this information can be brought to bear to reduce health disparities. I propose that making discrimination due to unconscious racism illegal—forbidden by explicit and enforceable law—will change the context, incentives, and outcomes in health care, and will thereby reduce health disparities. A legal prohibition against the unconscious racism that causes health and health care disparities would accomplish a paradigmatic and structural change in the way American health care is delivered in three ways.

An anti-implicit bias discrimination law would first signal a societal commitment to equality and justice in health care. This would be a paradigm shift, redefining the social norm around health disparities generally, but more specifically removing the ambivalence concerning the culpability of health disparities caused by unconscious racism. Laws effectively influence social norms by reflecting underlying social values that exist but about which there is incomplete information or uncertainty. Law serves to reflect commonly endorsed beliefs so that a community or society can live in accordance with collectively shared values. In health care, a law against unconscious racial discrimination would reflect the community consensus that we have seen among physicians who explicitly prefer equality and fairness in health care, but are surprised by the presence and influence of their unconscious biases. Moreover, an anti- implicit bias law in health care would extend the general disapprobation that Americans feel toward overt racial prejudice, bigotry, and discrimination. Conversely, an antidiscrimination law that accounts for implicit bias would endorse the generally shared value that favors equal rights and opportunity for all people of all racial and ethnic backgrounds. However, legal expression of these values is particularly important and necessary in health care where the discrimination arises from the unconscious biases that are not well understood by most.

In the health care context, this uncertainty arises in large part from the limited understanding that physicians and health care providers have about the connection between their implicit biases and the inequitable health outcomes that minorities suffer. As seen in the experiment by Dr. Alexander Green, physicians who are "clued into" the impact their implicit biases have on their medical decision-making want to change. Certainly anyone who reads this book or undertakes to systematically review the empirical social science literature about implicit bias in health care will have the information needed to understand the connection between unconscious racism and the inferior health care that minorities experience. However, only legal intervention will serve to generalize this information and signal to health providers and all others that the connection exists but will not be allowed to persist. A legal intervention prohibiting unconscious racism would serve the same purpose that legal bans and restrictions on smoking have served. To the extent that there was uncertainty or incomplete information about the health harms caused by second-hand smoke, legislative enactments sent a strong message that the dangers had been sufficiently proven to require legislative action to protect against a serious public health threat. Enacting prohibitory laws served as a collective signal to increase certainty.[42] The same collective signal is needed to establish a new contextual understanding of the devastating health harms caused by unconscious racism.

Secondly, an express, enforceable legal prohibition against unconscious racism in health care will incentivize behavior changes by health care providers who are in the best position to eliminate the effects of unconscious bias. Such a law would empower providers as a group to address discrimination from a position that economists describe as the "cheapest cost avoiders."[43] Providers occupy this position because they are best suited to bring about the changes in health care delivery that are required to minimize the harms being caused to patients. This is the essential role of a "cheapest cost avoider." Physicians seeking to conform to shared egalitarian values in order to enhance their personal standing and reputations, and institutional providers seeking to avoid second-order sanctions such as shaming or ostracizing by critics of discriminatory medical systems, are in a position to reform medical education curricula, change physician credentialing requirements, mandate stereotype negation training, meaningfully diversify all ranks of the health care workforce, and take other steps to structurally address unconscious bias in health care. Again, the case of legislative bans on smoking is instructive. These laws gave permission to nonsmokers to insist that smokers remove themselves or their cigarettes to conform their behavior to laws that government actors were nowhere in sight to enforce. Smokers themselves largely comply with designated smoking areas to avoid the hassle of personal chastisement. Similarly, empirical evidence presented in chapter 7 showed that a legal prohibition could operate as a Type C intervention to change the consensus signals that cause even overtly prejudiced individuals to check their discriminatory behavior. A law prohibiting unconscious racism in health care would also incentivize Type A training and Type B diversification interventions by raising the cost of remaining indifferent to the effects that unconscious racism has on minority health outcomes.[44] The goal of an antidiscrimination law directed at implicit biases would be to make discrimination due to unconscious racism so costly that a would-be discriminator would take steps to avoid the financial and reputational impact of being negatively perceived by his peers or penalized by the state. In short, legally prohibiting unconscious racism will make ignoring the prevalence of this form of discrimination an irrational choice.

Finally, an antidiscrimination law that expressly incorporates discrimination due to unconscious racism would provide a direct or first-order sanction by which the state could impose fines and penalties sufficient to disrupt the self-fulfilling prophecy of negative racial and ethnic stereotypes. For those whose preferences or tastes for unconscious discrimination remained unaltered by a legally communicated social norm against such attitudes and behavior, the law would interrupt the cycle of discrimination based on an erroneously perceived justification. According to the Biased Care Model, providers' negative perceptions of minority patients as noncompliant, uneducated, and uncooperative lead to inferior communication, minority patient dissatisfaction, statistical discrimination, and ultimately inequitable treatment decisions. All these mechanisms produce disparate health outcomes. Some advocates then use these disparate outcomes as license to argue biological, behavioral, and even genetic inferiorities that justify the discrimination and biased perceptions that feed into beginning the discriminatory cycle again. Law could interrupt this cycle of discriminatory behavior and outcomes, thereby reducing the social and moral costs that health care disparities impose on the provider, the patient, and society at large.[45]

There is no better time than now to abandon the failed educational, political, administrative, and self-regulatory approaches that have left health care disparities essentially unchanged for as long as they have been measured. There is no graver legal problem than saving the lives of tens of thousands of minority patients from the inequity of disparate outcomes in disease and death. We have seen that law can both harm and help the cause of health care equality. Although law has helped bring about some of the greatest successes in achieving equality, as in the case of desegregation during the civil rights era, the fact that it has done so does not argue convincingly for resorting to the same institution that also consigned blacks to segregated housing squalor, exposed Asians to dangerous vaccines, and facilitated the introduction of infectious diseases that wiped out entire populations of Native Americans in order to eradicate health discrimination today. But my argument here begins and ends with the conviction that only a radical and fundamental transformation of the context in which biased health care is currently practiced will undermine the Biased Care Model that dominates modern American health care, and only a well-conceived and enforced body of law can accomplish such a paradigm shift.

* * *

At the beginning of this chapter, I quoted the Reinhold Niebuhr's Serenity Prayer for the influence and inspiration it can bring to the challenge of eliminating race and ethnicity bias in health care. Lest anyone be fooled into thinking that a Protestant prayer is not a fitting inspiration for the social problems and solutions I discussed here, let me briefly remind you of the career of this prayer's author. One writer recently explained that due to his expansive influence over the religious and political discourse of the twentieth century, Niebuhr's name has become a synonym for American political realism.[46] Reinhold Niebuhr was an outspoken critic of moral complacency and a tireless advocate for justice. He supported Prohibition in 1916, decried workers' conditions at the Henry Ford plant in 1926, joined the Socialist Party in 1929, and then resigned that party in 1940 as he publicly announced his controversial support for America's coming confrontation with Hitler in World War II. He opposed the atomic bombing of Japan in 1945, McCarthyism in 1952, and the Vietnam War in 1955. Niebuhr published numerous influential essays and books, and received honorary doctorate degrees from Yale, Oxford, Princeton, and Harvard Universities. He endorsed Martin Luther King, Jr.'s civil disobedience and John F. Kennedy's bid for the presidency (albeit reluctantly). President Barack Obama called Niebuhr one of his favorite philosophers, saying, "I take away the compelling idea that there's serious evil in the world, and hardship and pain. And we should be humble and modest in our belief we can eliminate those things. But we shouldn't use that as an excuse for cynicism and inaction. I take away . . . the sense we have to make these efforts knowing they are hard, and not swinging from naïve idealism to bitter realism."[47] Surely, Niebuhr's invocation can help to guide the effort to remove implicit race and ethnicity bias in health care, and to eliminate their contribution to health care and health disparities.

A New Normal

The Restoration of Title VI

Title VI closes the gap between our purposes as a democracy
and our prejudices as individuals.
—Senator John O. Pastore, March 3, 1964

Of all the forms of inequality, injustice in health care is the
most shocking and inhumane.
—Reverend Martin Luther King, Jr., 1966

The Civil Rights Act of 1964 has been and could continue to be the most effective legal tool for eradicating racial and ethnic discrimination in American health care.[1] However, I began this book by surveying the ways in which law has failed to promote racial justice in this country. I return now to consider the nexus between a body of failed civil rights law and health inequality. My focus is on the currently impotent prohibitions of Title VI, which have not kept pace with the shift from explicit to implicit discrimination that has occurred over the last twenty-five years in American culture. This chapter proposes reforming federal antidiscrimination law to incentivize federally funded entities to institutionalize types of interventions that work to reduce discrimination due to implicit bias, particularly those described in chapter 7 as the Type A and Type B interventions. The proposed reforms will allow litigation of civil rights claims against the health care entities that continue to play host to physicians' implicit biases, as shown to operate through the six Biased Care Model mechanisms, and will reward those providers who take preemptive steps to stop unintentional discrimination. Specifically, I propose reforms to Title VI of the Civil Rights Act that will (1) expressly prohibit policies and practices that have a disparate impact on the basis of race, color, or national origin; (2) restore the private cause of action for disparate impact claims, read out of Title VI by the United States Supreme Court in *Sandoval*; and (3) introduce a new disparate impact claim, based on a negligence standard of care. This third reform will give federal contractors adequate incentive to make the structural changes to reduce unconscious discrimination. Thus, it is the most likely to have long-term impact on unconscious racism in health care and thereby reduce racial and ethnic health disparities.[2]

The changes to the Title VI statute that I propose will serve three objectives in reforming the delivery of health care. First, the substance of the new antidiscrimination law will accurately account for the copious scientific evidence that instructs how to control unconscious discrimination harms. Second, the proposed legal reform will incentivize evidence-based structural changes in health care practice that will mitigate the influence implicit biases have through each of the six mechanisms of the Biased Care Model. And third, reforming Title VI will leverage the expressive role of law to meaningfully shift the social norm that presently tolerates unconscious racism in health care. Overall, the reforms proposed here will operate to align provider and patient behavior with core American social values of equality and justice.

The Original Title VI

Title VI prohibits federally funded organizations from discriminating or denying benefits to any person on the ground of their race, color, or national origin. Similarly, Title VII of the Civil Rights Act of 1964 is a federal law that forbids employment discrimination based on race, color, religion, sex, or nationality.[3] Title VI and Title VII, both passed as part of the Civil Rights Act of 1964, have similar operative language and legislative histories and have been subject to similar interpretations by the courts. Numerous scholars have argued convincingly over the past ten years for the reform of the Title VII statute in light of the evidence that implicit rather than intentional bias is the source of most modern discrimination and resulting harmful injustice in the employment context. Title VI, however, has received considerably less scholarly attention. Therefore, this section reviews the Title VII literature and applies scholars' insights and recommendations for the reform of employment law to suggest reforming the provisions of the Title VI statute as well.

Lessons from Title VII Scholarship

There are two ways a lawsuit can be brought under Title VII. A plaintiff can either allege that he or she has been a victim of discriminatory *treatment* or assert that the defendant's practices have had a discriminatory *impact* on protected groups of people. Both legal claims, as currently permitted by law, are outdated. Disparate treatment cases require the plaintiff to prove a defendant's acts arose from *intentional* discrimination rather than also allowing recovery for the defendant's discriminatory acts that arise from *unintentional* bias. Disparate impact cases brought by private plaintiffs are now easily defeated when defendants show a nondiscriminatory reason for their challenged conduct. Several leading scholars have proposed adding a new ground for recovery in disparate treatment and disparate impact cases brought under Title VII; the new ground would add recovery in a disparate treatment case brought against a defendant employer who negligently discriminated against the plaintiff. I agree with the calls for revision in the outdated disparate treatment claims in order to allow the law to reach both conscious and unconscious racial and ethnic discrimination in disparate impact cases.

David Oppenheimer was the first to comprehensively propose applying a negligence standard of care to employment discrimination law under Title VII. In his landmark article arguing for the recognition of a claim against employers who fail to take all reasonable steps to prevent discrimination in the workplace, Oppenheimer argued that much of the Supreme Court's antidiscrimination jurisprudence already incorporates the underlying principles of negligence law without expressly acknowledging the claim. As proof, Oppenheimer pointed to several areas of antidiscrimination law where the reasonableness standards had already influenced courts' decisions. Examples include sexual harassment law ("reasonable discrimination victim" test); Equal Employment Opportunity Commission (EEOC) guidelines requiring employers to make "reasonable" religious accommodations; and the 1991 amendments to Title VII restoring the "less discriminatory alternative" test to Title VII, allowing plaintiffs to rebut a defendant's justification of discriminatory conduct when employers claim their discriminatory practices were required by a "business necessity." Citing what he called the "depth and depravity of racial stereotyping in America today,"[4] Oppenheimer argued for replacing the strict and intentional liability causes of action available under Title VII's antidiscrimination law with a theory of negligent discrimination.[5] Such a revision would carry several social benefits, which include eliminating the need to find moral wrongfulness before penalizing discrimination; encouraging greater care on the part of employers to avoid discrimination and discriminatory practices; and turning the law's focus to resolving discriminatory *outcomes* rather than discriminatory motives.

Marc Poirier drew an analogy between Oppenheimer's negligent discrimination model to the liability the law imposes on landowners who do not take reasonable measures to abate the risk of dangerous conditions on their land. Poirier pointed to provisions in the Comprehensive Environmental Response, Compensation, and Liability Act (CERCLA), also known as the Superfund statute, to reinforce the argument that no individual injury should be required to trigger liability for cleaning up and disposing of hazardous chemical substances. Similarly, Poirier argued that neither individualized injury nor causation on an individual level must necessarily precede the legal obligation for a defendant employer to supervise and control cognitive biases in the workplace.[6] Rather, Poirier argued, since cognitive bias operates as a precondition that leads to discrimination before the moment a discriminatory decision is made, and because discriminatory decisions are largely nondeliberate, a more appropriate model for workplace liability would be the law's precedent for assigning liability to landowners who knew or reasonably should have known about a dangerous condition on their land but failed to take steps to counteract the condition. Poirier calls for a structural redress to unintentional discrimination that would focus on "institutional responsibility instead of . . . individual intent" and "single-act moments of discrimination."[7]

Tristin Green expanded Oppenheimer's call for reform by arguing for a "structural account" of disparate treatment theory in order to hold employers accountable for business structures and institutional practices that enable discrimination. Green also extensively reviewed the subtle forms of discrimination that operate among those who believe sincerely in racial equality, but who are also subjected to psychological processes driven by their unavoidable internalization of stereotypes and prejudicial social beliefs. Green identified several aspects of the modern workplace that make individual discriminatory decisions harder to identify and less relevant than the overall dynamic of the diverse workplace. Therefore, to address the "systemic aspects of seemingly individual or personal conflicts,"[8] Green urged reform that would require employers to manage the diversity within their organizations and minimize the operation of discriminatory bias. Green's structural approach would allow courts to take a deeper look into workplace dynamics with the help of social psychology experts to find evidence of disparities and to question the "reasonableness" of the defendant's practices. Green would remove the requirement for the plaintiff to prove an individual injury and would instead recognize the harms caused by subtle and institutional forms of discrimination in the modern workplace as actionable. Green argued that her reforms would provide an impetus for structural change and more clarity for both plaintiffs and defendants who would be asked to participate in a contextualized inquiry into their workplaces.

However, another professor, Samuel Bagenstos, has questioned whether courts could realistically undertake the holistic scrutiny of workplace dynamics that Green's structural approach required.[9] Also, Professor Amy Wax argued that the cost of fixing "unpredictable and unavoidable" cognitive bias would be unproductively high.[10] Both Wax and Bagenstos point to the ubiquity and inevitability of implicit biases to argue they should escape legal scrutiny. Bagenstos distinguished between the courts' ability to focus on individual instances of discrimination with a fault-based approach and what he called "insubordination theory"—a name for the approaches of structural reformists like Tristin Green who focus on using the courts to achieve social change. Actually, Bagenstos's most damaging critique was that structural reform advocates lack a consensus vision of what "employment equality" looks like. According to Bagenstos, these advocates have not articulated an "operating theory" to describe what kinds of unconscious bias should count as unlawful or improper, thereby making it impossible for courts to penalize those who hold them. Thus, Bagenstos seems to claim that changing implicit biases rooted in widely held cultural norms is no match for courts of law.

In contrast to the views espoused by Bagenstos and Wax, Linda Krieger and Susan Fiske highlighted the fact that courts already make behavioral assumptions—sometimes untested and incorrect—when they apply current Title VII law. Krieger and Fiske challenged the notion that courts cannot or do not act to incentivize social and behavioral changes by attributing the success of the law and economics movement (an influential analytical approach that applies economic theory to understanding legal problems) to its "core insight" that "law can serve as a powerful tool for structuring . . . incentives in socially beneficial ways."[11] For example, they point to sexual harassment cases that permit defendant corporations to defeat a plaintiff's legitimate allegation that she worked in a hostile work environment by showing that the employer had instituted antiharassment policies, education programs, and grievance procedures that encouraged employees to complain early against escalating hostilities in the workplace. Pointing to the lack of empirical evidence that training and grievance programs actually work to reduce sexualized workplace hostility, Krieger and Fiske not only challenge the Supreme Court's presumptions based on a "behavioral world that does not in fact exist," but also cite cases in which the Supreme Court justices themselves stated their claim and aim to have their legal decisions "provide incentives . . . [that] will reduce the incidence of discrimination, thus furthering Title VII's goals."[12] Krieger and Fiske also answer Bagenstos's allegation that reform advocates lack an operating theory by summarizing the four key insights from social psychology that pertain to disparate treatment doctrine.[13] They conclude that behavioral realism requires courts to reject the intuitive social science conclusions they now use to justify antidiscrimination law decisions and to turn instead to empirical evidence from social psychologists to make normative antidiscrimination decisions.

Congress and Title VI

The social science record provides ample support for reforming civil rights law beyond the employment context covered by Title VII in order to broadly address how discriminatory behavior occurs throughout modern American society. Title VI of the Civil Rights Act provides the legal vehicle to reach all federally funded organizations where implicit bias operates to cause racial and ethnic discrimination and inequality. Moreover, the empirical record on malleability demonstrates the specific steps that responsible and reasonable recipients of federal funds—including medical providers—can take to mitigate, even eradicate, the discriminatory impact that implicit bias has on minority populations.

The plain language of Title VI prohibits racial and ethnic discrimination in health care delivery.[14] Section 601 of the Act says that "No person in the United States shall, on the ground of race, color, or national origin, be excluded from participation in, be denied the benefits of, or be subjected to discrimination under any program or activity receiving Federal assistance." In Section 602, Title VI goes on to say that "Each Federal department and agency . . . is authorized and directed to effectuate the provisions of section 2000d [Section 601] of this title,"[15] thus giving administrative agencies the authority to implement regulations consistent with the aims of the law. This language covers all health care providers who receive federal assistance from Medicare, Medicaid, and other federally funded health insurance.[16] Addressing health care inequity has been central to the procedural history of Title VI since its inception.

The legislative record from the Eighty-Eighth Congress's floor debate during the Senate's consideration of the bill proposing Title VI reveals that proponents repeatedly cited and quoted a watershed case involving hospital desegregation in their pleas for the bill's passage.[17] That watershed case was *Simkins v. Moses H. Cone Memorial Hospital*.[18] *Simkins* was brought by black physicians, dentists, and patients to challenge racial segregation in a publicly financed hospital. The defendant hospital had received funds under the Hill-Burton Act,[19] through which Congress had exercised its spending power authority to distribute federal grants for construction and renovation of racially segregated hospitals since 1946. The Fourth Circuit Court of Appeals held in *Simkins* that the separate but equal language contained in the Hill-Burton Act was unconstitutional. On March 2, 1964, the United States Supreme Court announced its decision to deny *certiorari* (that is, its decision to refuse to reconsider) – the lower court's decision in *Simkins*. On March 30, 1964, just after the Supreme Court declined to disturb this holding, the bill proposing Title VI came before the full Senate for debate. Senators regarded the Supreme Court's decision not to hear *Simkins* as a clear signal that the highest court in the land had concluded the "separate but equal" doctrine, as applied to hospitals and other recipients of public funding, violated the Equal Protection Clause.[20] Moreover, the Supreme Court's decision was seen both as validation of the important antidiscrimination goals set out in Title VI and as recognition that piecemeal litigation was insufficient to dismantle discrimination in the nation's hospitals.

As Senator John Pastore of Rhode Island explained:

> The Supreme Court declined to review that decision; so it is the law of our land. Yet despite the effort of the Court of Appeals to strike down discrimination in the *Simkins* case, the same court was forced last week to rule again in a Wilmington, N.C., suit that a private hospital operated with public funds must desist from barring Negro physicians from staff membership. That is why we need title VI of the Civil Rights Act, H.R. 7152—to prevent such discrimination where Federal funds are involved. Title VI intends to insure once and for all that the financial resources of the Federal Government—the commonwealth of Negro and white alike—will no longer subsidize racial discrimination.[21]

Thus, the Supreme Court's decision not to disturb the *Simkins* court's condemnation of the "massive use of public funds and extensive state-funding" that had supported hospital segregation[22] served both as a prelude to and an impetus for the enactment of Title VI.

More recently, Congress reiterated its intent to address health care inequity in the Patient Protection and Affordable Care Act of 2010 (the Affordable Care Act). The act contains a nondiscrimination provision that expressly incorporates Title VI both by name, and by repeating the plain language of the law.[23]

Today, fifty years after Title VI became law, Congress is still working to make its intent for the statute clear so that courts, agencies, and government contractors will give full effect to Title VI's antidiscrimination provisions. In June 2012, a proposed amendment[24] sought "to reconcile, restore, clarify and conform" Title VI and other provisions of the Civil Rights Act of 1964 to their original purpose and scope. The proposed language would have accomplished four objectives. First, the bill would have amended Section 601 of Title VI to clarify expressly that discrimination based on disparate impact is prohibited under the law. The proposal would have amended Section 602 to restore a private right of action to prosecute discrimination based on disparate impact, as well as discrimination based on disparate treatment, through civil litigation. Second, the bill would have provided a defense for any program that met its burdens of production and persuasion to show that its challenged activity was related and necessary to achieve a substantial and legitimate nondiscriminatory purpose. Third, the bill would have allowed recovery for a plaintiff who met the burdens of production and persuasion to show, after establishing a prima facie case, that the defendant rejected an existing less discriminatory practice or policy than the one challenged. Finally, the amendment would have allowed for compensatory damages in cases of intentional discrimination, punitive damages against nongovernmental entities in cases of intentional discrimination, and equitable remedies, including attorneys' fees, in all other Title VI cases. In short, the proposed law was intended to restore substantive protections and relief that the Supreme Court read out of Title VI in the 2001 case of *Alexander v. Sandoval*.[25] However, despite this restorative intent, the proposed amendments stopped short of strengthening Title VI to address unconscious racism, even though the proposed changes would have unraveled the tortuously schizophrenic string of Supreme Court decisions, which have retreated from Congress's original intent for the Title VI law.

The Supreme Court and Title VI

The United States Supreme Court is largely responsible for the confusion that has rendered Title VI impotent in the face of most modern forms of unconscious racial discrimination in America. The court's early decisions appeared to establish that Title VI reached cases of disparate impact—claims in which the defendant's liability was based on the discriminatory effects a program or policy caused, rather than proof that the defendant intentionally discriminated. Implicit bias claims, alleging the defendant's discrimination based on race or ethnicity was unconscious, seemed to fit within this disparate impact category, though the law has not ever been crystal clear on this point. Before explaining why both unintentional and unconscious discrimination should be actionable under Title VI, I will review the relevant Supreme Court cases to date.

The court confirmed in 1974 and again in 1983 that the provisions of Title VI can be read to prohibit unintentional discrimination, saying,

"The Court squarely held in *Lau v. Nichols*, that Title VI forbids the use of federal funds not only in programs that intentionally discriminate on racial grounds but also in those endeavors that have a disparate impact on racial minorities."[26] However, in 2001, the Supreme Court reversed this holding, up-ending over a quarter century of jurisprudence, in *Alexander v. Sandoval*.[27] In *Sandoval*, Justice Antonin Scalia wrote for the court to announce a new rule that Title VI applies only to disparate *treatment* cases where the plaintiff can show the defendant *intentionally* discriminated. This case now presents a nearly impossible proof problem for plaintiffs since few Americans are intentional racists who write, say, or do things that can be used in a court of law to prove they are bigots under the *Sandoval* standard. Justice Scalia's decision in that case went on to hold that Title VI does not provide a private cause of action to prosecute disparate *impact* cases where there is no showing of the defendant's intentional discrimination. The court opined that to the extent that disparate impact cases were prohibited, only the regulatory rules promulgated under Section 602 of Title VI address disparate impact causes of action, and therefore only administrative enforcement reaches these claims.[28]

As many commenters have written, Justice Scalia justified his holding in *Sandoval* by extending the reading of dicta in the court's decision in *Regents of the University of California v. Bakke* (1976),[29] in which the Supreme Court upheld affirmative action admissions on behalf of a white male applicant to medical school. Justice Scalia cited this case, notwithstanding the fact that Justice John Paul Stevens, joined by Justices David Souter, Ruth Bader Ginsburg, and Stephen Breyer, subsequently dissented from the very reading of *Bakke* that Scalia relied upon to decide *Sandoval*. In fact, *Bakke* cannot be read as a considered majority opinion on the intentionality issue for at least two reasons. First, of the five justices who joined the majority in *Bakke* to conclude that Section 601 of Title VI extended only as far as the Equal Protection Clause and therefore encompassed only intentional discrimination, two have subsequently written to denounce this view in *Guardians Association v. Civil Service Commission (1983)*, a later case involving the disparate impact that police examinations had on minority officers.[30] There, Justice Byron Raymond White rejected this limiting view, explaining that "disproportionate-impact discrimination is subject to the Title VI regime" and clarifying that "§ 601 does in fact reach some instances of unintentional discrimination."[31] Justice White flatly stated the question, writing that "The threshold issue before the Court is whether the private plaintiffs in this case need to prove discriminatory intent to establish a violation of Title VI," and he "conclude[d], as do four other Justices in separate opinions, that the Court of Appeals erred in requiring proof of discriminatory intent."[32] Justice White, of course, could not reach this conclusion without distancing himself from his ruling in *Bakke*. Therefore, he went further to say that although "I recognize that in *Bakke* five Justices, including myself declared that Title VI does not of its own force proscribe unintentional racial discrimination . . . [However h]olding that Title VI does not bar such affirmative action if the Constitution does not is plainly not determinative of whether Title VI proscribes unintentional discrimination in addition to the intentional discrimination that the Constitution forbids."[33] With this, Justice White was free to write, "It must be concluded that Title VI reaches unintentional, disparate-impact discrimination as well as deliberate racial discrimination."[34]

Similarly, Justice Thurgood Marshall denounced *Bakke's* narrow interpretation of Title VI in the *Guardians* case. He wrote, "I agree with Justice White that proof of discriminatory animus should not be required."[35] But in his agreement, Justice Marshall also went on to denounce the view expressed in *Bakke*. Justice Marshall wrote, "I frankly concede that our reasoning in *Bakke* was broader than it should have been. The statement that Title VI was 'absolutely coextensive' with the Equal Protection Clause was clearly superfluous to the decision in that case."[36] Justice Marshall then explained that his reasons for concluding that relief under Title VI may be justified without proof of discriminatory intent were pragmatic. He said, "the 'effects' test is far more practical than a test that focuses on the motive of the recipient [of federal funds] which is typically very difficult to determine."[37]

Following these opinions from *Guardians*, various members of the Supreme Court have repeatedly reaffirmed the view that unintentional discrimination is within the reach of Title VI. In *Alexander v. Choate*,[38] for example, a case in which plaintiff Medicaid recipients lost their challenge to revisions in Medicaid reimbursement rules, Justice Marshall explained that while Title VI did not directly prohibit unintentional discrimination, the *Guardians* case should be read to approve Title VI actions to remedy unintentional discrimination under the statute's regulatory scheme. He said, "In essence then, we held that Title VI had delegated to the agencies in the first instance the complex determination of what sorts of disparate impacts upon minorities constituted sufficiently significant social problems, and were readily enough remediable, to warrant altering the practices of the federal grantees that had produced those impacts." Justice Marshall later showed he understood the unconscious nature of discrimination and its sources and expected that Title VI would also address this form of discrimination when he noted, "discrimination against the handicapped is primarily the result of apathetic attitudes rather than affirmative animus."[39] Even Justice Clarence Thomas, writing to concur in *U.S. v. Fordice* (1992),[40] affirmed that Title VI reached unintentional discrimination through disparate impact claims. In *Fordice*, the court held that Mississippi's failure to dismantle its segregated higher education system violated the Constitution's Equal Protection Clause and Title VI.[41] Although Justice Thomas wrote separately in that case to pronounce his ideological objections to applying the same standard to facts not before the court, he did agree that "if policies traceable to the *de jure* system are still in force and have discriminatory effects, those policies too must be reformed to the extent practicable and consistent with sound educational practices."[42] In summary, several Supreme Court justices, speaking in several different cases, have admitted the disparate impact cause of action prohibits conduct and policies that have a harmful disparate impact on protected groups, even when the harm is unintentionally caused.

Implicit Bias Claims under Current Law

The Supreme Court's current disparate impact jurisprudence could and should be read to prohibit discrimination due to implicit bias under Title VI. Logically, unconscious racism fits squarely within the court's definition of an "unjustifiable disparate impact" subject to agency enforcement. One could scarcely doubt that Justice Marshall, writing for the court in *Alexander v. Choate*, encompassed unconscious racial discrimination as one of the "sorts of disparate impacts" which he said "constituted sufficiently significant social problems . . . to warrant altering the practices of federal grantees that had produced those impacts."[43] Justice Ginsburg has written with the most clarity of the justices on this point, repeatedly explaining that prohibited unintentional discrimination encompasses harms due to unconscious biases that are also prohibited under Title VI. For example, in her *Grutter v. Bollinger*[44] concurrence, Justice Ginsburg wrote, "It is well documented that conscious and unconscious race bias, even rank discrimination based on race, remain alive in our land, impeding realization of our highest values and ideals."[45] In *Gratz v. Bollinger*[46] she wrote, "Bias both conscious and unconscious, reflecting traditional and unexamined habits of thought, keeps up barriers that must come down if equal opportunity and nondiscrimination are ever genuinely to become this country's law and practice."[47] Notwithstanding the procedural uncertainty that *Sandoval* introduced, in numerous opinions, various members of the court have identified the problem that unintentional racial and ethnic discrimination presents and have acquiesced in the understanding that Title VI addresses this form of prejudice in disparate impact claims. Arguably, disparate impact claims also reach unconscious racial discrimination as well. Yet the Supreme Court, as well as lower courts, remain unsure of how to apply Title VI—whether through the courts or administratively—to mediate the harms caused when recipients of federal funding engage in either unintentional or unconscious racism.

Perhaps the judges and justices fear a slippery slope. Courts may be resistant to penalizing unconscious racism because they perceive that extending liability on these grounds may implicate enormously broad swaths of the American population. After all, the social science evidence reviewed earlier in this book confirms that the vast majority of Americans hold implicit racially biased attitudes. Thus, courts may conclude that attempts to penalize these views would be overly broad. Alternatively, courts may resist imposing liability on unintentional acts of racial discrimination because the analysis requires a skill set judges do not believe they possess. Identifying the evidence that a defendant acted from a prohibited attitude may seem like an exercise in mind reading,[48] but indeed the evidence reviewed in earlier chapters contradicts this view. In fact, neither of these concerns is well founded because the social science record demonstrates that the required statistical proofs, and the substantive limitations that would make only "unjustifiable" disparate impact actionable, can operate to sufficiently limit plaintiffs' recovery in disparate impact claims. Still, courts seem to genuinely wrestle with identifying exactly when implicit bias is the cause or even a contributing cause to injurious discrimination, as well as with the question of what, if any, legal liability is appropriate to assign to this type of racism.

The judicial construction rules academics have proposed to meet these concerns have, admittedly, been unwieldy. While no serious argument can support using IAT scores or other implicit bias measures as direct evidence of actionable bias, the important groundwork laid by proposed tests such as Charles Lawrence's Cultural Meaning Test,[49] Rachel Lenhardt's racial stigmatization test,[50] or Barbara Flagg's transparently white decision-making test[51] all laudably provide principles for distinguishing actionable unconscious bias from biased thinking that should not be legally penalized. Still, these tests share a level of practical infeasibility. Thus, in the absence of a pragmatic line-drawing mechanism, courts have limited Title VI liability to disparate treatment cases where requiring evidence of intentionality avoids the perceived unfairness of holding one accountable for behavior they cannot control, or have narrowed disparate impact enforcement to administrative agencies. Careful revision of the Title VI statute can expressly address all these concerns and coax administrative agencies, as well as private litigants, to hold government contractors fully accountable for unintentional as well as intentional discrimination. The next section proposes three specific steps to reforming Title VI. The first step is to return shared enforcement authority to both private and public plaintiffs for unintentional discrimination. The second step is to recognize an express prohibition against racial and ethnic discrimination due to implicit bias. The third step is to enact a negligence standard of care to apply to cases alleging unconscious racism in disparate impact cases under Title VI.

Fixing Title VI

I have shown that Congress originally intended to empower private parties and public officials in the fight against invidious racial and ethnic discrimination in the United States and that several Supreme Court cases have recognized the need to do so as well. Therefore, the first restorative step is to expressly prohibit unintentional discrimination under Section 601 of Title VI. In addition to reversing the *Sandoval* court's break with Supreme Court disparate impact precedent "in separate law-suits spanning several decades,"[52] restoring private causes of action for disparate impact cases will have important practical ramifications. Private enforcement will expand the government's ability to stretch scarce enforcement resources and provide needed assistance to uncover subtle forms of discrimination. In fact, most of the statutory language needed to restore private enforcement for disparate impact claims under Title VI has already been proposed before Congress, in June 2012, during the 112th Congress. In 2012, the Senate Committee on Veterans' Affairs considered but did not enact language to amend Title VI.[53]

Using that proposed language as a starting point, I next suggest creating a new cause of action to prohibit discrimination due to implicit bias by expressly adding "rights-creating language" to Section 601, based on a negligence standard of care. A new negligence cause of action will empower the government as well as private victims directly impacted by unconscious racism to challenge the policies and programs that result in discrimination against minorities. At the same time, such a measure would also provide an affirmative defense to protect federal aid recipients from liability by showing they took reasonable steps, based on the available scientific evidence of which interventions effectively combat discrimination from unconscious or implicit bias. Thus the negligence-based cause of action will fully incorporate the current knowledge scientists have amassed about preventing harms due to implicit biases or unconscious racism. A new negligence action will augment existing disparate impact claims. For example, in accordance with the current Title VI burden-shifting regime, the proposed amendments will leave current disparate impact jurisprudence in place, allowing plaintiffs to prevail by discharging the burdens of production and persuasion to show disparate impact from a policy for which there is no substantial and legitimate nondiscriminatory goal, or by making out a prima facie case that the defendant rejected an existing, less discriminatory practice or policy than the one challenged. Finally, I propose adding language to the end of Section 602 of Title VI to restore the public-private enforcement model for any and all Title VI causes of action authorized under Section 601.

In order to accomplish these reforms of Title VI, Congress must amend the legislative language to add a provision to Section 601 of the current statute, and add a provision to Section 602. After denoting the existing language in these Sections as subparagraph (a), I propose to delineate the additional provisions as Section 601(b) and Section 602(b)–(c). The text of the resulting amended statutes follows, with the additional language I proposed underlined.[54]

The proposed revised version of Section 601 would read as follows:

(a) No person in the United States shall, on the ground of race, color, or national origin, be excluded from participation in, be denied the benefits of, or be subjected to discrimination under any program or activity receiving Federal financial assistance.

(b) Discrimination based on disparate impact with respect to a program or activity is established under this section only if—

    (1) a Federal department or agency, or any person aggrieved, demonstrates that an entity subject to this title has a policy or practice with respect to the program or activity that causes a disparate impact on the basis of race, color, or national origin; and

    (2) the entity fails to demonstrate that it has taken reasonable steps to reduce discriminatory harms due to unconscious or unintentional biases; and

    (3) the entity fails to demonstrate that the challenged policy or practice is related to, and necessary to achieve, the substantial and legitimate nondiscriminatory goals of the program or activity; or

    (4) a Federal department or agency, or the person aggrieved, demonstrates that a less discriminatory alternative policy or practice exists, and the entity refuses to adopt such alternative policy or practice.

The revised version of Section 602 would read as follows:

(b) Any person aggrieved by the failure of an entity to comply with section 601 may bring a civil action in any Federal or State court of competent jurisdiction to enforce such person's rights and may recover equitable relief, reasonable attorney's fees (including expert fees), and costs. The aggrieved person may also recover legal relief (including compensatory and, from nongovernmental entities, punitive damages) in the case of noncompliance based on evidence of intentional discrimination. In an action brought by an aggrieved person based on evidence of disparate impact, the aggrieved person may recover equitable relief, reasonable attorney's fees (including expert fees), and costs.

(c) Nothing in subsection (b) limits the authority of a Federal department or agency to enforce Section 601.

These changes to the plain language of Title VI will fully restore the recovery and relief that Congress has consistently indicated it intended to provide under the Civil Rights Act of 1964, will add a negligence-based claim to prohibit discrimination due to implicit biases, and will encourage all government contractors to protect against the discriminatory injustice that Congress has historically deplored. The advantages and benefits of these reforms are worth reviewing in detail.

Benefits of Restoring the Public-Private Enforcement Model

The public-private litigation model has historically proved to be an indispensable weapon in the attack against subtle and complex racial discrimination.[55] However, one seminal case in Title VI jurisprudence provides a particularly vivid illustration of the importance and necessity of both public and private enforcement under this statute. In *United States v. Fordice* (1992),[56] the United States sued the governor of Mississippi, alleging that the state's failure to dismantle its racially segregated public university system violated Title VI and the Fourteenth Amendment. However, the United States only entered the lawsuit on a Motion to Intervene filed after black private citizens had initiated a class action lawsuit alleging violation of the Fifth, Ninth, Thirteenth, and Fourteenth Amendments, the civil rights statutes codified at 42 U.S.C. §§ 1981 and 1983, and Title VI. A close look at the tortured procedural history of that case reveals the importance of the public-private litigation model in prosecuting complex civil rights cases.

Initially, the Department of Health, Education, and Welfare (HEW)[57] filed suit against Mississippi in 1969, after its Title VI investigation had revealed persistent and pervasive segregation and after its administrative efforts to develop a satisfactory compliance plan had failed. HEW refused to continue to fund Mississippi's segregated school system under Title VI and then wrestled with a recalcitrant Mississippi Board of Trustees of State Institutions of Higher Learning over an eighteen-year period while the board repeatedly resisted desegregation. This bears repeating: The administrative process to integrate Mississippi schools lasted over eighteen years. For nearly two decades, the board submitted complicated but ineffective compliance agendas identifying missions, faculty hiring plans, intricate admissions targets, and elaborate changes in their degree programs. At one point, the board defiantly implemented a compliance program that had been twice rejected, despite HEW's prior objections to the plan. Yet, according to the *Fordice* court's description, by the mid-1980s, 99 percent of Mississippi's white students were still enrolled in the state's five white colleges, and 71 percent of the state's black students still attended one of the state's three segregated black institutions.[58]

Ultimately, the *Fordice* plaintiffs successfully challenged the State of Mississippi for failing to desegregate its state university system nearly forty years after *Brown v. Board of Education*. When Justice White wrote for the *Fordice* court, his decision, on the one hand, awarded the black citizens of Mississippi the integrationist goals they had fought to obtain through over twenty years of litigation. Justice White wrote, "To the extent that the State has not met its affirmative obligation to dismantle its prior dual system it shall be adjudged in violation of the Constitution and Title VI."[59] Reaching this decision took the combined effort of public and private litigators, and there can be no doubt that the desegregation objectives would not have been possible without the work of private black litigants pursing disparate impact claims directly to enforce Title VI. However, on the other hand, the legacy of the *Fordice* case remains deeply controversial and stands as an example of nuances of social change that litigation alone cannot achieve.[60] The court failed to equalize funding for Mississippi's historically black universities, and the litigation itself took years. Yet the case demonstrates that, to the extent that civil rights litigation successfully signals a change in social norms and incentivizes publicly funded actors to change, public and private action to enforce well-crafted civil rights law remains an important and necessary tool for achieving social justice and equality in America.

The Advantages of Aligning Title VI with Reality

Perhaps the chief advantage to reforming Title VI as proposed will be in clarifying the signals the law sends to health care providers and all recipients of federal funds. Changing the law will provide impetus to change health care delivery practices. Some examples from recent Title VI case law serve to illustrate this advantage. Courts currently focus on intentionality in Title VI cases to reach incongruous outcomes in both disparate treatment and disparate impact cases. Plaintiffs have tried to bring disparate impact cases disguised as disparate treatment cases in an attempt to prosecute invidious discrimination, despite *Sandoval*. In disparate treatment cases, courts have accepted very weak defenses to dismiss a plaintiff's claim that does not appear to rise to the level of outdated notions of explicit race bias. When these claims fail, not only do plaintiff harms go unaddressed, but defendant entities cannot know how to correct the discrimination that they may abhor, but that escaped legal liability.

A recent Indiana case provides an example. There, the court entered summary judgment for a defendant school where a multiracial high school student was expelled for allegations of sexual harassment after he had been subjected to five years of racial harassment. The plaintiff in that case put forth evidence that he was repeatedly called "Nigger" by other students in classes, on the playing field, during violent physical attacks, in hate notes, and even in multiple racially derogatory death threats. The plaintiff alleged school officials were liable of disparate treatment, the only Title VI cause of action available to private parties after *Sandoval*. Predictably, the court held that the school officials were not deliberately indifferent because they were not "definitely aware" of some incidents and that when they were, they took disciplinary action that was not "clearly unreasonable."[61] Reforming Title VI would change the outcome in this case and the signal it sends to future actors. First, restoring a private cause of action for disparate impact would allow the plaintiff in this case to allege the defendant school officials should be held liable for the deleterious effect that school disciplinary policies have when they are delayed and selectively directed only at victims of racial violence, but not preemptively at perpetrators. Second, introducing a negligence standard of care based on the social science record would allow courts to measure the reasonableness of a defendant's disciplinary action against objective standards empirically related to modern racism, rather than ambiguous notions of prejudice that lack scientific grounding. In sum, the defendant school officials in this case and educators nationwide would have reason to implement new disciplinary policies, provide training interventions for teachers and staff, suggest counseling alternatives for students and families, and take other steps that are attentive to reducing racial bias.

A recent New York case further demonstrates that reforming Title VI will influence business operations in a broad range of publicly funded activities. Under current law, a New York court simply ignored a plaintiff's evidence that the state's Department of Labor policies and procedures disadvantaged Hispanic customers because her complaints "focused on disparate impact on Hispanic LEP [limited English proficiency] customers, not intentional discrimination."[62] Under a reformed Title VI, the plaintiff in that case might not have needed to resort to litigation because the defendant Department of Labor may have had reason to prophylactically address unintended race bias against non-English speakers, because a revised Title VI law, by providing an affirmative defense to the charges, would credit the effort to undertake interventions that are proven effective.

A recent case from Pennsylvania provides another example of the advantages of reforming Title VI. In this case, a Pennsylvania court dismissed allegations of racial discrimination by a class of minority students who showed the defendant school district systematically removed black students from the mainstream educational curriculum by misidentifying them as disabled and unfairly assigning them to special needs classes.[63] The Pennsylvania plaintiffs presented statistical data sufficient to make out a prima facie case on disparate impact grounds, but due to *Sandoval*, these private litigants based their claim on disparate treatment doctrine. Consequently, the court concluded that the school did not act with "discriminatory purpose" to segregate minority students in inferior educational programs, despite abundant statistical data concerning the disproportionate representation of blacks in disabled classes, evidence of individual misdiagnoses, the school district's procedural irregularities in testing, evidence of disparate learning opportunities, and the underrepresentation of minority administrators throughout the school district.[64] The litigants' claims in this Pennsylvania case were essentially disparate impact allegations that fell victim to disparate treatment scrutiny of motive and intent. And here is the real concern: The law has done nothing whatsoever to help the Pennsylvania schools put an end to discrimination that will continue to harm students indefinitely. Reforming Title VI would permit such plaintiffs to allege that the school defendants acted unreasonably in light of the evidence that implicit race bias might unintentionally impact school administrators' discretionary decision-making. Moreover, reform would also allow the school officials to defend by showing they took evidence-based steps to mitigate implicit bias when assigning students to special education by using Type C interventions such as described in chapter 7 to train a group of teachers and administrators that included diverse leaders as visible counter-stereotypes. Schools will more likely construct meaningful interventions that mitigate unconscious discrimination if they wish to avail themselves of such a defense to potential Title VI actions.

The focus of Title VI litigation must be broadened beyond intentionality, not merely to change the outcomes in cases such as these, but most importantly to guide and motivate institutional and individual actors to take reasonable, evidence-based steps to avoid biased conduct where they do not intend to discriminate. Title VI reforms can achieve congruence between the factual evidence of discriminatory conduct and outcomes, as well as between the scientific evidence of human behavior and our national values that prohibit racial and ethnic discrimination. For years, scholars have pointed to the dissonance between antidiscrimination law and the contemporary behavior it seeks to regulate. Arguably, during the 1970s, 1980s, and 1990s, scholars lacked the basis for structuring more accurate rules to account for the subtle forms of racism that result from unintentional and unconscious conduct.

In 1995, Linda Krieger wrote a landmark article observing the futility of courts' search "for 'discriminatory motive or intent' without understanding the most prevalent form of discrimination today is not 'motivational rather than cognitive in origin.'"[65] Krieger stopped short of endorsing a negligence standard in order to reach discrimination driven by recent bias, saying that "unlike other scholars who advocate a 'negligence' approach to employment discrimination, I suggest that additional empirical and theoretical work must be done before the contours of such a duty can be precisely defined, let alone crafted into practical and effective legal rules."[66] Now, two decades later, the empirical record that Krieger sought has been developed. The scientific evidence reviewed throughout this book provides abundant proof that antidiscrimination law must be refined to fit the empirically supported social science record that demonstrates how unconscious racism causes discrimination and harm in health care and in other contexts as well. The scientific basis for legally distinguishing unconscious and implicit bias from intentional bias has eroded. In light of the evidence of malleability, the knowledge that individuals as well as institutions can take affirmative steps to intervene in and reverse implicit biases dissolves the notion that one who continues to act out of implicit racial biases lacks culpability. To further demonstrate the beneficial structural incentives that a behaviorally accurate Title VI jurisprudence will have in all federally funded contexts, it is useful to examine how the negligence standard would operate in the health care delivery context. The following hypothetical scenario is illustrative.

The Advantageous Incentive Effect of Reforming Title VI

Under a reformed Title VI, the entire record of social science knowledge will become relevant to informing changes in health care delivery by federally funded providers. A hypothetical plaintiff's claim will demonstrate how the revised law could be the catalyst for these institutional reforms. Under the new law, a plaintiff may contend that a provider's patient selection criteria, record-keeping practices, or failure to provide translation services systematically and disparately burdens minority patients in violation of Title VI. As part of her prima facie disparate impact case, the plaintiff in this hypothetical case may rely upon authoritative social science data to evince the association between the allegedly discriminatory practices and health outcomes for affected minority groups. This plaintiff will act as a private attorney general—an individual bringing a case to remedy a public harm, in her capacity as a private citizen—and call upon evidence from the implicit bias studies described in chapter 2 or the health disparities literature summarized in chapters 3, 4, and 5 to support allegations against the defendant health care provider. The objectives of raising such claims are fourfold. First, the plaintiff seeks to recover individual damages, and second the plaintiff may seek injunctive relief to stop the defendant's discriminatory practices from harming future patients. Third, this lawsuit would signal to other providers who wish to avoid liability that they too must stop discriminating. Fourth, the plaintiff's lawsuit will incentivize health care providers to enact ex-ante changes in their medical care delivery systems to address unconscious bias before litigation. As courts incorporate the evidence-based interventions into the negligence litigation model as defenses, the law will credit those providers who make anti-bias changes in their programs and practices, and will broadly signal the value of the reasonable efforts an institution may take to mitigate exposure to being sued for permitting unconscious racism to flourish.

Continuing this hypothetical case, the defendant provider would be able (and encouraged) to raise new defenses to the Title VI allegations by showing that the provider organization had implemented all reasonable interventions scientifically shown to combat discrimination due to implicit bias. Courts may examine the defendant's policies at each juncture of the health delivery process that the Biased Care Model identifies is relevant to the plaintiff's hypothetical claim. The effectiveness of these defenses will turn on the scientific record. In other words, to the extent that a defendant is able to show that reasonable steps were taken to implement the interventions supported by the malleability literature presented in chapter 7, that defendant would have satisfied the standard of care required of reasonable and similarly situated health care providers. As the social science evidence evolves to develop better interventions to alleviate bias-driven discrimination, the standard of reasonable care will also evolve. To use Tristin Green's parlance again, by reforming Title VI as I propose, we can expect health providers to adopt best practices identified by social scientists, because we have framed the law to embed social science as a social and legal authority.[67]

A defendant under a reformed Title VI could identify these evidence-based best practices as part of a defense that would replace the generalized assertion that has guided the burden-shifting analysis in disparate impact cases historically. In an evidence-based approach to disparate impact under a reformed Title VI, the plaintiff would bear the initial burden of showing that the defendant health care organization had a facially neutral practice that resulted in a racially disparate impact on minorities. Then, the defendant health provider could respond by show-ing that it had acted reasonably to reduce health disparities by taking steps that have been empirically demonstrated to reduce implicit bias. A showing that matches the scientific evidence would replace the vague and self-serving representations that the defendant provider had a "le-gitimate nondiscriminatory reason" or a "substantial, legitimate justifi-cation" for its policy. Instead, challenged practices must be reasonable in light of the scientific evidence in order to pass muster. If the defendant provider discharges the burden to show evidence-based reasonableness, then the burden would return to the plaintiff, who could prevail in a dis-parate impact case only by showing that the defendant health provider's actions were unreasonable based on the social science evidence of what steps mitigate implicit bias-driven disparities, as well as on what other similarly situated organizations have done.

This new addition to the Title VI burden-shifting regime would be evidence-based and reflect the prevailing standard of care in light of available scientific knowledge. Examples of effective defenses may in-clude evidence the defendant provided stereotype-negation training for physicians, made doctors aware of their personal implicit bias scores using an IAT (or other scientifically valid, personalized instrument), and educated providers concerning the demonstrated impact their biases are likely to have on health care delivery. These defenses would be based on evidence that increasing awareness of biasing potential may evoke self-correction.[68] Stereotype-negation training should specifically address each of the Biased Care Model's six mechanisms, which describe the pathways through which implicit bias travels to affect health dispari-ties; it should also include training specifically directed toward exposure to counter-stereotypes based on the evidence that this type of training weakens racial, ethnic, and gender stereotypes.[69]

The defendant provider could show it took reasonable steps to pro-mote workforce diversity through programs to hire, promote, and retain physicians from racial and ethnic minority backgrounds in positions of leadership and authority. This defense would be based upon the evi-dence that fewer negative stereotypes operate following interactions with minority physicians and others in authority.[70] Alternatively, were the defendant provider to base its defense on evidence that implicit biases are related to high cognitive load, another intervention that would demonstrate reasonableness may be related to efforts to reduce workloads placed on health care providers. A defendant may show that implicit biases have been addressed by clinical scheduling changes, employing the well-documented evidence that physicians will reduce their dependence on negative stereotypes when they are able to spend adequate time to focus and learn about the attributes of the individual patient with whom they are interacting.[71] These are examples of actions that could form the basis of a sea change in the way that physicians, hospitals, clinics, and indeed all federally funded actors address unconscious racism. The contours of changes in delivery, as well as legal actions and defenses, will take shape based on evolving scientific evidence.

Anticipating Objections

Understandably, courts have been reluctant to extend Title VI liability to penalize conduct that most previously believed defendants could not control. Though their prejudices may have been repugnant, they were assumed to be no more harmful than mere bad thoughts. Until now, the commonsense limits of antidiscrimination law have steered clear of unconscious racism, which legislators deemed an apparently small and thorny space, unfit for judicial regulation. Again, based on the generally accepted misconception of implicit bias, principles of basic fairness seemed to counsel that discrimination due to unconscious racism was not culpable conduct. Although these commonsense principles of basic fairness do not any longer square with the scientific record, some may nevertheless resort to them to challenge my proposal to reform Title VI.

For example, critics unfamiliar with the fact that unconscious racism is malleable may argue against extending Title VI to cover implicit liability on the ground that legal liability should be avoidable to be just; this is an objection about fairness. Moreover, critics may argue that culpability is appropriate only where individuals and institutions have chosen not to comply with clearly articulated legal standards and their contrary choice may fairly give rise to liability; this is an objection about predictability. Further, the critique may assert that antidiscrimination law should not penalize discriminatory behavior that is helpful, reasonable, or that is not harmful in the health care context, where crafting a narrow and precise enough standard of care is crucial; this is an objection about proportionality. Physicians, of course, must not ever be penalized at times when they appropriately consider race or ethnicity—whether intentionally or unintentionally—as a relevant factor in medical decision-making, as, for example, when diagnosing Cohn's Disease or sickle-cell anemia. Yet, even critics will concede that a just legal standard must isolate and penalize providers whose institutional or individual considerations of race or ethnicity *wrongly* influence the delivery of medical care and expend public funds to cause discrimination. The crux of these objections will turn, however, on a misunderstanding of when implicit bias discrimination is "wrong." The answer to this line of principled objection lies in the hundreds—perhaps thousands—of reports providing scientific evidence that unconscious racism causes[72] legally cognizable injury and that it stems from attitudes that are subject to individual and institutional controls. In other words, jurists must understand the science of unconscious racism, as well as the stories of those who are its victims in health care. That is the mission of this book—namely, to organize the scientific record beside the narratives of those affected by unconscious bias in health care, for law- and policy-makers to fully appreciate the grave impact that health care discrimination has on real lives. Those who will painstakingly engage with the scientific record will find the scientifically proven truth that imposing liability for unconscious discrimination indeed satisfies the common sense principles of fairness, predictability, and proportionality. Moreover, those who consider the health impacts on the lives of minority men and women in America cannot escape the moral imperative to address health inequality.

Critics of a Title VI reform that accounts for unconscious racism may also cite the risk of over-inclusiveness. The ubiquity of implicit biases poses an interesting challenge to the important goal of applying Title VI litigation to address discrimination that is prohibited because it is harmful and unjust, while protecting decision-makers' ability to acknowledge differences that are substantive, rational, and not injurious. However, the fact that the vast majority of Americans evince some degree of implicit racial and ethnic bias does not mean that discrimination due to bias is a tolerable norm or that efforts to curb the harmful discriminatory effects of these biases will necessarily overreach to include innocent behavior. In fact, my proposal to extend Title VI addresses the threat of over-inclusiveness by directing legal sanction only against those who *unreasonably* refuse to protect against unintentional harms, not simply those who unavoidably cause such harms. In the regime I propose, culpability is not imposed on those who merely discriminate based on their implicit biases, but liability is reserved for those who discriminate based on their implicit biases without taking reasonable, evidence-based precautions available to prevent the foreseeable harms their discrimination causes. For this very reason, another critique of my proposed reforms may be that they do not go far enough. Some may argue the proposals I advance are under-inclusive because they are not entirely free from the chance that odious and objectionable discrimination will escape liability and continue unabated. I must concede this point to these critics, but I do so with the belief that the scientific knowledge of and evidence for the malleability of implicit bias will continue to develop and over time will extend an even more refined and comprehensive basis for responsible providers to take progressively broader, reasonable steps to combat unconscious racism. Legal and provider institutions will respond to the legal reforms, I believe, by more precisely identifying culpable conduct under the reasonableness standard that I have proposed. Flexibility, after all, is the point of incorporating an evolving scientific standard into antidiscrimination law.

I anticipate that some may question the soundness of the social science that I have relied upon to recommend evidence-based legal reforms. Of course, not all social science research is created equal. Fortunately, information about the quality of the research findings for any given study is usually reported with the research findings. In selecting the research that I have highlighted and relied upon throughout this book, I have paid close attention to those quality measures in the same way that courts or legislators will when implementing the evidence-based proposals presented here. For example, I considered sample sizes, research methodology, and the measures of statistical significance reported for each study cited. Where studies included regression analysis, I generally selected articles that reported statistically significant results evidenced by P-values $< .05$ and R^2 values closer to 1.0. Moreover, when selecting articles to rely upon for my models and proposals, I also considered the extent to which other social scientists have cited and relied upon those studies. Finally, I reviewed the research designs, hypotheses tested, and results reported for each of the major studies I cited with experienced social scientists to confirm the quality, and identify limita-tions, of study results. Indeed, the methods for evaluating the quality of the science that I relied upon here are similar to the approaches that courts could use when comparing the reasonableness of a defendant's antidiscrimination efforts to the current scientific reports of implicit bias interventions available to that defendant.

Some may object to fashioning any legal solution at all to the prob-lem of implicit bias in health care or elsewhere. Specifically, the notion of regulating thoughts and intentions may be abhorrent to some, espe-cially where the complexities of medical decision-making confound the race and ethnicity discrimination targeted by my proposals. Others will prefer to leave physicians and other providers to self-regulate, rightly noting that the vast majority of providers are well intentioned and caring about all patients. Finally, some may object to additionally burdening health providers who are already weighed down by an irrational legal malpractice system that randomly and inefficiently imposes liability on physicians.[73] To these objections I point first to the abject failure of the range of legislative and regulatory tools surveyed in chapter 8, next to the prevalence of injustice that degrades the quality and longevity of minority American's lives in this country, and finally to the dogged persistence of inequitable health disparities that have been the focus of sincere and determined efforts that have repeatedly fallen far short of the goal of eradicating ethnic and racial health disparities entirely. The proposals to reform Title VI set forth here represent a new threshold in the relationship between law and social science and address new forms and levels of inequality.[74] I propose using social science evidence as an authoritative ground for creating a new set of Title VI rules. I further propose to embed social science in Title VI defenses by giving litigants access to social science facts about implicit bias to define a reasonable standard of care. In the specific case of health care delivery, I offer the Biased Care Model, which provides a roadmap for targeted interven-tions that reasonable providers may undertake based on social science facts in order to reduce disparities due to unconscious racism.

Litigation under an updated version of Title VI will signal the efficacy of aligning health care delivery policies and practice with the social sci-ence facts. Nevertheless, changing this particular law is merely a first step in the direction of achieving health justice. Equally as important is that reforming Title VI for health care will inspire providers to fundamentally and structurally change health care delivery in ways that will directly impact minority health. And perhaps most importantly, reforming Title VI for health care will impact and improve civil rights law implementation and enforcement for all recipients of federal funding throughout the United States.

Conclusion

Beyond Title VI

[A]n individual shall not on the ground prohibited under title VI of the Civil Rights Act of 1964, . . . title IX of the Education Amendments of 1972 (20 U.S.C. 1681 et seq.), the Age Discrimination Act of 1975 (42 U.S.C. 6101 et seq.), or section 50 of the Rehabilitation Act of 1973 (29 U.S.C. 794), be excluded from participation in, be denied the benefits of, or be subjected to discrimination under, any health program or activity, any part of which is receiving Federal financial assistance, including credits, subsidies, or contracts of insurance, or under any program or activity that is administered by an Executive Agency or any entity established under this title.
—Section 1557, Affordable Care Act, 2010

When the 111th Congress enacted the Patient Protection and Affordable Care Act of 2010, the national legislature once again affirmed its commitment to a health care system free of discrimination and a strong civil rights law to ensure it. Section 1557 of the Affordable Care Act contains the nation's first civil rights provision that specifically prohibits discrimination in health care.[1] Although this new civil rights law leaves Title VI and its implementation of regulations as written in place, the new statute significantly enlarges Title VI protections in at least four ways. First, Section 1557 prohibits discrimination based not only on race, color, and national origin, but also on age, disability, and sex. In fact, this is the first civil rights law to prohibit sex discrimination in health care, including a prohibition against discrimination based on sex stereotyping and gender identity.[2] Second, the Affordable Care Act's civil rights provision covers a larger range of participants in the health care industry than

Title VI alone does. Covered entities under Section 1557 include health insurers, hospitals, and the newly created health insurance exchanges, thus prohibiting discrimination in health insurance activities by all insurance entities authorized under the act. Any entities that received federal funds are covered by this health care civil rights provision. The act gives the Office of Civil Rights authority to investigate complaints under this provision and use the breadth of this new antidiscrimination tool to address institutional bias and discrimination such as the ways in which insurers and health plans organize networks, selectively contract with providers, and make coverage decisions. Third, the Affordable Care Act's Section 1557 grants individuals the right to file administrative complaints alleging violations of the nondiscrimination provision. Indeed, this new section plausibly might be read to acknowledge a private right of action to protect civil rights; however the restoration of such a right is by no means clear. Moreover, although Section 1557's incorporation of "the enforcement mechanisms provided for and available under"[3] the civil rights provisions in Title VI, Title IX, § 504, and the Age Discrimination Act, should be read to prohibit both intentional disparate treatment and unintentional disparate impact discrimination under all these landmark civil rights laws, neither the secretary of the DHHS nor the courts have adopted this broad reading.

Section 1557 enforcement has already begun in earnest and reported cases are revealing. The first complaint filed alleging violation of the new nondiscrimination provision involved a male who alleged sex discrimination in violation of Section 1557. This complaint was resolved when, on December 6, 2013, the HHS Office for Civil Rights announced a corrective action taken against the Louisiana hospital where staff had discriminated against male victims of domestic violence. Moreover, the named hospital revised its abuse protocol and provided training to emergency department staff to ensure equal treatment to domestic violence victims regardless of their sex.

The second Section 1557 complaint also alleged gender bias. This claim was against an Arkansas provider that automatically assigned male spouses as financial guarantors of their wives' medical bills but not the reverse. The administrative investigation resulted in the Arkansas medical center changing its policy to ensure equal treatment of male and female recipients of medical services.

In June 2013, the National Women's Law Center filed a series of complaints with the Office of Civil Rights alleging Section 1557 violations by institutions that exclude pregnancy coverage from their health benefit plans. The resolution of these claims will be watched closely. From these early cases, two important observations emerge about Section 1557 enforcement. First, thus far, the new civil rights provision is being heavily litigated to control gender but not racial or ethnic discrimination. Second, the nondiscrimination provision can provide an effective incentive for health institutions to change their discriminatory practices and policies.

The efficacy of Section 1557 provisions in changing structural inequities is further evident from a recently resolved class action suit filed in Louisiana. John East filed suit against Blue Cross and Blue Shield of Louisiana, individually and on behalf of all HIV/AIDS patients, alleging that the insurer violated Section 1557 by refusing to accept Ryan White funds[4] to subsidize the cost of insurance premiums for low-income HIV/AIDS patients. The *East* suit alleged that "Even if Defendants did not act with discriminatory intent, Defendants' refusal to accept premium payments from third parties . . . has a disparate impact on individuals with a disability, namely their HIV or AIDS diagnosis, . . . who as a result of Defendants' policy necessarily will be denied meaningful access to, excluded from participation in and denied the benefits of any health program or activity, any part of which is receiving Federal financial assistance, in violation of Affordable Care Act section 1557(a)."[5] Based on the likelihood the plaintiff class would succeed on the merits, the Louisiana court entered a temporary restraining order and later set a hearing for a preliminary injunction. The defendant insurers relented and agreed to begin accepting payments at least temporarily in response to the class action disparate impact claim. The *East* suit outcome bodes well for the argument that Section 1557 restores private causes of action for disparate impact civil rights claims.

Section 1557 is not a panacea, however. For one thing, the new statute does not have a tested body for implementing regulations that will guide administrative and judicial enforcement of the law. These regulations are under development, but even once promulgated, they will remain nascent for some time. Although the Department of Health and Human Services issued a request for information in June 2013 and will soon issue the draft regulations for this new civil rights provision for notice and comment, the process of establishing firm legal and administrative precedent for enforcement of Section 1557 promises to be long and complex. Section 1557, then, is an unprecedented and encouraging civil rights law, but the statute's language and application so far provide a potential, but not yet a proven, weapon against unconscious racism in health care. Therefore, to the extent that the Affordable Care Act incorporates and indeed relies upon the language of Title VI, the task of reforming that civil rights statute remains vital. Indeed, given the apparent focus on gender and sexual orientation litigation under Section 1557 currently, reforming Title VI as I have proposed stands out as the single reform with the greatest potential to fundamentally change the way health care is delivered to minority patients in this country.

* * *

It is fitting to close this book with a call for reform that goes well beyond Title VI or any legal solutions to health inequality generally. Even after the sweeping and radical recommendations for legal reform made here, and even when the legislative and judicial branches adopt an evidence-based approach to making civil rights law reflect behavioral reality, truly achieving sustainable racial and ethnic justice will require still more work and more far-reaching change. Health care providers seeking to deliver the highest quality of medical care must creatively fashion solutions to implicit bias that fit the medical needs of all their patients in all health care settings. The social science community must provide more targeted research to reveal details of the extent and methods by which each Biased Care Model mechanism operates to influence health outcomes. In reliance on the empirical record, policy-makers must continue to implement and require intervention strategies that are effective and narrowly tailored. Patients will learn increasingly to trust providers as the systemic discrimination in health care abates. In sum, this book begins what I hope will result in a long and dramatically improved relationship among providers, patients, jurists, and social scientists committed to eradicating racial and ethnic health disparities. Toward that end, I close with three appeals.

First, based on the vital role that social science has thus far played in uncovering the true scope and scale of unconscious racism, I am especially hopeful that this book will impact researchers' future study agenda, and that policy-makers will pay close attention to the fruits of these scientists' labor. The social science literature should become increasingly contextualized. Researchers who in the past have failed to appreciate the systemic racist structures that have fueled, and even caused, the implicit biases they study, must broaden the scope of their inquiry. I challenge social science scholars to recognize the importance of the racially biased ideology that informs all Americans' social knowledge and therefore enlarge the isolated cognitive corrections currently suggested in the literature. Chapter 1 demonstrates that where health and health care are concerned, racial discrimination was historically and structurally built into the American fiber and psyche, and I hope that more research will reflect this reality. Admittedly, the structure of racial discrimination built into the most powerful tool of the American state—the law—confirms that to the extent that racism is a part of the American political economy, its tentacles will not be dislodged solely by passing stronger laws. But I do believe that passing *better* laws can significantly help to dismantle discrimination due to unconscious racism. However, better laws will require better social science.

My second appeal follows directly from the first. By ignoring the continuing influence of our historical, national consciousness of discrimination against minorities, the individualized focus almost exclusively on physicians as implicitly biased actors within the discriminatory health care system is shortsighted, incomplete, and unfair. I have argued that this focus exaggerates the power of physicians' and patients' agency over structure to address health inequities related to unconscious racism. I appeal to health care providers to begin to act collectively, at systemic and institutional levels, to address the extent to which inequality and racial discrimination diminish the quality of health care in America. It is not only interpersonal interaction and factors such as disparate physician diagnosis, treatment, or communication that produce health disparities. Health inequality is also determined by systemic ways in which powerful health institutions, including providers, insurers, and the state, interact with groups of underclass patients as populations, not merely as individuals. Thus, only changes to the overarching environment and these social systems will interrupt the flow of messages that inform the stereotypes, class stratification, and inequality that distorts interactions between individual physicians and patients. And only such a fundamental disruption will confer upon individuals the agency to acknowledge and then take steps to reject implicit biases completely. I believe this disruption is the responsibility of legal, medical, social, political, and scientific institutions, not only of doctors, hospitals, and health care providers.

My third appeal challenges these responsible communities to endeavor in all policies and programs to address the socioeconomic factors represented in the bottom tier of Thomas Frieden's health impact pyramid. This appeal arises from the breadth and complexity of the structural discrimination that arises from implicit racial and ethnic biases to adversely affect the health of minority and low-income populations. This structural discrimination includes inequities in housing opportunities, employment, and education, as well as the enormous income disparities that underlie unconscious biases against patients. By viewing the psychological determinants of implicit bias and the discriminatory behavior it produces in isolation, we will continue to fall short of addressing the multidimensional discrimination that feeds and reinforces health disparities. While this book has focused narrowly on the clinical environment, changes in that setting alone cannot combat unconscious bias and the harm it causes minority patients. We must consider that physicians' implicit biases grow out of inequities in power and wealth that separate physicians from their patients in virtually every aspect of their lives. Indeed, as David Williams and Toni Rucker observe, "effectively addressing health care disparities will require comprehensive efforts by multiple sectors of society in order to address inequities in major societal institutions. There is clearly a need for concerted society-wide efforts to confront and eliminate discrimination in education, employment, housing, criminal justice, and other areas of society which will improve the socioeconomic status (SES) of disadvantaged minority populations and indirectly provide them with greater access to medical care."[6]

In conclusion, I return to the conviction that reforming civil rights law to account for unconscious racism is an indispensible step in the journey toward achieving equality in health care and beyond. While the health gaps between minorities and whites have been slowly shrinking in a few categories such as overall life expectancy, the fact remains that over the past twenty-five years, in every racial and ethnic category, the number and proportion of all quality measures for which disparities are tracked show the vast majority of differences in health and health care quality are not changing and in many cases are worsening.[7] These tragic differences remain notwithstanding an era of self-regulation, substantial expenditures, and extensive investment in research and programs aimed at reducing disparities. The fact is that without a new approach to civil rights law—one based on the evidentiary record that addresses implicit bias directly, which I submit is the single determinant that no prior efforts have forthrightly addressed—minority health and health care disparities will persist. More to the point, patients whose skin color or ethnicity is not white or Caucasian will continue to die quicker and live sicker than those who have white skin or ancestors. My hope is that the models and methods introduced in this book will reach far beyond health care to remove all reasonable excuses for failure to take action against unconscious racism. Failure, in health care and in all other contexts where implicit biases devastate lives and life chances, is no longer an acceptable scientific, legal, or ethical option.

NOTES

INTRODUCTION

1 David Satcher et al., "What If We Were Equal? A Comparison of the Black-White Mortality Gap in 1960 and 2000," *Health Affairs* 24, no. 2 (2005): 459–64.

2 Brian D. Smedley et al., *Unequal Treatment: Confronting Racial and Ethnic Disparities in Health Care* (Washington, DC: National Academies Press, 2003).

3 M. Marmot et al., "Closing the Gap in a Generation: Health Equity through Action on the Social Determinants of Health," *Lancet* 372 (2008): 1661–69.

4 P. Lantz et al., "Socioeconomic Factors, Health Behaviors, and Mortality," *Journal of American Medical Association* 279, no. 21 (1998): 1703–8.

5 David R. Williams et al., "Racial Differences in Physical and Mental Health," *Journal of Health Psychology* 2, no. 3 (1997): 335–51.

6 R. S. Phillips et al., "Race, Resource Use, and Survival in Seriously Ill Hospitalized Adults" *Journal of General Internal Medicine* 11 (1996): 387–96.

7 Pamela A. Meyer, Paula W. Yoon, and Rachel B. Kaufmann, "CDC Health Disparities and Inequalities Report—United States, 2013," *Centers for Disease Control and Prevention Morbidity and Mortality Weekly Report* 62, no. 3 (2013).

CHAPTER 1. BAD LAW MAKES BAD HEALTH

1 Epigraphs from Nancy Scheper-Hughes and Margaret M. Lock, "The Mindful Body: A Prolegomenon to Future Work in Medical Anthropology," *Medical Anthropology Quarterly* 1, no. 1 (1987): 6–41; *Akenbrandt v. Richards*, 504 U.S. 689 (1992) (Justice Stevens concurring in judgment).

2 Thomas R. R. Cobb, *An Inquiry into the Law of Negro Slavery in the United States* (Athens: University of Georgia Press, 1858) (citing the Slave Trade Act of 1788, also known as Dolben's Act).

3 See, e.g., Frederick Douglass, "The Constitution of the United States: Is It Pro-Slavery or Anti-Slavery?" Speech at Glasgow, Scotland, March 26, 1860, summarizing the "slaveholding provisions" of the Constitution: Article 1, Section 9 (continuing slavery until 1808), Article 4, Section 9 (recovery of fugitive slaves), Article 1, Section 8 (military to be used to suppress slave insurrection as invasion), Article 1, Section 2 (slave states accord a slave 3/5 of a person for representation).

4 Alexander Falconbridge, *An Account of the Slave Trade on the Coast of Africa* (London, 1788), available at http://www.learnnc.org/lp/editions/nchist-colonial/1904.

5 See, Henry Wiencek, *Master of the Mountain: Thomas Jefferson and His Slaves*, (New York: Macmillan, 2012); see also *Thomas Jefferson and Slavery*, available at http://www.monticello.org/site/plantation-and-slavery/thomas-jefferson-and-slavery.

6 Chief Justice John Marshall, *Johnson and Graham's Lessee v. William M'Intosh*, 21 U.S. 543 (1823).

7 President Andrew Jackson, Fifth Annual Message, December 3, 1833, available at http://indiancountrytodaymedianetwork.com/2013/07/17/nice-day-genocide-shocking-quotes-indians-us-leaders-pt-2-150465.

8 See *Johnson and Graham's Lessee v. M'Intosh*, 21 U.S. 543 (1823).

9 Joseph William Singer, "Original Acquisition of Property: From Conquests and Possession to Democracy and Equal Opportunity," *Harvard Law School Public Law and Theory Working Paper Series,* paper no. 10–28 (2010).

10 *Johnson and Graham's Lessee v. William M'Intosh*, 21 U.S. 543 (1823) (Chief Justice John Marshall).

11 David S. Jones, "The Persistence of American Indian Health Disparities," *American Journal of Public Health* 96 (2006): 2122–34.

12 See, e.g., Janette Beals et al., "Prevalence of Mental Disorders and Utilization of Mental Health Services in Two American Indian Reservation Populations: Mental Health Disparities in a National Context," *American Journal of Psychiatry* 162 (2005): 1723, 1731 (Southwest women as carriers of tradition in matrilineal culture may have less risk for alcohol use disorders because of closer ties to Native ways).

13 *Dred Scott v. John F. A. Sandford*, 60 U.S. 393 (1856) (the Constitution of the United States recognizes Negros of the African race as articles of property not citizens).

14 See University of Virginia, "Patients' Voices in Early 19th Century Virginia," in Historical Collections at the Claude Moore Health Sciences Library, available at http://carmichael.lib.virginia.edu/story/slavecare.html.

15 Ibid.

16 T. L. Savitt, "Black Health on the Plantation: Owners, the Enslaved, and Physicians," *Organization of American Historians Magazine of History* 19, no. 5 (2005): 14–16.

17 See, e.g., Todd Savitt, *Medicine and Slavery: The Disease and Health Care of Blacks in Antebellum Virginia* (Urbana: University of Illinois Press, 1978), 60; for the role of physicians in debates about the health of black slaves, see Nancy Krieger, "Shades of Difference: Theoretical Underpinnings of the Medical Controversy on Black/White Difference in the United States, 1830–1870," *International Journal of Health Sciences* 17 (1987): 259–78.

18 *In re Ah Yup*, 5 Sawy. 155 (1878).

19 But see *In re Lee Sing et al.*, 43 F. 359 (C.C.N.D. Cal. 1890) (declaring one such ordinance unconstitutional).

20 *United States v. Morrison*, 109 F. 891 (1901) (J. McPherson).

21 David J. LaVigne, "Immigrants," in *Industrial Revolution—People and Perspectives*, ed. Jennifer L. Goloboy (Santa Barbara, CA: ABC-CLIO, Inc., 2008), 147.

22 See Teresa M. Gorman, "Back on the Chain Gang: Why the Eighth Amendment and the History of Slavery Proscribe the Resurgence of Chain Gangs," *California Law Review* 85 (1997): 441. See also Donald G. Nieman, *To Set the Law in Motion: The Freedmen's Bureau and the Legal Rights of Blacks, 1865–1868* (Millwood, NY: KTO Press, 1979); Recent Legislation, "Criminal Law—Prison Labor—Florida Reintroduces Chain Gangs," *Harvard Law Review* 109 (1996): 876, 880; Alan R. Madry, "Accountability and the Fourteenth Amendment: State Action, Federalism and Congress," *Missouri Law Review* 59 (1994): 499, 534.

23 *Cal. Sat.* 175 (1855).

24 See, generally, Clement E. Vose, *Caucasians Only: The Supreme Court, the NAACP, and the Restrictive Covenant Cases* (Berkeley and Los Angeles: University of California Press 1973). See also Eric J. Branfman et al., "Measuring the Invisible Wall: Land Use Controls and the Residential Patterns of the Poor," *Yale Law Journal* 82 (1973): 483.

25 See, e.g., Richard J. Lazarus, "Environmental Justice: The Distributional Effects of Environmental Protection," *Northwestern University Law Review* 87 (1993): 787; Robert D. Bullard, "Environmental Justice for All: It's the Right Thing to Do," *Journal of Environmental Law and Litigation* 9 (1994): 281. Compare U.S. Environmental Protection Agency, *Environmental Equity, Reducing Risks for all Communities*, Workgroup Report to the Administrator 2 (EPA230-R-92-008) (1992), available at http://www.epa.gov/compliance/ej/resources/reports/annual-project-reports/reducing_risk_com_vol2.pdf.

26 Rolf Pendall, "Local Land Use Regulation and the Chain of Exclusion," *Journal of the American Planning Association* 66, no. 2 (2000): 125–42; Marc Settles, "The Perpetuation of Residential Racial Segregation in America: Historical Discrimination, Modern Forms of Exclusion, and Inclusionary Remedies," *Journal of Land Use and Environmental Law* 14, no. 1 (1998): 89-124.

27 Stanley Lebergott, "Wages and Working Conditions," in *Fortune Encyclopedia of Economics* (New York: Warner Books, 1993), available at http://www.econlib.org/library/Enc1/WagesandWorkingConditions.html.

28 W. E. B. Du Bois, *Black Reconstruction: An Essay toward a History of the Part which Black Folk Played in the Attempt to Reconstruct Democracy in America 1860–1880* (New York: Harcourt, Brace and Co., 1935).

29 Susan Lynn Smith, *Sick and Tired of Being Sick and Tired: Black Women's Health Activism in America, 1890–1950* (Philadelphia: University of Pennsylvania Press 1995).

30 Nancy Krieger, "Embodying Inequality: A Review of Concepts, Measures, and Methods for Studying Health Consequences of Discrimination," *International Journal of Health Services* 29, no. 2 (1999): 295–352.

31 *Wong Wai v. Williamson*, 103 F. 1 (1900).

32 *Jew Ho v. Williamson*, 103 F. 10 (1900).

33 Natalia Molina, "Borders, Laborers, and Racialized Medicalization," *American Journal of Public Health* 101 (2011): 1024.

34 Ibid., 1026.

35 See Kevin Outterson, "Tragedy and Remedy: Reparations for Disparities in Black Health," *DePaul Journal of Health Care Law* 9 (2005): 735.

36 William H. Williams, "The Early Days of Anglo-America's First Hospital: The Pennsylvania Hospital, 1751–1775," *Journal of the American Medical Association* 220, no. 1 (April 3, 1972): 115–19.

37 163 U.S. 537 (1896).

38 See the "Hospital Discrimination in Detroit in the 1950s," special exhibit by Kellogg African American Health Care Project, originally created in 1995 at the University of Michigan, available at http://www.med.umich.edu/haahc/hospitals/special.htm (showing NAACP, Urban League, and grassroots organizations fighting to end discrimination in hospitals and drawing connections between higher mortality rates for blacks versus whites and the limited, segregated, inferior health services provided to blacks).

39 W. E. B. Dubois, "The Health and Physique of the Negro American," Eleventh Conference for the Study of the Negro Problems, Atlanta University, May 1906 (a systematic study of data on black and white health statistics written to contradict the assertion that inequalities in infant mortality, disease, and death were due to the biological inferiority of blacks).

40 *Johnson v. Crawfis*, 128 F.Supp. 230, 235 (#.D. Ark. 1955)

41 Ibid.

42 261 F.2d 521 (1958).

43 Importantly, since *Alexander v. Sandoval* was decided in 2001, three federal courts of appeals have held that no private cause of action is available to private litigants under 42 U.S.C. § 1983 to enforce Title VI's disparate impact regulations. This is despite the fact that the dissent in *Sandoval* expressly pointed out that private parties might still be able to sue under 42 U.S.C. § 1983 to enforce Title VI. See Christopher Dunn, "Time to Fix Civil Rights Act of 1965 Race Discrimination Protections," *New York Law Journal* 3 (February 2, 2009), (col 1), available at http://academic.udayton.edu/race/02rights/civilrights04.htm.

44 *Eaton v. Board of Managers of James Walker Memorial Hospital*, 261 F.2d 521, 522. See 42 U.S.C.A. §§ 1981, 1983.

45 323 F.2d 959 (1963).

46 45 C.F.R. Part 80 et seq.

47 297 F. Supp. 291 (M.D. Ala. 1969).

48 *Marable v. Alabama Mental Health Board*, 297 F.Supp. 291 (M.D. Ala. 1969).

49 *Atakpa v. Perimeter OB-GYN Assoc.*, 912 F.Supp. 1566 (N.D. Ga. 1994).

50 *United States v. Harris Methodist Fort Worth*, 970 F.2d 94 (5th Cir. 1992).

51 *Linton v. Commissioner of Health and Environment of Tennessee*, 65 F.3d 508 (6th Cir. 1995).

52 *Doe v. St. Joseph's Hospital*, 788 F.2d 411 (7th Cir 1986).

53 See, e.g., *National Association for Advancement of Colored People v. Medical Center, Inc.*, 599 F.2d 1247 (3rd Cir. 1979); *Bryan v. Koch*, 627 F.2d 612 (2nd Cir. 1980), *United States v. Bexar County*, 484 F.Supp. 855 (D.C. Tex. 1980).

54 627 F.2d 612 (2nd Cir. 1980).

55 491 F.Supp. 290 (1980).

56 David B. Smith, "The Racial Segregation of Hospital Care Revisited: Medicare Discharge Patterns and Their Implications," *American Journal of Public Health* 88 (1998): 461–63.

57 *Alexander v. Sandoval*, 532 U.S. 275 (2001).

58 David K. Hampton, "Title VI Challenges by Private Parties to the Location of Health Care Facilities: Toward a Just and Effective Action," *Boston College Law Review* 37 (1996): 517.

59 Vernella R. Randall, "Racial Discrimination in Health Care in the United States as a Violation of the International Convention on the Elimination of All Forms of Racial Discrimination," *University of Florida. Journal of Law and Public Policy* 14 (2002): 45, 72.

60 See *St. Joseph's Hosp. of Fort Wayne*, 788 F.2d 411, on remand 113 F.R.D. 677 (7th Cir. 1986).

61 80 F.3d 1121 (6th Cir. 1996).

62 Title VI still requires federally funded health care organizations to provide translated documents and skilled interpreters for non-English speaking patients. However, these provisions are seldom enforced. Some hospitals must still comply with the Hill-Burton community service obligation. Also, all fifty states have enacted civil rights provisions, and each state in the country has passed legislation that requires equal language access for non-English speaking patients in hospitals. However, as I will discuss later, the mere presence of laws on our "books" does not alone ensure these laws will be followed.

63 See chapter 3 for a detailed review of health disparities data.

64 Despite some progress in disparities such as life expectancy, there is data confirming widening health disparities in most measured categories; see chapter 8 for details.

65 Kathleen M. Harris et al., "Longitudinal Trends in Race/Ethnic Disparities in Leading Health Indicators from Adolescence to Young Adulthood," *Archives of Pediatric and Adolescent Medicine* 160, no. 1 (2006): 74–81.

66 Ibid., 76.

67 Carlos Blanco et al., "National Trends in Ethnic Disparities in Mental Health Care," *Medical Care* 45 (2007): 1012–19.

68 Ibid.

69 John F. Dovidio and Susan T. Fiske, "Under the Radar: How Unexamined Biases in Decision-Making Processes in Clinical Interactions Can Contribute to Health Care Disparities," *American Journal of Public Health* 102, no. 5 (2012): 945–52.

70 J. F. Dovidio and S. L. Gaertner, "Aversive Racism," in *Advances in Experimental Social Psychology*, ed. M. P. Zanna (San Diego: Academic Press, 2004), 36: 1–51.

71 Pew Research, Social and Demographic Trends, "King's Dream Remains an Elusive Goal; Many Americans See Racial Disparities," August 22, 2013, available at http://www.pewsocialtrends.org/2013/08/22/ kings-dream-remains-an-elusive-goal-many-americans-see-racial-disparities/.

72 The Henry J. Kaiser Family Foundation, "Race, Ethnicity, and Medical Care: A Survey of Public Perceptions and Experiences," September 30, 1999, available at http://kff.org/disparities-policy/poll-finding/race-ethnicity-medical-care-a-survey-of/.

CHAPTER 2. IMPLICIT BIAS AND HEALTH DISPARITIES

1 In preparation for writing this book, I spoke to scores of physicians, nurses, and former patients. While these conversations were not a part of any formal research project or protocol—for example, I did not record or transcribe every conversation, most people interviewed were friends or referred by friend, and I did not ask the same questions of everyone with whom I spoke—I did in each conversation ask about experiences with implicit bias. Also, for each conversation quoted in this book, I obtained written consent.

2 John F. Dovidio, Samuel L. Gaertner, and Keri Kawakami, "Implicit and Explicit Prejudice and Interracial Interaction," *Journal of Personality and Social Psychology* 82 (2002): 62.

3 K. Fiscella et al., "Inequality in Quality: Addressing Socioeconomic, Racial, and Ethnic Disparities in Health Care," *Journal of the American Medical Association* 283 (2000): 2579–84.

4 For example, physicians may reasonably take a patient's race into consideration to diagnose a disease more prevalent among members of that patient's racial group. Nothing can be wrong with a provider taking account of traditional cultural values when making the decision to enter or communicate a DNR order for a patient from a Chinese or Latino family whose culture values collaborative rather than individual medical decision-making at the end of life. These are examples of racial and ethnic distinctions that providers may appropriately introduce when exercising medical discretion. Yet, the use of negative racial and ethnic stereotypes and prejudices continues to occur and continues to contribute to inequities in health outcomes.

5 See E. G. Burchard et al., "The Importance of Race and Ethnic Background in Biomedical Research and Clinical Practice, *New England Journal of Medicine* 348, no. 12 (2003): 1170–75.

6 See N. Krieger, "Stormy Weather: Race, Gene Expression, and the Science of Health Disparities," *American Journal of Public Health* 95 (2005): 2155.

7 B. A. Nosek, M. R. Banaji, and A. G. Greenwald, "Harvesting Implicit Group Attitudes and Beliefs from a Demonstration Website," *Group Dynamics* 6, no. 1 (2002): 101–15.

8 Laurie A. Rudman, Richard D. Ashmore, and Melvin L. Gary, "'Unlearning' Automatic Biases: The Malleability of Implicit Prejudice and Stereotypes," *Journal of Personality and Social Psychology* 81 (2001): 856.

9 Ronald Deitsch, Bertram Gawronski, and Fritz Strack, "At the Boundaries of Automaticity: Negation as Reflective Operation," *Journal of Personality and Social Psychology* 91 (2006): 385.

10 M. W. Chee et al., "Dorsolateral Prefrontal Cortex and the Implicit Association of Concepts and Attributes," *Neuroreport* 11 (2000): 135.

11 See Charles M. Blow, "Newt Gingrich and the Art of Racial Politics," *New York Times,* January 17, 2012, available at http://campaignstops.blogs.nytimes. com/2012/01/17/newt-gingrich-and-the-art-of-racial-politics/.

12 See "What Did Rick Santorum Say? Welfare Comments Scrutinized," ABC News, January 3, 2012, available at http://abcnews.go.com/blogs/politics/2012/01/ what-did-rick-santorum-say-welfare-comments-scrutinized/.

13 United States Department of Agriculture, Food and Nutrition Service, "Characteristics of Supplemental Nutrition Assistance Program Households: Fiscal Year 2013" (Report No. SNAP-14-CHAR December 2014), available at http://www.fns. usda.gov/sites/default/files/ops/Characteristics2013.pdf.

14 Ibid.

15 United States Department of Health and Human Services, "2013 CMS Statistics," available at: http://www.cms.gov/Research-Statistics-Data-and-Systems/Statistics-Trends-and-Reports/CMS-Statistics-Reference-Booklet/Downloads/ CMS_Stats_2013_final.pdf.

16 United States Department of Agriculture, Food and Nutrition Service, "Characteristics of Supplemental Nutrition Assistance Program Households: Fiscal Year 2013," Report No. SNAP-14-CHAR, Washington, DC, December 2014, available at http://www.fns.usda.gov/sites/default/files/ops/Characteristics2013.pdf.

17 See, e.g., Charles R. Berg, "Stereotyping in Films in General and of the Hispanic in Particular," *Howard Journal of Communications* 2, no. 3 (1990) 286–300; Linda P. Rouse and Jeffery R. Hanson, "American Indian Stereotyping, Resource Competition, and Status-Based Prejudice," *American Indian Culture and Research Journal* 15, no. 3 (1991): 1–17; Yuki Fujioka, "Television Portrayals and African-American Stereotypes: Examination of Television Effects when Direct Contact Is Lacking," *Journalism and Mass Communication Quarterly* 76, no. 1 (1999): 52–75.

18 For a discussion of other measures of implicit attitudes and the prevalent use of the IAT, see Kristin A. Lane et al., "Understanding and Using the Implicit Association Test: IV," in *Implicit Measures of Attitudes*, ed. Bernd Wittenbrink and Norbert Schwarz (New York: Guilford Press 2007), 59–102.

19 Janice Sabin et al., "Physicians' Implicit and Explicit Attitudes about Race by MD Race, Ethnicity, and Gender," *Journal of Health Care for the Poor and Undeserved* 20 (2009): 896–913.

20 Ibid., 901. Gender preferences seen among MD test-takers was similar for JD and PhD test-takers; however, JDs and PhDs showed weaker preferences for whites over blacks than physicians.

21 Ibid., 906.

22 Gregory Mitchell and Philip Tetlock, "Antidiscrimination Law and the Perils of Mindreading," *Ohio State Law Journal* 67 (2006): 1023.

23 See Samuel R. Bagenstos, "Implicit Bias, 'Science,' and Antidiscrimination Law," *Harvard Law and Policy Review* 1 (Summer 2007): 477.

24 See Anthony G. Greenwald and Linda Hamilton Krieger, "Implicit Bias: Scientific Foundations," *California Law Review* 94 (July 2006): 945.

25 However, researchers point out that understanding automatic stereotyping was a logical extension of "a century's worth of research on perception, memory, and learning" that established the cognitive principle that knowledge is organized in a person's memory by virtue of associations based on personal experiences, societal norms, and familiar procedures. See John Jost et al., "The Existence of Implicit Bias Is Beyond Reasonable Doubt: A Refutation of Ideological and Methodological Objections and Executive Summary of Ten Studies that No Manager Should Ignore," *Research in Organizational Behavior* 29 (2009): 39–69.

26 Other methodologies for measuring implicit bias include cognitive accessibility, which is based on subliminal priming; semantic priming, which evaluates the speed and efficiency of the linkage of social attitudes to semantically related concepts; and evaluative (or sequential) priming, which exposes study participants to photographs and then asks them to categorize subsequent words as either positive or negative.

27 Robert J. Smith and Justin D. Levinson, "The Impact of Implicit Racial Bias on the Exercise of Prosecutorial Discretion," *Seattle University Law Review* 35 (2012): 795.

28 Ian F. Haney-Lopez, "Intentional Blindness," *New York University Law Review* 87 (2012): 1779.

29 Jonathan C. Ziegert and Paul J. Hanges, "Employment Discrimination: The Role of Implicit Attitudes, Motivation, and a Climate for Racial Bias," *Journal of Applied Psychology* 90 (2005): 553–62.

30 Todd Rudd, "Racial Disproportionality in School Discipline—Implicit Bias Is Heavily Implicated," *Kirwan Institute Issue Brief* (Columbus: Ohio State University, February 2014).

31 Joshua Correll et al., "Across the Thin Blue Line: Police Officers and Racial Bias in the Decision to Shoot," *Journal of Personality and Social Psychology* 92 (2007): 1006–23.

32 Justin D. Levinson, Robert J. Smith, and Danielle Young, "Devaluing Death: An Empirical Study of Implicit Racial Bias on Jury-Eligible Citizens in Six Death Penalty States," *New York University Law Review* 89 (2014): 513–79.

33 Kurt Hugenberg and Galen V. Bodenhausen, "Facing Prejudice: Implicit Prejudice and the Perception of Facial Threat," *Psychological Science* 14 (2003): 640–43.

34 Laurie Rudman, "The Validity of the Implicit Association Test Is a Scientific Certainty," *Industrial and Organizational Psychology* 1 (2008): 426–29.

35 Laurie A. Rudman, "Sources of Implicit Attitudes," *Current Directions in Psychological Science* 13 (2004): 79–82.

36 Gregory Mitchell and Philip E. Tetlock, "Antidiscrimination Law and the Perils of Mindreading," *Ohio State Law Journal* 67 (2006): 1023.

37 See Jost et al., "The Existence of Implicit Bias is Beyond Reasonable Doubt."

38 Thu Quach et al., "Experiences and Perceptions of Medical Discrimination among a Multiethnic Sample of Breast Cancer Patients in the Greater San Francisco Bay Area, California," *American Journal of Public Health* 102, no. 5 (March 12, 2012): 1027–34.

CHAPTER 3. PHYSICIANS' UNCONSCIOUS RACISM

1 Brian D. Smedley et al., *Unequal Treatment: Confronting Racial and Ethnic Disparities in Health Care* (Washington, DC: National Academies Press, 2003).

2 Contessa Fincher et al., "Racial Disparities in Coronary Heart Disease: A Sociological View of the Medical Literature on Physician Bias," *Ethnicity and Disease* 14 (Summer 2004): 360–71.

3 Pamela Sankar et al., "Genetic Research and Health Disparities," *Journal of the American Medical Association* 291 (2004): 2985.

4 Vilma E. Cokkinides et al., "Racial and Ethnic Disparities in Smoking Interventions," *American Journal of Preventative Medicine* 34 (2008): 404.

5 Donald H. Gemson et al., "Difference in Physician Prevention Practice Patterns for White and Minority Patients," *Journal of Community Health* 13 (1988): 53.

6 Ashish K. Jha et al., "Differences in Medical Care and Disease Outcomes among Black and White Women with Heart Disease," *Circulation* 108 (2003): 1089.

7 Ali F. Sonel et al., "Racial Variations in Treatment and Outcomes of Black and White Patients with High-Risk Non-ST-Elevation Acute Coronary Syndromes," *Circulation* 111 (2005): 1225.

8 Edward L. Hannan et al., "Access to Coronary Artery Bypass Surgery by Race/Ethnicity and Gender among Patients Who Are Appropriate for Surgery," *Medical Care* 37 (1999): 68.

9 Katherine L. Kahn, "Health Care for Black and Poor Hospitalized Medicare Patients," *Journal of the American Medical Association* 271 (1994): 1169.

10 See, e.g., John Z. Ayanian, "Determinants of Racial and Ethnic Disparities in Surgical Care," *World Journal of Surgery* 32 (2008): 509; Stuart E. Sheifer et al., "Race and Sex Differences in the Management of Coronary Artery Disease," *American Heart Journal* 139 (2000): 848.

11 Michelle van Ryn et al., "Physicians' Perceptions of Patients' Social and Behavioral Characteristics and Race Disparities in Treatment Recommendations for Men with Coronary Artery Disease," *American Journal of Public Health* 96 (2006): 351.

12 Michelle van Ryn and Jane Burke, "The Effect of Patient Race and Socioeconomic Status on Physicians' Perceptions of Patients," *Social Science and Medicine* 50 (2000): 813.

13 Black Americans are at substantially greater risk for end-stage renal disease (ESRD) than white Americans; they represent one third of all ESRD patients, but only 12 percent of the total U.S. population.

14 John Z. Ayanian, "Determinants of Racial and Ethnic Disparities in Surgical Care," *World Journal of Surgery* 34, no. 4 (2008): 509–15.

15 Michelle van Ryn, "Research on the Provider Contribution to Race/Ethnicity Disparities in Medical Care," *Medical Care* 40, no. 1 (2002): 1–140.

16 See, e.g., L. Ebony Boulware et al., "Preferences, Knowledge, Communication and Patient-Physician Discussion of Living Kidney Transplantation in African American Families," *American Journal of Transplantation* 5 (2005): 1503.

17 See, e.g., Alexander K. Smith et al., "Racial/Ethnic Disparities in Liver Transplant Surgery and Hospice Use: Parallels, Differences, and Unanswered Questions," *American Journal of Hospice and Palliative Medicine* 25 (2008): 285.

18 Elisa J. Gordon et al., "Disparities in Kidney Transplant Outcomes: A Review," *Seminars in Nephrology* 30 (2010): 81.

19 Karen Yeates et al., "Similar Outcomes among Black and White Renal Allograft Recipients," *Journal of American Social Nephrology* 20 (2009): 172.

20 Peter B. Bach et al., "Survival of Blacks and Whites after a Cancer Diagnosis," *Journal of the American Medical Association* 287, no. 16 (2002): 2106.

21 Taylor S. Riall, "Dissecting Racial Disparities in the Treatment of Patients with Locoregional Pancreatic Cancer: A Two-Step Process," *Cancer* 116 (2010): 930.

22 Nina A. Bickell et al., "Missed Opportunities: Racial Disparities in Adjuvant Breast Cancer Treatment," *Journal of Clinical Oncology* 24 (2006): 1357.

23 For example, in a study sponsored by the National Cancer Institute, survival rates for blacks and whites with colon, breast, uterus, and bladder cancer found that poorer rates persisted for blacks with all four types of cancer, even after adjusting for clinical and socioeconomic characteristics. Agency for Health Care Research and Quality, "Blacks Have Worse Colorectal Cancer Survival Rates than Whites," March 2011, available at http://www.ahrq.gov/news/newsletters/research-activities/mar11/0311RA19.html; Richard M. Elledge et al., "Tumor Biologic Factors and Breast Cancer Prognosis among White, Hispanic, and Black Women in the United States," *Journal of the National Cancer Institute* 86, no. 9 (1999): 705–12; Kathleen Settle et al., "Racial Survival Disparity in Head and Neck Cancer Results from Low Prevalence of Human Papillomavirus Infection in Black Oropharyngeal Cancer Patients," *Cancer Prevention Research* 2, no. 9 (2009): 776–81.

24 Bach et al., "Survival of Blacks and Whites after a Cancer Diagnosis."

25 Paula Diehr et al., "Treatment Modality and Quality Differences for Black and White Breast-Cancer Patients Treated in Community Hospitals," *Medical Care* 27 (1989):

26 Carrie N. Klabunde, "Trends and Black/White Differences in Treatment for Nonmetastatic Prostate Cancer," *Medical Care* 36 (1998): 1337.

27 See Vickie L. Shavers et al., "Racial and Ethnic Disparities in the Receipt of Cancer Treatment," *Journal of the National Cancer Institute* 94 (2002): 334; James A. Lee et al., "Medicare Treatment Differences for Blacks and Whites," *Medical Care* 35 (1997): 1173.

28 Peter B. Bach et al., "Differences in the Treatment of Early-Stage Lung Cancer," *New England Journal Medicine* 341 (1999): 1198.

29 See Smedley et al., *Unequal Treatment.*

30 Institute of Medicine, Committee on Advancing Pain Research, Care, and Education, "Pain as a Public Health Challenge," in *Relieving Pain in America: A Blueprint for Transforming Prevention, Care, Education, and Research* (Washington, DC: National Academies Press, 2011), 55–111, available at http://www.ncbi.nlm.nih.gov/books/NBK92516/.

31 Tiffani J. Johnson et al., "Association of Race and Ethnicity with Management of Abdominal Pain in the Emergency Department," *Pediatrics* 132, no. 4 (2013): e851–58, available at: http://pediatrics.aappublications.org/content/132/4/e851.full.pdf.

32 Edwin D. Boudreaux, "Race/Ethnicity and asthma Among Children Presenting to the Emergency Department: Differences in Disease Severity and Management," *Pediatrics* 111 (2003): e615.

33 But cf. Tracy A. Lieu et al., "Racial/Ethnic Variation in Asthma Status and Management Practices among Children in Managed Medicaid," *Pediatrics* 109 (2002): 857 (disease management processes of asthma equal to whites or better for minorities).

34 Genevieve M. Kenney et al., *Racial and Ethnic Differences in Access to Care and Service Use for Children with Coverage through Medicaid and the Children's Health Insurance Program* (Washington, DC: Urban Institute, 2013), 12.

35 Smedley et al., *Unequal Treatment*, 64.

36 See, e.g., D. E. Fleck et al. "Differential Prescription of Maintenance Antipsychotics to African American and White Patients with New-Onset Bipolar Disorder," *Journal of Clinical Psychiatry* 63 (2002): 658.

37 T. S. Durazzo et al., "Influence of Race on the Management of Lower Extremity Ischemia: Revascularization vs. Amputation," *Journal of the American Medical Association* 148 (2013): 617.

38 Benjamin Le Cook et al., "Measuring Trends in Racial/Ethnic Health Care Disparities, *Medical Care Research and Review* 66, no. 1 (February 2009): 23–48.

39 Ibid., 33.

40 Ibid., 1–25.

41 Ibid., 20.

42 Kevin A. Schulman, Jesse A. Berlin, and Jose J. Escarce, "Correspondence—Race, Sex, and Physicians' Referrals for Cardiac Catheterization," *New England Journal of Medicine* 341 (1999): 285–87.

43 But note that the African American physicians studied did not show a demonstrable implicit race bias for or against either their black or white patients. See Alexander R. Green et al., "Implicit Bias among Physicians and Its Prediction of Thrombolysis Decisions for Black and White Patients," *Journal of Internal Medicine* (2007): 1231–38.

44 Ibid., 1235.

45 Diana Burgess et al., "Patient Race and Physicians' Decisions to Prescribe Opioids for Chronic Low Back Pain," *Social Science and Medicine* 67 (2008): 1853.

46 See Hal R. Arkes and Neal V. Dawson, "Race-Based Bias in Physician Decision Making," presented to Society for Judgment and Decision-Making, November 2008. However, another criticism raised by Arkes and Dawson is legitimate. These researchers point out that Green failed to describe criteria for the appropriateness of thrombolysis as a treatment for African American patients especially since racial differences between patients may represent real epidemiological or clinical differences. Indeed, Green did not examine the reasons behind physicians' decisions. Yet this omission has little bearing on the relationship between bias and treatment that Green did examine and find.

47 Janice A. Sabin and Anthony G. Greenwald, "The Influence of Implicit Bias on Treatment Recommendations for Four Common Pediatric Conditions: Pain, Urinary Tract Infection, Attention Deficit Hyperactivity Disorder, and Asthma," *American Journal of Public Health* (May 2012).

48 Gordon B. Moskowitz, Jeff Stone, and Amanda Childs, "Implicit Stereotyping and Medical Decisions: Unconscious Stereotype Activation in Practitioners' Thoughts about African Americans," *American Journal of Public Health* 102, no. 5 (2012): 996–1001.

49 Ibid., 1000.

50 Ibid.

51 Adil H. Haider et al., "Association of Unconscious Race and Social Class Bias with Vignette-Based Clinical Assessments by Medical Students," *Journal of the American Medical Association* 306, no. 9 (September 7, 2011): 942–51.

52 Irene V. Blair et al., "An Investigation of Associations between Clinicians' Ethnic or Racial Bias and Hypertension Treatment, Medication Adherence, and Blood Pressure Control," *Journal of General Internal Medicine* 29, no. 7 (2014): 987–95.

53 Joseph Ravenell and Gbenga Ogedegbe, "Unconscious Bias and Real-World Hypertension Outcomes: Advancing Disparities Research," *Journal of General Internal Medicine* 29, no. 7 (2014): 973–75.

54 Smedley et al., *Unequal Treatment*, 166.

CHAPTER 4. FROM IMPRESSIONS TO INEQUITY

1 Brian D. Smedley et al., *Unequal Treatment: Confronting Racial and Ethnic Disparities in Health Care* (Washington, DC: National Academies Press, 2003), 166.

2 See, Jackie Green, "The Role of Theory in Evidence-Based Health Promotion Practice," *Health Education Research* 15 (2000): 125–29, for support of the view that "without reference to . . . theoretical principles we risk being submerged by a post-modern morass of empirical evidence, which, on its own can do little to guide practice" (125).

3 My Biased Care Model builds upon on the excellent work and hypotheses presented in Michelle van Ryn, "Research on the Provider Contribution to Race/Ethnicity Disparities in Medical Care," *Medical Care*, 40, no. 1, supplement (2002): I-140–51, and in Irene V. Blair, John F. Steiner, and Edward P. Havranek, "Unconscious (Implicit) Bias and Health Disparities: Where Do We Go from Here?" *Permanent Journal* 15, no. 2 (Spring 2011): 71.

4 I further identify implicit racial and ethnic bias as a meta-mechanism that operationalizes discrimination in this model. See Bruce G. Link and Jo Phelan, "Social Conditions as Fundamental Causes of Disease," *Journal of Health and Social Behavior* 35 (1995): 80–94.

5 Richard L. Street, Jr., Howard Gordon, and Paul Haidet, "Physicians' Communication and Perceptions of Patients: Is It How They Look, How They Talk, or Is It Just the Doctor?" *Social Science and Medicine* 65 (2007): 586.

6 John F. Dovidio and Susan T. Fiske, "Under the Radar: How Unexamined Biases in Decision-Making Processes in Clinical Interactions Can Contribute to Health Care Disparities," *American Journal of Public Health* 102, no. 5 (2012): 945–52.

7 Scott K. Aberegg and Peter B. Terry, "Medical Decision-Making and Healthcare Disparities: The Physician's Role," *Translational Research* 144, no. 1 (2004): 11–17.

8 P. R. Reilly, *The Surgical Solution: A History of Involuntary Sterilization in the United States* (Baltimore: John Hopkins University Press, 1991).

9 Gordon B. Moskowitz et al., "Implicit Stereotyping and Medical Decisions: Unconscious Stereotype Activation in Practitioners' Thoughts about African-Americans," *American Journal of Public Health* 102 (2012): 999.

10 Michelle van Ryn and Jane Burke, "The Effect of Patient Race and Socio-Economic Status on Physicians' Perceptions of Patients," *Social Science and Medicine* 50 (2000): 813–28.

11 Diana J. Burgess et al., "Patient Race and Physicians' Decisions to Prescribe Opioids for Chronic Low Back Pain," *Social Science and Medicine* 67 (2008): 1852–60.

12 See, e.g., J. L. Eberhardt et al. "Looking Death Worthy: Perceived Stereotypicality of Black Defendants Predicts Capital-Sentencing Outcomes," *Psychological Science* 17 (2006): 383–86; J. L. Eberhardt, "Imaging Race," *American Psychologist* 60 (2005): 181–90; J. L. Eberhardt et al., "Seeing Black: Race, Crime, and Visual Processing," *Journal of Personality and Social Psychology* 87 (2004): 876–93.

13 See Janice A Sabin et al. "Physicians' Implicit and Explicit Attitudes about Race by MD Race, Ethnicity, and Gender," *Journal of Health Care for the Poor and Underserved* 20 (2009): 896–913.

14 Ibid. Like the Penner study, this research presents a sampling concern in that the participants were volunteers rather than randomly chosen. Therefore, the group's diversity is only with respect to what you can see and measure as diverse; socioeconomic diversity may or may not be present in this sample. Therefore, inferences from this study can be made based only on the people who agreed to take the tests.

15 Sabin et al., "Physicians' Implicit and Explicit Attitudes about Race," 906.

16 See Janice A. Sabin et al., "Physician Implicit Attitudes and Stereotypes about Race and Quality of Medical Care," *Medical Care* 46, no. 7 (July 2008): 678–85.

17 Van Ryn and Jane, "The Effect of Patient Race and Socioeconomic Status on Physicians' Perceptions of Patients."

18 Ibid., 823.

19 See A. H. Haider et al., "Association of Unconscious Race and Social Class Bias with Vignette-Based Clinical Assessments by Medical Students," *Journal of the American Medical Association* 306, no. 9 (September7, 2011): 942–51.

20 Shelley White-Means et al. "Cultural Competency, Race, and Skin Tone Bias among Pharmacy, Nursing, and Medical Students: Implications for Addressing Health Disparities," *Medical Care Research and Review* 66 (2009): 436–55.

21 Sadly, White-Means did not study the same students throughout the three year period of her research. This means that the differences she failed to find over time may represent only the fact that she tested different groups of students with different levels of bias. But her results cannot properly be read to say anything about how students' biases changed over time. Moreover, the researchers in this study changed the alpha values for significance when showing their T-test results for the measures of bias White-Means reported.

22 White-Means, "Cultural Competency, Race, and Skin Tone Bias," 441.

23 See Adil Haider, "Association of Unconscious Race and Social Class Bias by Medical Students," *Journal of the American Medical Association* 306 (2011): 942–51.

24 Ibid.

25 See generally, Ana I. Balsa and Thomas G. McGuire, "Statistical Discrimination in Health Care," *Journal of Health Economics* 20 (2001): 881–907.

26 See Ana I. Balsa, Thomas G. McGuire, and Lisa S. Meredith, "Testing for Statistical Discrimination in Health Care," *Health Services Research* 40, no. 1 (February 2005): 227–52.

27 Ibid., 231.

28 Brian Rubineau and Yoon Kang, "Bias in White: A Longitudinal Natural Experiment Measuring Changes in Discrimination," *Management Science*, November 4, 2011, 1–18.

29 Thomas G. McGuire et al., "Testing for Statistical Discrimination by Race/Ethnicity in Panel Data for Depression Treatment in Primary Care," *Health Services Research* 43, no. 2 (2008): 531–51.

30 Diana J. Burgess, Steven S. Fu, and Michelle van Ryn, "Why Do Providers Contribute to Disparities and What Can Be Done about It?" *Journal of General Internal Medicine* 19 (2004): 1154–59.

31 Rubineau and Kang, "Bias in White," 3.

32 Balsa, McGuire, and Meredith, "Testing for Statistical Discrimination," 248–49.

CHAPTER 5. IMPLICIT BIAS DURING THE CLINICAL ENCOUNTER

1 See, e.g., Rachel L. Johnson et al., "Patient Race/Ethnicity and Quality of Patient-Physician Communication During Medical Visits," *American Journal of Public Health* 94, no. 12 (2004): 2084–90; Lisa A. Cooper et al., "Patient-Centered Communication, Ratings of Care, and Concordance of Patient and Physician Race," *Annals of Internal Medicine* 139 (2003): 907–15.

2 Lisa A. Cooper et al., "The Associations of Clinicians' Implicit Attitudes about Race with Medical Visit Communication and Patient Ratings of Interpersonal Care," *American Journal of Public Health* 102, no. 5 (2012): 979–87.

3 Ibid. See also Richard L. Street et al., "How Does Communication Heal? Pathways Linking Clinican-Patient Communication to Health Outcomes," *Patient Education and Counseling* 74, no. 3 (2009): 295–301; Moira A. Stewart, "Effective Physician-Patient Communication and Health Outcomes: A Review," *Canadian Medical Association Journal* 152, no. 9 (1995): 1423–33.

4 Diana Burgess, Steven S. Fu, and Michelle van Ryn, "Why Do Providers Contribute to Disparities and What Can Be Done about It?" *Journal of General Internal Medicine* 19 (2004): 1156.

5 Elizabeth M. Hooper et al., "Patient Characteristics that Influence Physician Behavior," *Medical Care* 20 (1982): 630–38.

6 Hooper did find that the nonverbal attention, courtesy, and information content did not vary significantly by ethnicity.

7 Rachel L. Johnson et al., "Patient Race/Ethnicity and Quality of Patient-Physician Communication during Medical Visits," *American Journal of Public Health* 94, no. 12 (2004): 2084–90.

8 Moria Stewart et al., "The Impact of Patient-Centered Care on Outcomes," *Journal of Family Practice* 49, no. 9 (September 2000): 796–804.

9 Johnson et al., "Patient Race/Ethnicity and Quality of Patient-Physician Communication," 2087.

10 Warren Ferguson and Lucy Candib, "Culture, Language, and the Doctor-Patient Relationship," *Family Medicine* 35, no. 4 (2002): 353–61.

11 Klea Bertakis et al., "Physician Practice Styles and Patient Outcomes: Differences between Family Practice and General Internal Medicine," *Medical Care* 36, no. 6 (1998): 879–91.

12 Howard S. Gordon et al., "Racial Differences in Trust and Lung Cancer Patients' Perceptions of Physician Communication," *Journal of Clinical Oncology* 24, no. 6 (February 20, 2006): 904–9.

13 Ibid., 907. See also C. M. Ashton et al., "Racial and Ethnic Disparities in the Use of Health Services: Bias, Preferences, or Poor Communication?" *Journal of General Internal Medicine* 18 (2003): 146–52.

14 Ibid.

15 Jonathan Klick and Sally Satel, *The Health Disparities Myth—Diagnosing the Treatment Gap* (Washington, DC: American Enterprise Institute for Public Policy Research, 2006).

16 H. S. Gordon, D. A. Paterniti, and N. P. Wray, "Race and Patient Refusal of Invasive Cardiac Procedures," *Journal of General Internal Medicine,* 19 (2004): 962–66; S. S. Rathore, D. L. Ordin, and H. M. Krumholz, "Race and Sex Differences in the Refusal of Cardiac Catheterization among Elderly Patients Hospitalized with Acute Myocardial Infarction," *American Heart Journal* 144 (2002): 1052–56; J. Z. Ayanian et al., "The Effect of Patients' Preferences on Racial Differences in Access to Renal Transplantation," *New England Journal of Medicine* 341 (1999): 1661–69.

17 V. N. Gamble, "Under the Shadow of Tuskegee: African-Americans and Health Care," *American Journal of Public Health* 87 (1997): 1773–78.

18 T. L. Savitt, "Black Health on the Plantation: Owners, the Enslaved, and Physicians," *Organization of American Historians Magazine of History* 19, no. 5 (2005): 14–16.

19 H. Devlin et al., "Our Lives Were Healthier Before: Focus Groups with African American, American Indian, and Hmong People with Diabetes" *Health Promotion Practice* 7, no. 1 (2006): 47–55.

20 See Derald Wing Sue, *Microaggressions in Everyday Life: Race, Gender and Sexual Orientation* (Hoboken, NJ: John Wiley and Sons, 2010).

21 Judith Hall, Debra Roter, and Nancy Katz, "Meta-Analysis of Correlates of Provider Behavior in Medical Encounters," *Medical Care* 27, no. 7 (July 1988): 657–75.

22 Hooper et al., "Patient Characteristics that Influence Physician Behavior."

23 Howard S. Gordon et al., "Racial Differences in Doctors' Information-Giving and Patients' Participation," *Cancer* 107, no. 6 (August 14, 2006): 1313–20.

24 Louis Penner et al., "Aversive Racism and Medical Interactions with Black Patients: A Field Study," *Journal of Experimental Social Psychology* 46 (2010): 436–40.

25 Jennifer A. Richeson and Nalni Ambady, "Effects of Situational Power on Automatic Racial Prejudice," *Journal of Experimental Social Psychology* 39 (2003): 177–83.

26 Ibid., 181.

27 John F. Dovidio and Susan T. Fiske, "Under the Radar: How Unexamined Biases in Decision-Making Processes in Clinical Interactions Can Contribute to Health Care Disparities," *American Journal of Public Health* 102, no. 5 (2012): 945–52.

CHAPTER 6. IMPLICIT BIAS BEYOND THE CLINICAL ENCOUNTER

1 The classic oath is from National Institutes of Health, National Medical Library, History of Medicine Division, "Greek Medicine—the Hippocratic Oath" (2012), available at http://www.nlm.nih.gov/hmd/greek/greek_oath.html. A modern version is found at Johns Hopkins Sheridan Libraries, "Hippocratic Oath, Modern Version," (2014), available at http://guides.library.jhu.edu/content.php?pid=23699&sid=190964. However, neither version of the Oath is without controversy. To quote from the *Annals of Internal Medicine*, "For many residents, fatigue cultivates anger, resentment, and bitterness rather than kindness, compassion, or empathy" (Michael J. Green, "What [If Anything] Is Wrong with Residency Overwork?" *Annals of Internal Medicine* 123 [1995]: 512–17). How are we to provide compassionate care to others when our own educational system is the model of abuse? *Primum non nocere* indeed—the hypocrisy of this oath is that we can't even manage to muster non-maleficence to practitioners of our own profession, let alone our patients. For other examples of critique that the oath is outdated and irrelevant, see, PBS NOVA Online, "Hippocratic Oath Today: Doctors' Responses," 2001, message posted to http://www.pbs.org/wgbh/nova/doctors/oath_doctors.html.

2 Alexander R. Green et al., "Implicit Bias among Physicians and Its Prediction of Thrombolysis Decisions for Black and White Patients," *Journal of Internal Medicine* 22 (2007): 1231–38

3 Janice A. Sabin and Anthony G. Greenwald, "The Influence of Implicit Bias on Treatment Recommendations for Four Common Pediatric Conditions: Pain, Urinary Tract Infection, Attention Deficit Hyperactivity Disorder, and Asthma," *American Journal of Public Health* 102, no. 5 (May 2012): 988–95.

4 Irene V. Blair et al., "An Investigation of Associations between Clinicians' Ethnic or Racial Bias and Hypertension Treatment, Medication Adherence, and Blood Pressure Control," *Journal of General Internal Medicine* 29 (2014): 987.

5 Laura M. Bogart et al., "Factors Influencing Physicians' Judgments of Adherence and Treatment Decisions for Patients with HIV Disease," *Medical Decision Making* 21 (2001): 28–36.

6 U.S. Department of Health and Human Services, Agency for Healthcare Research and Quality, National Healthcare Disparities Report, 2006, AHRQ Publication No. 077-0012, Rockville, MD, December 2006, available at: http://archive.ahrq.gov/qual/nhdr06/nhdr06report.pdf. For updated data, see also, U.S. Department of Health and Human Services, Agency for Healthcare Research and Quality, National Healthcare Disparities Report, 2013, AHRQ Publication No. 14-006, Rockville, MD, May 2014, available at: http://www.ahrq.gov/research/findings/nhqrdr/nhdr13/2013nhdr.pdf.

7 P. B. Bach et al., "Primary Care Physicians Who Treat Blacks and Whites, *New England Journal of Medicine* 351, no. 6 (August 5, 2004): 575–84.

8 A. Donovan et al. "Two-Year Trends in the Use of Seclusion and Restraint among Psychiatrically Hospitalized Youths," *Psychiatric Services* 54, no. 7 (July 2003): 987–93.

9 Cathy J. Bradley et al., "Race, Socioeconomic Status, and Breast Cancer Treatment and Survival," *Journal of the National Cancer Institute* 94, no. 7 (2002): 490–96.

10 E. Bradley et al., "Racial and Ethnic Differences in Time to Acute Reperfusion Therapy for Patients Hospitalized with Myocardial Infarction," *Journal of the American Medical Association* 292, no. 13 (October 6, 2004): 1563–72.

11 Melissa M. Farmer et al., "Are Racial Disparities in Health Conditional on Socioeconomic Status?," *Social Science and Medicine* 60 (2005): 191–204.

12 T. A. LaVeist, "Disentangling Race and Socioeconomic Status: A Key to Understanding Health Inequalities," *Journal of Urban Health: Bulletin of the New York Academy of Medicine* 82, no. 2, supplement 3 (2005): 26–34.

13 David R. Williams, "Race, Socioeconomic Status, and Health: The Added Effects of Racism and Discrimination," *Annals of the New York Academy of Sciences* 896, no. 1 (1999): 173.

14 Michelle van Ryn and Steven S. Fu, "Paved with Good Intentions: Do Public Health Providers Contribute to Racial/Ethnic Disparities in Health? *American Journal of Public Health* 93 (2003): 248.

15 John F. Dovidio et al., "Disparities and Distrust: The Implications of Psychological Processes for Understanding Racial Disparities in Health and Health Care," *Social Science and Medicine* 67 (2008): 478.

16 Bruce G. Link and Jo Phelan, "Social Conditions as Fundamental Causes of Disease," *Journal of Health and Social Behavior* 35 (1995): 80–94.

17 David R. Williams and Toni D. Rucker, Understanding and Addressing Racial Disparities in Health Care," *Heath Care Financing Review* 21, no. 4 (2000): 75–90.

18 Karen Lutfey and Jeremy Freese, "Toward Some Fundamentals of Fundamental Causality: Socioeconomic Status and Health in the Routine Clinic Visit for Diabetes," *American Journal of Sociology* 110 (2005): 1326–72.

19 Ibid., 1330.

20 See, e.g., Scott E. Maxwell and Harold D. Delaney, *Designing Experiments and Analyzing Data* (New York: Psychology Press, Taylor & Francis Group, 2004) 9–10.

21 See Donald T. Campbell and Julian C. Stanley, *Experimental and Quasi-Experimental Designs for Research* (Chicago: Rand McNally College Publishing, 1977), 34–37.

22 Thu Quach et al., "Experiences and Perceptions of Medical Discrimination among a Multiethnic Sample of Breast Cancer Patients in the Greater San Francisco Bay Area, California," *American Journal of Public Health* 102, no. 5 (May 2012): 1027–34.

23 Pamela J. Sawyer et al., "Discrimination and the Stress Response: Psychological and Physiological Consequences of Anticipating Prejudice in Interethnic Interactions," *American Journal of Public Health* 102, no. 5 (May 2012): 1020–26.

24 L. Cooper-Patrick et al., "Race, Gender, and Partnership in the Patient-Physician Relationship," *Journal of the American Medical Association* 282 (1999): 583–89.

25 L. M. Cooper, et al., "Delving Below the Surface—Understanding How Race and Ethnicity Influence Relationships in Health Care," *Journal of General Internal Medicine* 21 (2006): S21–27.

26 Michelle van Ryn and Jane Burke, "The Effect of Patient Race and Socioeconomic Status on Physicians' Perceptions of Patients," *Social Science and Medicine* 50 (2000): 823.

27 Jaya K. Rao et al., "Visit-Specific Expectations and Patient-Centered Outcomes," *Family Medicine* 9 (November/December 2000): 1148–55.

28 Dara Sorkin et al., "Racial/Ethnic Discrimination in Health Care: Impact on Perceived Quality of Care," *Journal General Internal Medicine* 25, no. 5 (2010): 390–96.

29 Ibid. The study was based on the 2003 California Health Interview Survey (CHIS), a random-digit dial telephone survey in the state of California.

30 Ibid., 392.

31 See Louis Penner et al., "The Experience of Discrimination and Black-White Health Disparities in Medical Care," *Journal of Black Psychology* 35, no. 2 (May 2009): 180–203.

32 See Diana J. Burgess et al., "Understanding the Provider Contribution to Race/Ethnicity Disparities in Pain Treatment: Insights from Dual Process Models of Stereotyping" *Pain Medicine* 7, no. 2 (2006): 119. See also Vence L. Bonham, "Race, Ethnicity, and Pain Treatment: Striving to Understand the Causes and Solutions to the Disparities in Pain Treatment," *Journal of Law, Medicine, and Ethics* 52 (2001).

33 Burgess et al., "Understanding the Provider Contribution," 119, 123.

34 David Moskowitz et al., "Is Primary Care Providers' Trust in Socially Marginalized Patients Affected by Race?" *Journal of General Internal Medicine* 26, no. 8 (2011): 846–51.

35 Ibid.

36 See M. Crowley-Matoka, "Political and Moral Economies of Managing Pain," American Anthropological Association Annual Meeting (Washington, DC, 2005) (cited in Moskowitz, et al., "Is Primary Care Providers' Trust in Socially Marginalized Patients Affected by Race?"). See also M. Crowley-Matoka and Gala True, "No One Wants to Be the Candy Man: Ambivalent Medicalization and Clinician Subjectivity in Pain Management," *Cultural Anthropology* 27, no. 4 (November 2012): 689–712.

37 See Louis A. Penner et al., "Aversive Racism and Medical Interactions with Black Patients: A Field Study," *Journal of Experimental Social Psychology* 46 (2010): 436–40.

38 Thomas A. LaVeist et al., "Attitudes about Racism, Medical Mistrust, and Satisfaction with Care among African American and White Cardiac Patients," *Medical Care Research and Review* 7 (2000): 146.

39 Moira A. Stewart, "Effective Physician-Patient Communication and Health Outcomes: A Review," *Canadian Medical Association Journal* 152, no. 9 (1995) 1423–33

40 Burgess et al., "Understanding the Provider Contribution to Race/Ethnicity Disparities in Pain Treatment," 119.

CHAPTER 7. FROM INEQUITY TO INTERVENTION

1 Epigraph based on a clinical vignette in Alexander R. Green et al., "Implicit Bias among Physicians and Its Prediction of Thrombolysis Decisions for Black and White Patients," *Journal of Internal Medicine* 22 (2007): 1231–38.

2 See early studies by Daniel T. Gilbert and J.Gregory Hixon, "The Trouble of Thinking: Activation and Application of Stereotypic Beliefs," *Journal of Personality and Social Psychology* 60, no. 4 (1991): 509–17 (comparing the effect of cognitive busyness introduced before stereotype activation and after on Asian stereotypes); see also C. Neil Macrea et al., "Stereotypes as Energy-Saving Devices: A Peek Inside the Cognitive Toolbox," *Journal of Personality and Social Psychology* 66 (1994): 37–47 (including seminal experiment introducing the "ironic effect" that skinhead stereotypes strengthened following suppression).

3 Nilanjana Dasgupta and Shaki Angara, "Seeing Is Believing: Exposure to Counter-Stereotypic Women Leaders and Its Effect on the Malleability of Automatic Gender Stereotyping," *Journal of Experimental Social Psychology* 40 (2004): 642 (reviewing forty studies). See also Irene V. Blair, "The Malleability of Automatic Stereotypes and Prejudice," *Personality and Social Psychology Review* 6 (2002): 242 (citing fifty malleability studies in 2002).

4 See Alison P. Lenton, Martin Bruder, and Constantine Sedikides, "A Meta-Analysis on the Malleability of Automatic Gender Stereotypes," *Psychology of Women Quarterly* 33 (2008): 184.

5 Ibid.

6 For example, see John A. Bargh, Mark Chen, Lara Burrows, "Automaticity of Social Behavior: Direct Effects of Trait Construct and Stereotype Activation in Action," *Journal of Personality and Social Psychology* 771, no. 2 (1996): 230–44.

7 Patricia G. Devine, "Stereotypes and Prejudice: Their Automatic and Controlled Components," *Journal of Personality and Social Psychology* 56, no. 1 (1989): 5–18.

8 Irene Blair, "The Malleability of Automatic Stereotypes and Prejudice," *Personality and Social Psychology Review* 6 (2002): 256.

9 Ibid., 255.

10 Ana J. Balsa and T.G. McGuire, "Prejudice, Clinical Uncertainty, and Stereotyping as Sources of Health Disparities," *Journal of Health Economics* 22 (2003): 89–116.

11 Ibid. Devine, "Stereotypes and Prejudice," 16 (study 3 in which low-prejudice individuals chose non-prejudiced thoughts to record in contradiction to a list of stereotypes about blacks they had earlier generated).

12 Ibid., 15.

13 Joseph R. Betancourt et al., "Cultural Competence and Health Care Disparities: Key Perspectives and Trends," *Health Affairs* 24 (2005): 499.

14 See, e.g., Office of Minority Health website, http://minorityhealth.hhs.gov, which offers several certificate courses for health care providers to learn cultural competency. *The Physicians' Guide to Cultural Competency,* available at https://cccm.thinkcultural-health.hhs.gov/, provides an interactive online course that took me approximately two hours to complete. It contained important and accurate data about health disparities, case studies followed by "self-exploration" questions that ask about the responder's feelings, and aspirational goals for "respectful" and "equitable" care. The training includes no mention of implicit biases or automatic stereotypes, prejudices, beliefs, or attitudes of any kind.

15 Désirée A. Lie et al., "Does Cultural Competency Training of Health Professionals Improve Patient Outcomes? A Systematic Review and Proposed Algorithm for Future Research," *Journal of General Internal Medicine* 3 (2011): 317.

16 Kerry Kawakami et al., "Just Say No (to Stereotyping): Effects of Training in the Negation of Stereotype Associations on Stereotype Activation," *Journal of Personality and Social Psychology* 78, no. 5 (2000): 871–88.

17 Ibid., 884.

18 Ibid.

19 Laurie A. Rudman, Richard D. Ashmore, and Melvin L. Gary, "'Unlearning' Automatic Biases: The Malleability of Implicit Prejudice and Stereotypes," *Journal of Personality and Social Psychology* 8 (2001): 856 (these studies were quasi- experiments because participants were volunteers, not randomly selected or assigned).

20 The Lexical Decision Task (LDT) first exposes subjects to an event that is expected to activate a stereotype (e.g., a black man enters the room). Next, participants are shown a series of words and phrases that are non-words. The subjects must decide quickly whether each item is a word or a non-word. A faster response to stereotype words than to non-stereotypic attributes is defined as and measures an automatic stereotype.

21 See, e.g., Kerry Kawakami et al., "(Close) Distance Makes the Heart Grow Fonder: Improving Implicit Attitudes and Interracial Interactions through Approach Behaviors," *Journal of Personality and Social Psychology* 92 (2007): 957 (showing that individuals trained to approach rather than avoid blacks using a computer joystick showed significantly reduced implicit anti-black attitudes).

22 See, e.g., Roland Deutsch, Bertram Gawronski, and Fritz Strack, "At the Boundaries of Automaticity: Negation as Reflective Operation," *Journal of Personality and Social Psychology* 91 (2006): 385 (negation can change associative representations but procedural and rule-based negations are not effective while associative representations are).

23 See Karen Gonsalkorale et al., "Accounting for Successful Control of Implicit Racial Bias: The Roles of Association Activation, Response Monitoring, and Overcoming Bias," *Personality and Social Psychology Bulletin* 37 (2011): 1534 (showing that self-motivated individuals are more responsive to reducing implicit biases).

24 Nilanjana Dasgupta and Anthony Greenwald, "On the Malleability of Automatic Attitudes: Combating Automatic Prejudice with Images of Admired and Disliked Individuals," *Journal of Personality and Social Psychology* 81 (2001): 800.

25 Laurie A.Rudman, Richard D. Ashmore, Melvin L. Gary, "Unlearning Automatic Biases: The Malleability of Implicit Prejudice and Stereotypes," *Journal of Personality and Social Psychology* 81, no. 5 (2001): 856 (prejudice and conflict seminar taught by admired black professor).

26 Irene V. Blair, Jennifer E. Ma, and Allison P. Lenton, "Imagining Stereotypes Away: The Moderation of Implicit Stereotypes through Mental Imagery," *Journal of Personality and Social Psychology* 81 (2001): 828 (imagining strong women).

27 Claire Cullen et al., "The Implicit Relational Assessment Procedure (IRAP) and the Malleability of Ageist Attitudes," *Psychological Record* 49 (2009): 591.

28 Nilanjana Dasgupta, Shaki Asgari, "Seeing Is Believing: Exposure to Counterstereotypic Women Leaders and Its Effect on the Malleability of Automatic Gender Stereotyping," Journal of Experimental Social Psychology 40, no. 5 (2004): 642–58.

29 Ibid., 654.

30 Bernd Wittenbrink, Charles M. Judd, and Bernadette Park, "Spontaneous Prejudice in Context: Variability in Automatically Activated Attitudes," *Journal of Personality and Social Psychology* 81 (2001): 815. See also Bernd Wittenbrink et al., "Evaluative versus Conceptual Judgments in Automatic Stereotyping and Prejudice," *Journal of Experimental Social Psychology* 37 (2001): 244.

31 Irene V. Blair, Jennifer E. Ma, Alison P. Lenton, "Imagining Stereotypes Away: The Moderation of Implicit Stereotypes through Mental Imagery," *Journal of Personality and Social Psychology* 81, no. 5 (2001): 828.

32 The fourth experiment used a "Go/No-Go Association Test" (GNAT), which works to examine implicit associations within a single category instead of between categories as the IAT does. The fifth experiment used a Deese-Roediger-McDermott (DRM) false memory paradigm that is a well-recognized memory association test of implicit attitudes.

33 Gregory Mitchell and Philip E. Tetlock, "Antidiscrimination Law and the Perils of Mindreading," *Ohio State Law Journal* 67 (2006): 1023–21.

34 Brian S. Lowery, Curtis D. Hardin, and Stacey Sinclair, "Social Influence Effects on Automatic Racial Prejudice," *Journal of Personality and Social Psychology* 81 (2001): 842.

35 See, e.g., David M. Amodio, Eddie Harmon-Jones, and Patricia G. Devine, "Individual Differences in the Activation and Control of Affective Race Bias as Assessed by Startle Eyeblink Response and Self Report," *Journal of Personality and Social Psychology* 84 (2003): 738–53; see also Gordon Moskowitz et al., "Preconscious

Control of Stereotype Activation through Chronic Egalitarian Goals," *Journal of Personality and Social Psychology* 77, (1999): 167.

36 Gretchen B. Sechrist and Charles Stangor, "Perceived Consensus Influences Intergroup Behavior and Stereotype Accessibility," *Journal of Personality and Social Psychology* 80 (2001): 645

37 Ibid., 651.

38 See Rudman, Ashmore, and Gary, "Unlearning Automatic Biases," 856–57.

39 Diana Burgess et al., "Reducing Racial Bias among Health Care Providers: Lessons from Social Cognitive Psychology," *Society of General Internal Medicine* 22 (2007): 882.

40 Terence M. Davidson and Christopher P. Guzelian, "Evidence-Based Medicine (EBM): The (Only) Means for Distinguishing Knowledge of Medical Causation from Expert Opinion in the Courtroom," unpublished manuscript (on file with author).

41 See, e.g., Ray Pawson et al., "Realist Review—A New Method of Systematic Review Designed for Complex Policy Interventions," *Journal of Health Services Research and Policy* 10, supplement 1 (2005): 21–34.

42 See Brian S. Lowery, Curtis D. Hardin, and Stacey Sinclair, "Social Influence Effects on Automatic Racial Prejudice," *Journal of Personality and Social Psychology* 81, no. 5 (2001): 842–55.

43 Jennifer A. Joy-Gaba and Brian A. Nosek, "The Surprisingly Limited Malleability of Implicit Racial Evaluation," *Social Psychology* 41 (2010): 137.

44 Joy-Gaba and Nosek increased the number and types of exposures, as well as the prior day-to-day familiarity study participants had with the people in photographs. They added photographs of admired whites to their study and had participants complete their studies online as well as in laboratories. Although Joy-Gaba and Nosek did see reductions in implicit racial biases in two of their experiments, their results were not as robust as prior studies. Their third study showed no reduction in implicit biases. Yet it would be foolish to generalize from these three experiments that varied numerous factors pertaining to counter-stereotypes in laboratory experiments. The "surprising" limits these researchers found are limited to the laboratory conditions they produced.

45 Alden P. Gregg, Beate Seibt, and Mahzarin R. Banaji, "Easier Done than Undone: Asymmetry in the Malleability of Implicit Preferences," *Journal of Personality and Social Psychology* 90 (2006): 1.

46 H. Anna Han et al., "Malleability of Attitudes or Malleability of the IAT?," *Journal of Experimental Social Psychology* 46 (2010): 286.

47 Laurie A. Rudman, "The Validity of the Implicit Association Test Is a Scientific Certainty," *Industrial and Organizational Psychology* 1 (2008): 426.

CHAPTER 8. A STRUCTURAL SOLUTION

1 Thurgood Marshall, Liberty Medal Acceptance Speech, National Constitution Center, Independence Hall, Philadelphia, July 4, 1992,, available at http://constitution-center.org/libertymedal/recipient_1992_speech.html.

2 For Niebuhr's own account of his authorship of this prayer, see Reinhold Niebuhr, "Epilogue: A View of Life from the Sidelines," in *The Essential Reinhold Niebuhr: Selected Essays and Addresses*, ed. Robert McAfee Brown (New Haven, CT: Yale University Press, 1986).

3 Thomas R. Frieden, "A Framework for Public Health Action: The Health Impact Pyramid," *American Journal of Public Health* 100, no. 4 (April 2010): 590–95.

4 See Elisabeth Rosenthal, "Pre-Med's New Priorities: Heart and Soul and Social Science," *New York Times*, April 13, 2012, available at http://www.nytimes.com/2012/04/15/education/edlife/pre-meds-new-priorities-heart-and-soul-and-social-science.html?_r=0.

5 John F. Dovidio and Susan T. Fiske, "Under the Radar: How Unexamined Biases in Decision-Making Processes in Clinical Interactions Can Contribute to Health Care Disparities," *American Journal of Public Health* 102, no. 5 (2012): 945–52 (more work bridging psychology literature and medical practice needed).

6 See, e.g., Alexander Green, "Implicit Bias among physicians and Its Prediction of Thrombolysis Decisions for Black and White Patients," *Journal of Internal Medicine* 22 (2007): 1231–38 (new approaches to disparities might include confidentially making physicians aware of their privately administered IAT results).

7 Cf. Lisa Cooper et al., "The Associations of Clinicians' Implicit Attitudes about Race with Medical Visit Communication and Patient Ratings of Interpersonal Care," *American Journal of Public Health* 102 (2012): 979–87 (health professionals can serve as influential advocates for social justice by opening discourse about bias in health care).

8 Bernd Wittenbrink, Charles M. Judd, and Bernadette Park, "Evidence for Racial Prejudice at the Implicit Level and Its Relationship with Questionnaire Measures *Journal of Personality and Social Psychology* 72 (1997): 262.

9 Dovidio and Fiske, "Under the Radar," 102.

10 Gordon B. Moskowitz et al., "Implicit Stereotyping and Medical Decisions: Unconscious Stereotype Activation in Practitioners' Thoughts about African-Americans," *American Journal of Public Health* 102 (2012): 996.

11 U.S. Department of Health and Human Services, Office of Minority Health, "National Standards for Culturally and Linguistically Appropriate Services in Health Care Executive Summary," Final Report (March 2001), available at http://minority-health.hhs.gov/assets/pdf/checked/finalreport.pdf. See also enhanced version of CLAS standards launched by DHHS in April 2013, available at http://www.hhs.gov/news/press/2013pres/04/20130424b.html.

12 For the Federal Register that contains publication of the final national standards on Culturally and Linguistically Appropriate Services in Health Care (CLAS), see 65 FR 80685-03 (December 22, 2000).

13 DHHS, OMH, Final Report, 3.

14 Ibid.

15 Ibid., 28.

16 See U.S. Department of Health and Human Services Office of Minority Health, Agency for Healthcare Research and Quality, "Setting the Agenda for Research on

Cultural Competence in Health Care," Contract No. 00T061242, August 2004, available at: http://archive.ahrq.gov/research/findings/factsheets/literacy/cultural/cultural.pdf.

17 Ibid.

18 Lisa C. Diamond et al., "Do Hospitals Measure Up to the National Culturally and Linguistically Appropriate Services Standards?" *Medical Care* 48, no. 12 (December 2010): 1080–87.

19 Jo Ann Kaires et al., "Caring for Diverse Populations: Do Academic Family Medicine Practices Have CLAS?" *Family Medicine* 38, no. 3 (2006): 196–205.

20 American Hospital Association Comments to the Senate Finance Committee on Expanding Health Care Coverage: Proposals to Provide Affordable Coverage to All Americans, May 21, 2009, available at http://www.aha.org/testimony/2009 (explaining that the CLAS standards are not the regulatory standards but are guidelines issued outside the Administrative Procedures Act and prior to government-wide guidelines on language access issued by the DOJ and interpreted by HHS. The CLAS standards were not updated and do not reflect flexibility provisions to tailor standards to different size health care organizations.).

21 See, e.g., The Joint Commission, "Advancing Effective Communication, Cultural Competence, and Patient- and Family-Centered Care: A Roadmap for Hospitals" (Oakbrook Terrace, IL: Joint Commission, 2010), 57, available at http://www.jointcommission.org/assets/1/6/ARoadmapforHospitalsfinalversion727.pdf.

22 See "The Joint Commission's Draft Standards of Patient-Provider Communication," August 23, 2009, available at www.patientprovidercommunication.org/article_5.htm.

23 Ibid., The Joint Commission, "A Roadmap for Hospitals," 51, available at http://www.jointcommission.org/assets/1/6/ARoadmapforHospitalsfinalversion727.pdf.

24 See, e.g., ibid., Appendix C: New Joint Commission Standards for Patient Centered Communication, 57.

25 Ibid. The Joint Commission, "A Roadmap for Hospitals," New Joint Commission RI Requirements, RI.01.01.01, at 61.

26 See, generally, The Joint Commission, "A Roadmap for Hospitals," 14, 27, 55, 74,

27 See American Medical Association, "Report on Racial and Ethnic Disparities in Health Care," Board of Trustees Report 50 (I-95), available at http://www.ama-assn.org/ama/pub/about-ama/our-people/member-groups-sections/minority-affairs-section/news-resources/racialethnic-health-care-disparities/report-racial-ethnic.page.

28 See Council on Ethical and Judicial Affairs, CEJA Opinion 7-I-05, presented by Priscilla Ray, "Racial and Ethnic Health Care Disparities," available at http://www.allhealth.org/briefingmaterials/AMA-OpinionoftheCouncilonEthicalandJudicialAffairs-63.pdf. See also, AMA Code of Medical Ethics, available at http://www.ama-assn.org/ama/pub/physician-resources/medical-ethics/code-medical-ethics.page.

29 AMA Code of Medical Ethics, "Opinion 1.02—The Relation of Law and Ethics," available at http://www.ama-assn.org/ama/pub/physician-resources/medical-ethics/code-medical-ethics/opinion102.page.

30 Ibid. Frieden, "A Framework for Public Health Action," 592.

31 See Progressive Party Platform, "Social and Industrial Strength," August 7, 1912, available at http://www.pbs.org/wgbh/americanexperience/features/primary-resources/tr-progressive/.

32 Harry S. Truman, Special Message to the Congress Recommending a Comprehensive Health Program, November 19, 1945, Public Papers of the Presidents from the Harry S. Truman Library & Museum, available at http://www.trumanlibrary.org/publicpapers/index.php?pid=483.

33 "Lyndon Johnson's Remarks upon Signing the Medicare Bill, July 30, 1965," in *The United States Since 1945: A Documentary Reader*, ed. Robert P. Ingalls and David K. Johnson (Malden, MA: Blackwell Publishing Ltd., 2009), 117–19.

34 Richard Nixon, Special Message to Congress Proposing a Comprehensive Health Insurance Plan, February 6, 1974, The Nixon Foundation, available at http://nixon-foundation.org/news-details.php?id=621.

35 Jimmy Carter, National Health Plan Message to the Congress on Proposed Legislation," June 12, 1979 available at http://www.presidency.ucsb.edu/ws/?pid=32466.

36 William J. Clinton, Address of the President to the Joint Session of Congress,(September 22, 1993, in Joseph Antos, "Lessons from the Clinton Plan: Incremental Market Reform, Not Sweeping Government Control," *Health Affairs* 27, no 3 (2008): 705–10. , available at http://content.healthaffairs.org/content/27/3/705.full#ref-1.

37 The White House, Office of the Press Secretary, Remarks by the President on the House Vote on Health Insurance Reform, March 22, 2010, available at http://www.whitehouse.gov/the-press-office/remarks-president-house-vote-health-insurance-reform.

38 Norman Daniels, "Health Care Needs and Distributive Justice," *Philosophy and Public Affairs* 10, no. 2 (Spring 1981): 146–79.

39 Thomas A. LaVeist, Darrell, J. Gaskin, and Patrick Richard, "The Economic Burden of Health Inequalities in the United States," Joint Center for Political and Economic Studies, September 2011, available at http://jointcenter.org/sites/default/files/Economic%20Burden%20of%20Health%20Inequalities%20Fact%20Sheet.pdf.

40 David Satcher et al., "What If We Were Equal? A Comparison of the Black-White Mortality Gap in 1960 and 2000," *Health Affairs* 24, no. 2 (2005): 459–64.

41 Still, improvements should not be overlooked. Infant mortality rates among whites and blacks have fallen consistently since 1935, yet in 2009, the infant mortality rate in the United States was 12.5 infant deaths per 1,000 live black births, as compared to 5.3 among whites. Similarly, birth outcomes for white babies born to highly educated white women are better than outcomes for highly educated black women of the same age. Indeed, black mothers who are college educated and hold advanced degrees have higher infant mortality rates than white mothers who have not finished high school. See Laudy Y. Aron, "Despite Fifty Years of Improvements in Infant Mortality, Large Black-White Gap Remains Unchanged," *Urban Wire: Poverty, Vulnerability, and the Safety Net*, August 26, 2013, available at http://www.urban.org/

urban-wire/despite-fifty-years-improvements-infant-mortality-large-black-white-gap-remains-unchanged. The black-white life expectancy gap in the United States has improved. See Sam Harper et al., "Trends in the Black-White Life Expectancy Gap in the United States, 1983–2003," *Journal of the American Medical Association* 297, no. 11 (2007): 1224–32. However, when race and education are combined, the gap has been widening. See Bruce A. Carnes et al., "Differences in Life Expectancy Due to Race and Educational Differences Are Widening, and Many May Not Catch Up," *Health Affairs* 31, no. 8 (2012): 1803–13; see also Sabrina Tavernise, "Racial Disparities in Life Spans Narrow, but Persist," *New York Times*, July 18, 2013, available at http://www.nytimes.com/2013/07/18/health/racial-disparities-in-life-spans-narrow-but-persist.html.

42 See Dhammika Dharmapala and Richard McAdams, "The Condorcet Jury Theorem and The Expressive Function of Law: A Theory of Informative Law," University of Illinois Law and Economics Research Paper No. 00-19, February 2001, available at http://ssrn.com/abstract=260996 or http://dx.doi.org/10.2139/ssrn.260996.

43 See Guido Calabresi, *The Cost of Accidents: A Legal and Economic Analysis* (New Haven, CT: Yale University Press, 2008).

44 Richard McAdams, "An Attitudinal Theory of Expressive Law," *Oregon Law Review* 79 (2000): 339.

45 See generally, Eric A. Posner, *Law and Social Norms*, (Cambridge, MA: Harvard University Press, 2002), chap. 8.

46 Paul Elie, "A Man for All Reasons," *Atlantic*, November 1, 2007, available at http://www.theatlantic.com/magazine/archive/2007/11/a-man-for-all-reasons/306337/. "Political realism" has been defined as the belief that politics, like society, is governed by objective laws rooted in human nature and subject to a rational theory that distinguishes truth from opinion. See Hans J. Morgenthau, "A Realist Theory of International Politics," in Hans J. Margenthau, *Politics Among Nations: The Struggle for Power and Peace*, 7th rev. ed., (New York: McGraw-Hill Publishing Company, 1985), 3.

47 See David Brooks, "Obama, Gospel and Verse," *New York Times*, April 26, 2007, available at http://www.nytimes.com/2007/04/26/opinion/26brooks.html.

CHAPTER 9. A NEW NORMAL

1 See chapter 1.

2 See Tristin Green, "Discrimination in Workplace Dynamics: Toward a Structural Account of Disparate Treatment Theory," *Harvard Civil Rights–Civil Liberties Law Review* 38 (2003): 91.

3 Section 2000e-2. [Section 703] provides:

(a) . . . It shall be an unlawful employment practice for an employer—

(1) to fail or refuse to hire or to discharge any individual, or otherwise to discriminate against any individual with respect to his compensation, terms, conditions, or privileges of employment, because of such individual's race, color, religion, sex, or national origin; or

(2) to limit, segregate, or classify his employees or applicants for employment in any way, which would deprive or tend to deprive any individual of employment

opportunities or otherwise adversely affect his status as an employee, because of such individual's race, color, religion, sex, or national origin.

4 See David Benjamin Oppenheimer, "Negligent Discrimination," *University of Pennsylvania Law Review* 141 (January 1993): 899, 902–14 (explaining that before the IAT became available, one of the best ways to test whether whites held stereotypes about blacks was to ask them). Researchers such as those at the University of Chicago's National Opinion Research Center (NORC) and others produced solid evidence that anti-black stereotypes held by whites were pervasive and long-standing. For example, in 1990, the NORC published a report showing that while 53 percent of whites opined that African Americans were not as intelligent as whites in 1942, and 23 percent of white respondents continued to hold that view in 1968; by 1990, when the question was rephrased to ask for relative ratings of intelligence among the races, a hefty 53.3 percent of white respondents said blacks are generally less intelligent than whites.

5 Ibid.

6 Marc R. Poirier, "Is Cognitive Bias at Work a Dangerous Condition on Land?" *Employee Rights and Employee Policy Journal* 7 (2003): 459.

7 Ibid., 494.

8 Green, "Discrimination in Workplace Dynamics," 91.

9 Samuel R. Bagenstos, "The Structural Turn and the Limits of Antidiscrimination Law," *California Law Review* 94 (2006): 1.

10 Amy Wax, "Discrimination as Accident," *Indiana Law Journal* 74 (1999): 1129.

11 Linda Hamilton Krieger and Susan T. Fiske, "Behavioral Realism in Employment Discrimination Law: Implicit Bias and Disparate Treatment," *California Law Review* 94 (2006): 997, 1016.

12 Ibid., 1018.

13 Ibid., 1027. In section II, Krieger and Fiske describe a "Behavioral Realist Critique of Disparate Treatment Doctrine": (1) Most discrimination is "mindless," proceeding on automatic pilot; (2) biases such as stereotypes affect intergroup perception and social judgments and impair people's ability to accurately understand the social world around them; (3) the desire to conform to one's social surroundings has an enormous impact on individual behavior; and (4) varying even a minor aspect of a situation or context in which actors make social judgments and behave can completely change individuals' patterns of social behavior.

14 Although Title VI prohibits discrimination broadly by any recipient of federal assistance, I focus in this chapter on the law's application to the health care delivery system as the chosen exemplar for analytical purposes for reasons described earlier. The analysis here extends beyond the health care sector.

15 42 U.S.C.A. § 2000d-1(1964).

16 In 2009, this funding totaled $715 billion. Last year, the United States government paid 36.4 percent of this nation's national health care expenditures. See, National Center for Health Statistics, U.S. Department of Health and Human Services, Centers for Disease Control and Prevention, *Health, United States 2011: With Special Feature on Socioeconomic Status and Health* (2012), table 129, at 376.

17 I refer here to the views of the majority that prevailed in enacting this legislation, but do not mean to imply that Congress displayed unanimity of thought and mind in passing this law. The congressional coalitions that reached compromise to enact Title VI were not homogeneous. In their account, Daniel Rodriguez and Barry Weingast explain there were ardent supporters (mostly northern Democrats), ardent opponents (mostly southern Republicans) and a number of moderates who eventually passed Title VI. Daniel B. Rodriguez and Barry R. Weingast, "Positive Political Theory of Legislative History: New Perspectives on the 1964 Civil Rights Act and Its Interpretation," *University of Pennsylvania Law Review* 151 (2003): 1417.

18 *Simkins v. Moses H. Cone Memorial Hospital*, 323 F.2d 959, 969 (4th Cir. 1963), *certiorari* denied, 376 U.S. 938 (1964).

19 The full title of the statute known as "The Hill-Burton Act" is the Hospital Survey and Construction Act, codified at 42 U.S.C.A. 291 (c)(e)(2).

20 For a legislative history and discussion of the impact the *Simkins* case had on Title VI floor debate, see David Barton Smith, *Health Care Divided: Race and Healing a Nation* (Ann Arbor: University of Michigan Press 1999), 101–5.

21 *Congressional Record*, Senate, March 3, 1964, 88th Congress, 2nd Session, 4183.

22 "But we emphasize that this is not merely a controversy over a sum of money. Viewed from the plaintiffs' standpoint it is an effort by a group of citizens to escape the consequences of discrimination in a concern touching health and life itself. . . . Such involvement in discriminatory action it was the design of the Fourteenth Amendment to condemn." *Simkins*, 323 F.2d, at 969.

23 Patient Protection and Affordable Care Act, Nondiscrimination at 42 U.S. C. s. 18116, Section 1557(a): "Except as otherwise provided for in this title (or an amendment made by this title), an individual shall not, on the ground prohibited under title VI of the Civil Rights Act of 1964 (42 U.S.C. 2000d et seq.), . . . be excluded from participation in, be denied the benefits of, or be subjected to discrimination under, any health program or activity, any part of which is receiving Federal financial assistance, including credits, subsidies, or contracts of insurance, or under any program or activity that is administered by an Executive Agency or any entity established under this title (or amendments). The enforcement mechanisms provided for and available under such title VI . . . shall apply for purposes of violations of this subsection."

24 Original cosponsors included U.S. Senators John Kerry, Patrick Leahy, Christopher Coons, Tom Harkin, Richard Blumenthal, Barbara Mikulski, Sheldon Whitehouse, Al Franken, and Jeanne Shaheen. Later, Senator Amy Klobuchar of Minnesota was added as a tenth cosponsor. See 158 *Congressional Record* S4460–03.

25 The preamble of S3322 states the bill was introduced in the Senate to amend the Uniformed and Overseas Citizens Absentee Voting Act and to "reconcile, restore, clarify, and conform similar provisions in other related civil rights statutes, and for other purposes." See 112th Congress, 2nd Session (2011) US S3322 (June 20, 2012). If S3322 passed as proposed, the amended Section 601 of Title VI would read as follows:

(a) No person in the United States shall, on the ground of race, color, or national origin, be excluded from participation in, be denied the benefits of, or be subjected to discrimination under any program or activity receiving Federal financial assistance.

(b) (1) Discrimination based on disparate impact with respect to a program or activity is established under this section only if—

a. a Federal department or agency, or any person aggrieved, demonstrates that an entity subject to this title has a policy or practice with respect to the program or activity that causes a disparate impact on the basis of race, color, or national origin; and

b. (i) the entity fails to demonstrate that the challenge policy or practice is related to, and necessary to achieve, the substantial and legitimate nondiscriminatory goals of the program or activity; or

c. (ii) the Federal department or agency, or the person aggrieved, demonstrates that a less discriminatory alternative policy or practice exists, and the entity refuses to adopt such alternative policy or practice

(2) In this subsection, the term 'demonstrates' means meets the burdens of production and persuasion.

S3322, if passed, would add the following language to the end of Section 602 of Title VI:

(b) Any person aggrieved by the failure of an entity to comply with section 601 may bring a civil action in any Federal or State court of competent jurisdiction to enforce such person's rights and may recover equitable relief, reasonable attorney's fees, and costs. The aggrieved person may also recover legal relief (including compensatory and, from nongovernmental entities, punitive damages) in the case of noncompliance that is intentional discrimination.

(c) Nothing in subsection (b) limits the authority of a Federal department or agency to enforce section 601.

26 *Guardians Ass'n. v. Civil Service Com'n. of City of New York*, 463 U.S. 582, 589(1983) (citing *Lau v. Nichols*, 414 U.S. 563 [1974]).

27 532 U.S. 275 (2001).

28 See Note, "After Sandoval: Judicial Challenges and Administrative Possibilities in Title VI Enforcement," *Harvard Law Review* 116 (April 2003): 1774. Justice Scalia went further, strongly hinting that Section 602 of Title VI might not support disparate impact claims alleging unintentional discrimination, though he declined to decide the question in *Sandoval*.

29 *Regents of the University of California v. Bakke*, 438 U.S. 265 (1976).

30 463 U.S. 582 (1983).

31 *Sandoval*, 532 U.S., at 308.

32 *Guardians Ass'n*, 463 U.S., at 584.

33 Ibid., at 590.

34 Ibid., at 593.

35 Ibid., at 615.

36 Ibid., at 623–24.

37 Ibid., 622.

38 *Alexander v. Choate*, 469 U.S. 287 (1985).

39 469 U.S., at 718.

40 505 U.S. 717 (1992).

41 Ibid., at 743.

42 Ibid., at 745 (citing *ante* at 2736).

43 *Alexander v. Choate*, 469 U.S., at 293–94.

44 539 U.S. 306 (2003).

45 Ibid., at 345.

46 539 U.S. 244 (2003).

47 Ibid., at 300.

48 See Gregory Mitchell and Philip Tetlock, "Antidiscrimination Law and the Perils of Mindreading," *Ohio State Law Journal* 67 (2006): 1023.

49 See Charles R. Lawrence, "The Id, the Ego, and Equal Protection: Reckoning with Unconscious Racism," *Stanford Law Review* 39 (1987): 317.

50 R. A. Lenhardt, "Understanding the Mark: Race, Stigma, and Equality in Context," *New York University Law Review* 79 (2004): 803.

51 See Barbara Flagg, "Fashioning a Title VI Remedy for Transparently White Subjective Decision-Making," *Yale Law Journal* 104 (1995): 2009.

52 *Alexander v. Sandoval*, 532 U.S. 275, 294 (J. Stevens, dissenting).

53 See 158 *Congressional Record* S4, 460–03 (daily ed. June 25, 2012) (statement of Sen. Sherrod Brown).

54 See Dayna Bowen Matthew, "Health Care, Title VI, and Racism's New Normal," *Georgetown Journal of Law and Modern Critical Race Perspectives* 6 (Spring 2014): 3. In that article I published an earlier proposal to amend Title VI language. This amended language has been updated and revised in response to many helpful comments I received on that earlier draft.

55 For analysis of the of both the limitations and strength of public and private enforcement to protect civil rights, see Olatunde C. A. Johnson, "The Private Attorney General: Equality Directives in American Law," *New York University Law Review* 87 (2012): 1339; see also Michael Waterstone, "A New Vision of Public Enforcement," *Minnesota Law Review* 92 (2007): 434.

56 505 U.S. 717 (1992).

57 Predecessor to the Department of Health and Human Services (DHHS).

58 In reading the *Fordice* case, I am struck by the correctness of Ralph Banks's and Richard Ford's call for focus on the alleviation of substantive educational, housing, and employment inequalities that plagued Mississippi long before black students applied for admission to the state's white universities, notwithstanding Banks's and Ford's misunderstanding of the social psychology behind the IAT and their misguided understanding of the importance of addressing subconscious bias in the pursuit of equal civil rights for ethnic and racial minorities. See Ralph Richard Banks and Richard Thompson Ford, "(How) Does Unconscious Bias Matter?: Law, Politics, and Racial Inequality," *Emory Law Journal* 58 (2009): 1053.

59 505 U.S. at 743.

60 The *Fordice* court failed to equalize funding for Mississippi's historically black universities. See Alex M. Johnson, Jr., "*Bid Whist, Tonk, and United States v. Fordice*: Why Integrationism Fails African-Americans Once Again," *California Law Review* 81 (1993): 1401 (given American history, the only appropriate result in Fordice should have been the maintenance of HBCUs at improved funding level, while also protecting equal opportunity to attend predominantly white institutions).

61 *C.S. v. Couch*, 843 F. Supp.2d 894, 916 (2011).

62 *Morales v. NYS Department of Labor*, F.Supp.2d (2012) (2012 WL 1097318).

63 *Blunt v. Lower Merion School District*, 826 F. Supp.2d 749 (2011).

64 Ibid., at 761.

65 Linda Krieger, "The Content of Our Categories: A Cognitive Bias Approach to Discrimination and Equal Employment Opportunity," *Stanford Law Review* 47 (1995): 1161, 1164.

66 Ibid., 1166.

67 Tristin K. Green, "'It's Not You, It's Me': Assessing an Emerging Relationship between Law and Social Science," *Connecticut Law Review* 46 (2013): 287.

68 See, e.g., Bertram Gawronski, "Implicit Bias in Impression Formation: Associations Influence the Construal of Individuating Information," *European Journal of Social Psychology* 33 (2003): 573, 585.

69 See, e.g., Kerry Kawakami et al., "Effects of Training in the Negation of Stereotype Associations on Stereotype Activation," *Journal of Personality and Social Psychology* 78 (2000): 871; Irene V. Blair and M. R. Banaji, "Automatic and Controlled Processes in Stereotype Priming," *Journal of Personality and Social Psychology* 70 (1996): 1142; and N. Dasgupta and A. Greenwald, "On the Malleability of Automatic Attitudes: Combating Automatic Prejudice with Images of Admired and Disliked Individuals," *Journal of Personality and Social Psychology* 81 (2001): 800.

70 See, e.g., Lisa Sinclair and Ziva Kunda, "Reactions to a Black Professional: Motivated Inhibition and Activation of Conflicting Stereotypes, *Journal of Personality and Social Psychology* 77 (1999): 885.

71 Susan T. Fiske, "Stereotyping, Prejudice, and Discrimination," in *The Handbook of Social Psychology,* ed. Susan T. Fiske, Daniel T. Gilbert, and Gardner Lindzey (Hoboken, NJ: Wiley, 1998), 357.

72 Another criticism bears brief mention. The objection that rests on an assertion that the social science record I have cited proves only a mere association rather than a causal relationship between unconscious racism and discriminatory harms is specious. See, e.g., Joshua Stone, "Reaction to 'Health Care, Title VI, and Racism's New Normal,'" *Georgetown Journal Law and Modern Critical Race Perspectives* 6 (2014): 67. Proof of causation under the law by circumstantial as well as direct evidence, such as the copious scientific record of the association between unconscious racism and health disparities, is as accepted and longstanding as the law itself. Therefore resorting to the scientific standard of causation in order to defeat a legal claim is incongruous at best, and disingenuous at worse.

73 See, e.g., David M. Studdert et al. "Medical Malpractice," *New England Journal of Medicine* 350, no. 3 (January 15, 2004): 283–92.

74 Green, "'It's Not You, It's Me,'" 287.

CONCLUSION

1 See Department of Health and Human Services, Section 1557 of the Patient Protection and Affordable Care Act, available at http://www.hhs.gov/ocr/civilrights/understanding/section1557/.

2 Matthew Heinz and Juliet K. Choi, "Enhancing Health Care Protections for LGBT Individuals," April 15, 2014, available at http://www.hhs.gov/healthcare/facts/blog/2014/04/health-care-protections-lgbt-individuals.html.

3 42 U.S,C, §18116(a) (2010).

4 First authorized in 1990, the Ryan White HIV/AIDS program is administered by the U.S. Department of Health and Human Services, Health Resources and Services Administration, and HIV/AIDS Bureau to provide services to people without sufficient health insurance coverage or financial resources to cope with HIV disease. See the U.S. Department of Health and Human Services Ryan White HIV/AIDs Program website, avaiable at http://hab.hrsa.gov/abouthab/aboutprogram.html.

5 Complaint—Class Action, *John East v. Blue Cross and Blue Shield of Louisiana et al.* No. 3:14CV00115, United States District Court, M.D. Louisiana (February 20, 2014), available at https://a.next.westlaw.com/Document/I61be15729acc11e39ac8bab74931929c/View/FullText.html?originationContext=document&contextData=(sc.DocLink)&cacheScope=null&transitionType=DocumentItem&searchWithinQuery=impact&chunkSize=L&docSource=5c17168843664556ae473f38f52687fc&needToInjectTerms=False&searchWithinHandle=ioad82350000001461efad61f911d3ec4.

6 David R. Williams and Toni D. Rucker, "Understanding and Addressing Racial Disparities in Health Care," *Heath Care Financing Review* 21 (2000): 75.

7 See Agency for Healthcare Research and Quality, National Healthcare Disparities Report 2011, AHRQ Publication No. 12-0006 (Rockville, MD: U.S. Department of Health and Human Services, 2012), 6.

INDEX

Adherence, 50, 72, 77, 111, 113, 118, 127, 132, 140, 144–45, 183; non-adherence, 4

Affordable Care Act. *See* Patient Protection and Affordable Care Act

African-Americans, 19, 20, 28, 30, 44, 47–50, 57–61, 65, 69, 70, 81, 84, 87, 90, 91, 93, 110, 116, 119, 125, 126, 130, 141, 143, 144, 152, 160, 161, 163, 166, 167, 177, 187, 188

Agency for Healthcare Research and Quality (AHRQ), 180, 187

AHRQ. *See* Agency for Healthcare Research and Quality

Alexander v. Choate, 205

Alexander v. Sandoval, 27, 196, 203–4, 208, 213–14

American Hospital Association, 181

American Medical Association, 141, 181, 183

Americans with Disabilities Act (ADA), 28

Amygdala, 42

Anterior Cingulate Cortex (ACC), 42

Antidiscrimination law, 3, 6–7, 11, 22, 26, 28, 30, 46, 56, 189, 191–92, 195–98, 200, 215–16, 219, 221

Ashmore Richard, 161

Attitudes, 11, 32, 34, 38, 39, 41, 42, 45, 46, 74–77, 79, 82, 85, 89, 91–96, 99, 101, 102, 106, 119, 120, 125, 127, 130, 132, 141, 156, 157, 160, 161–63, 165–67, 170, 177, 185, 192, 206, 207, 220

Automaticity, 157

Aversive: racism, 87, 125–26; racist, 88, 125–26

Bach, Peter, 60

Bagenstos, Samuel R., 199–200

Bakke. See *Regents of the University of California v. Bakke*

Balsa, Ana, 103, 105, 158

Bertakis, Klea, 113

Biased Care Model, 4–5, 75–79, 106, 110, 120, 123, 129, 131, 138–40, 146, 148–53, 158, 171, 190, 192, 193, 195, 196, 217, 222, 228

Black codes, 17, 27

Blair, Irene V., 72–73, 131, 157, 164

Blanco, Carlos, 29

Breyer, Justice Stephen, 204

Brown v. Board of Education, 28, 212

Bryan v. Koch, 26

Burgess, Diana, 104, 150, 151, 152, 167

Burke, Jane, 85, 86, 93

Candib, Lucy, 113

Carmichael, Doctr James or Doctr Edwd H, 14

Carter, President Jimmy, 184

Centers for Medicare and Medicaid (CMS), 44

Chinese, 15, 18, 84, 147; laborers, 15; immigrants, 15; immigration, 16

Civil War, 17, 19

CLAS Standards, 179–182

Clinton, President William J., 184

Cobb, Thomas R. R., 12

ABOUT THE AUTHOR

Dayna Bowen Matthew holds a joint appointment at the University of Colorado Law School and Colorado School of Public Health and serves on the faculty of the University of Colorado Center for Bioethics and Humanities. She is Co-founder of the Colorado Health Equity Project, a medical-legal partnership whose mission is to remove barriers to good health for low-income clients by providing legal representation, research, and policy advocacy with law, medical, and public health students and faculty. Her articles on health and public health law topics have appeared in numerous law and policy journals. Most recently, Professor Matthew has enjoyed the privilege of public service as a Senior Advisor to the Director of the Office of Civil Rights for the Environmental Protection Agency, and as a 2015–2016 Robert Wood Johnson Health Policy Fellow.